JACKIE COCHRAN

JACKIE COCHRAN

An Autobiography

JACQUELINE COCHRAN &
MARYANN BUCKNUM BRINLEY

BANTAM BOOKS
TORONTO · NEW YORK · LONDON · SYDNEY · AUCKLAND

Author's Note
I would like to thank Vi Strauss Pistell, Ann Wood, Yvonne Smith, and Aldine Tarter
for opening up their personal photo albums of Jackie memorabilia and letting me
browse to borrow.

PHOTO CREDITS

National Air and Space Museum (NASM): Insert 1, p. 1 (top), p. 7.

Northrop Corporation: Insert 1, p. 1 (bottom), p. 6; Insert 2, p. 4 (inset), p. 7 (inset);
Insert 3, p. 3, p. 5 (top), p. 6 (bottom), p. 7.

San Diego Aero-Space Museum: Insert 1, p. 2 (top right); Insert 2, p. 3.

Rudy Arnold/LaGuardia Field: Insert 1, p. 2 (bottom).

M. D. Bradshaw: Insert 2, p. 1.

Don Ornitz: Insert 3, p. 1.

Robert E. Burke: Insert 3, p. 5 (bottom).

99's: Insert 3, p. 6 (top).

JACKIE COCHRAN: AN AUTOBIOGRAPHY
A Bantam Book / August 1987

Library of Congress Cataloging-in-Publication Data
Cochran, Jacqueline.
  Jackie Cochran: an autobiography.

  Includes Index.
  1. Cochran, Jacqueline. 2. Air pilots—United States—
Biography. I. Brinley, Maryann Bucknum. II. Title.
TL540.C63A3 1987 629.13′092′4 [B] 86-47908
ISBN 0-553-05211-X

Published simultaneously in the United States and Canada

PRINTED IN THE UNITED STATES OF AMERICA

0 9 8 7 6 5 4 3 2 1

CONTENTS

At the time of her death on August 9, 1980, Jacqueline Cochran held more speed, altitude, and distance records than any other pilot, male or female, in aviation history. Her career spanned 40 years, from the Golden Age of the 1930s as a racing pilot, through the turbulent years of World War II as founder and head of the Women's Airforce Service Pilot (WASP) program, into the jet age, when she became the first female pilot to fly faster than the speed of sound. She was a 14-time winner of the Harmon trophy for the outstanding female pilot of the year and was accorded numerous other awards and honors in addition to the trophies she won with her flying skills.

—National Air and Space Museum exhibit, Smithsonian Institution, 1981

AUTHOR'S NOTE

This book could not have been written without the help of Jackie's friends, all of whom gave me patiently and generously of their time and memories. Their names and voices follow here.

But I am also overwhelmingly indebted to Jackie herself, for she was a classic "pack rat"—as all of her friends agree. As a result, her race notes, the drafts of an early autobiography published as *The Stars at Noon*, (along with its follow-up which was never completed), her own oral histories, articles, interviews, clippings, copies of speeches and correspondence—all survive intact. In addition, the Dwight D. Eisenhower Presidential Library guards a mass of written items connected with Jacqueline Cochran, as does the Lyndon B. Johnson Presidential Library. Other prestigious institutions and people hold oral, written, and filmed material. These include the Columbia University oral history project, the United States Air Force Oral History Program, Northrop Aviation's historian Ira Chart, and most particularly the National Air and Space Museum and the Smithsonian Institution, where Jay Spenser and especially Curator Claudia Oakes were of enormous help in contributing to this "close-up" autobiographical biography of a very remarkable woman. My thanks to all.

Traditional biographies often place the writer/researcher looking over the shoulder of the person about whom they are writing, whose words they are interpreting. The autobiography, on the other hand, places the reader directly in the mind of the chief protagonist, seeing the world through that person's eyes, living events as they occurred, experiencing the thrills and shocks, the joys and sorrows, as the subject experienced them. The combination of autobiography and "Other Voices" permits the biographer to widen the point of view, to get some perspective on the person playing the lead, to see the biographee as the world saw him—or, in this instance, very much her.

Jacqueline Cochran was a self-named, self-created phenomenon. Whatever the circumstances of her birth, she must have been born fighting. And she never stopped. True, she had a poverty-stricken background, but somehow I think that wherever or whoever she was at birth, her native acumen, extraordinary energy, talent, and sheer guts would inevitably have driven her to the very top.

Jackie was an irresistible force. Time and time again in the many, many interviews I was so kindly granted, the repeated theme was "Jackie just could not be stopped." And indeed, this driving, cussed determination is signally evident in Jackie's own writings. Her unremitting persistence is clear in everything she did, from regaining the doll of which she was robbed at the age of six to her need to be the world's top aviatrix. Generous, egotistical, penny-pinching, compassionate, sensitive, aggressive —indeed, an explosive study in contradictions—Jackie was consistent only in the overflowing energy with which she attacked the challenge of being alive. Always passionately convinced of any viewpoint she happened to hold (nothing Jackie ever did was by halves), she raced through life, making lifelong friends and unforgetting enemies, surely breaking all records in the sheer volume of her living on this earth—as she did in the air.

This is a biography of an authentic, native-born American heroine—a real life "Li'l Orphan Annie"—who battled her way through adventures that Annie never even dreamed. It is built on autobiographical scenes from a life lived flat out. Jackie was loved and hated probably just about equally in her seventy-some years of living. But no one who encountered her was indifferent, or indeed ever forgot her. In her own writing, sometimes she is almost chronological. Sometimes she is not. But whatever she did was done her way. And Jackie believed in jumping into any adventure feetfirst. To begin at the beginning, you often need to go to the middle.

—Maryann Bucknum Brinley

MAKING IT
IN A MAN'S WORLD

The engine was experimental
and turned out later to be aerodynamically out of balance. I didn't
know that at the time. I installed it in my airplane, a Northrop
Gamma. The airplane was fairly fast with it, but that darn engine
would not hold its temperature down. The whole plane would start
vibrating terribly. It had a buffeting in the tail, and that can be serious if it is too bad or continues for very long. It'll make the plane
fall apart on you. And I didn't want that to happen.

I wasn't the first woman to be allowed to enter one of the
National Air Racing events, but I was in a particularly sensitive
spot that year. A young woman, Florence Klingensmith, had been
killed in '33, and racing officials wanted no more female blood on
their hands. It had taken every ounce of my persuasive and political powers to earn my spot there on the starting line in 1935. In
fact, I had been forced to get okays from all the other male pilots
entered in that Bendix cross-country race. I painted a "13" on the
side of my airplane for good luck.

We were flying from Los Angeles to Cleveland, west to east.
Some years the Bendix racers flew east to west. But believe me, no
matter which direction, those races were a big deal in those days.
To be excluded from them simply because I was a woman would
have been criminal. And because of my own stubbornness, at the
last minute my friend Amelia Earhart threw her name and plane
into the Bendix race. She and her copilot, Paul Mantz, took fifth
that year in the Lockheed Vega. I felt good about that.

1

What I didn't feel so good about was the weather. It was so bad you couldn't see across the airport. Most of the other planes in the race were lucky to get off the ground before the fog rolled in around midnight or a little after. Since starting times for each contestant in the race were staggered and I had wanted to take advantage of as much daylight flying time as possible, I had chosen 3 A.M. It was a bad choice.

Thousands of people were milling about. Photographers were flashing cameras, and from time to time their lights would blind me temporarily. I lost the yellow rosebud my fiancé Floyd Odlum always gave me for good luck at the start of a hard race. Floyd had gone ahead to meet me in Cleveland. Automobile headlights discovered the bud a hundred feet away from my plane on the runway but not before I spent some tense, terrible moments. Not just because of a missing rosebud, however.

I remember that Bill Gwinn, a field representative for Pratt & Whitney engines, came up to me and asked me not to take off.

"Are you willing to say to the public that that motor is malfunctioning?" I asked him.

"I can't afford to say that," he said.

"Then," I answered, "I can't afford not to take off. If I don't take off, probably no woman will be allowed to fly in a race again."

A representative of Northrop came over to me, too, and explained that Mr. Northrop didn't want me to take off.

"Are you willing to say that the plane is malfunctioning?" I asked. They weren't.

"Then go away and hush," I told him.

Next, an official from the Civil Aeronautics Administration came over and pleaded with me not to take off. I asked him if he had the right to ground me, hoping a little that perhaps he did. But he said that he didn't have that right. This was a race and everything was up to the pilot's discretion.

About twenty minutes before I was scheduled to take off, a boy by the name of Cecil Allen, who was in a Gee Bee, took off and crashed at the end of the runway. He was completely decapitated. I know that because I was sitting in a police car at the time and the policeman took me down in his car and showed me. Perhaps he had something in mind about discouraging me. Whatever, shortly thereafter I parted company with my "cookies" out behind the airport hangar. Maybe it was the Mexican food I had eaten earlier in

the evening or the soda pop I had drunk. Maybe it was my nerves.
Anyway, I telephoned Floyd before I went back to the plane.
   "What should I do?" I asked him.

In later years, after Floyd and I were married, he would head
the company that built the B-36 intercontinental bomber and
Convair Lines, but in those days his only thrills and adventures
in the field of aviation were vicarious ones he had through my
escapades. That night I needed to hear his calm voice of reason
more than anything. And he was there for me. He told me that
there was a fine line between a course of action determined by
logic and one dictated by great emotional urge. No one, he said
to me, could quite draw that line for someone else. In his opinion, it simmered down to a philosophy of life.

This time I decided to satisfy my emotional urge. I walked
back outside and climbed into the plane. It had been rolled out
to the starting line and 600 gallons of gas now weighted it down.
That's nearly two extra tons of weight. Would it get off the
ground? I couldn't see the end of the field for the fog, and I
heard the starter say, "It's not too late to quit. I hate to see you
kill yourself."

The engine roars and I head down the runway. A fire truck
and ambulance follow. Half the way gone, I see no sign of lift.
Two thirds of the way gone and not a fraction of an inch
between my wheels and the ground. The fence at the end of the
runway and I are destined to meet, it seems, if not, well—there
are two telephone posts and wires just beyond.

I shave that fence so closely it catches my radio antenna and
tears off the trailing wire. Pulling high enough to get over the
telephone wire, I nose slightly down again to gain speed. Nothing but fog around me. I'm still struggling through really bad,
bad weather. My airspeed is so poor that I don't dare turn the
plane around. The race is eastward, of course, but I'm heading
west in the same direction I had taken off. It's unsafe to turn an
airplane with such a big load and so little altitude or speed. The
thought crosses my mind that I probably won't get to wear the
two new dresses I bought that afternoon when I should have
been taking a nap.

But this story doesn't end in the Pacific.

I finally did get that plane turned and flew back toward the coast, the airport, and the mountains, slowly gaining altitude. I was worried about running into the mountains I knew were less than five miles ahead somewhere in that fog. So I doubled back over the ocean and then made another shallow turnback, heading for the mountains again. I kept repeating this maneuver until I caught sight of the stars at about 9,000 feet. Never have they looked so bright and friendly.

About two hours later, over the Grand Canyon, the engine started to sputter.

I know nothing more beautiful than a plane's-eye view of the Grand Canyon and Painted Desert. The softness of the colorings seems to temper the hardness of that deep wonderful gash in the earth. Sometimes it looks like a bed of pastel-shaded flowers from the air when the sun is bright and all's well. But in the dark of night, with a hot sputtering engine and a ship that's about to shake apart, the beauties of the Grand Canyon got no appreciation from me.

The engine temperature was, as they say, "right off the boards." The airplane was vibrating very badly. I couldn't move faster than 160 miles per hour and this was a ship supposed to be doing 220 mph. I knew I was going to be forced down. It was just a matter of when. The radio wasn't working, having lost its antenna on the fence, and I could see a line of squalls, or violent electrical storms, advancing toward me. It felt as though the plane was going to shake apart. The only airport I could imagine reaching was the one at Kingman, Arizona, the one I had just passed back across the Grand Canyon. To keep going in the other direction meant 400 miles of wild peaks and canyons. There were no airports ahead for me because I had been flying a direct route to Cleveland, not a regular air line with stops along the way. At that point, discretion took the better part of my 3 A.M. valor away.

I turned back and on the way decided to use the gasoline dump valves designed for exactly the kind of emergency landing I was going to make. Landing a plane with the load of gas I still had on board is very dangerous. The dump valves had never been tested.

A flip of the switch. The valves are open and they work. But oh God. Four hundred gallons of gasoline suddenly mixed with the exhaust fumes, almost causing a fire, and then some sort of suction drew the mixture into the plane's cockpit for a nerve-racking minute or two. I hardly knew what had happened to me, and I stopped cursing God long enough to thank him for the leather flying suit I was wearing. I was saturated with gas and threw open the canopy to get my face into the wind stream so I could breathe. But the force of the air nearly took my head off. It's a wonder I never lost consciousness.

Then I spotted Kingman and went ahead to land, assuming now that if I got a spark anywhere, even from a rock hitting my gasoline-soaked ship, we'd be on fire in an instant. That frightened me because I used to think that I feared death less than the thought of living the rest of my life burned, in pain, or with horribly disfiguring injuries. Perhaps that's only something a woman would worry about, but I doubt it. Anyway, male or female, if you ponder such possibilities too long or too often, you'll never risk anything. And to live without risk for me would have been tantamount to death.

I put that plane down at Kingman as smooth as is humanly possible, taxied up, piled out at the hangar, and ran to the ladies' room to strip off my clothes and wash up. I had no dry clothes to put on. Somebody gave me an overcoat. And as the morning light lengthened, somebody went into town to buy me dry trousers and a shirt—anything—clothes.

OTHER VOICES:

General Chuck Yeager
(A CLOSE PERSONAL FRIEND AND FELLOW FLYER)

She didn't have the word *consequences* in her makeup. She had no fear at all and never considered the consequences of not riding a plane real good. She just didn't worry about dying. The way she looked at it, it didn't make a whole hell of a lot of difference—that's just the way it would go. She was a remarkable person and she was a competitor. You've got to be aggressive to do that and you've got to have guts to go out and get exactly what you want. Jackie was damn well aggressive enough and she got what she wanted. And she wasn't dumb. She was a very smart gal with a lot of horse sense. Her formal education may not have been much, but she sure had a tremendous amount of horse sense....

BEGINNINGS

SOMEWHERE AROUND 1906

I'm a refugee of what I like to call "Sawdust Road" and if you aren't sure just where that is, let me tell you. There's a Tobacco Road you may have heard of because of the nasty notoriety it achieved in a movie. But my Sawdust Road was just as bad. Until I was eight years old I had no shoes. My bed was usually a pallet on the floor and sometimes just the floor. I'd always choose the latter over the option of sleeping with my foster sister Myrtle because Myrtle was usually a dirty, sloppy sort and I've had a cleanliness fetish for as long as I can remember. I still can recall my sisters making fun of me because I would carry buckets of cold water from a pump to give myself a good icy scrubbing in the washtub on the floor of our house. They laughed at me but I kept right on. I wanted to be clean. They said I was putting on airs. I liked being different from them, stronger in fact. And I used my strength to get what I wanted.

Food at best consisted of the barest essentials—sometimes nothing except what I foraged for myself in the woods of the Northern Florida sawmill towns my foster family called home. I remember eating a lot of mullet and beans, with an occasional bit of sowbelly added when we were in clover. Blackeyed peas were for very special occasions. No butter. No sugar. My dresses were made from cast-off flour sacks.

My first clear recollection—and I couldn't have been much more than four years old—is of my foster father being sick with typhoid fever. We lived in a house then in Sampson, Florida, which didn't have any windows in it. I can still see paper pinned up to the openings to keep the cold out. The house was in some kind of marshy area, and there was a dark, dank, abandoned mill nearby. It had been an ice-manufacturing operation for fishermen but was quite abandoned and quite stinky. A big creek, or branch, as we called them, ran behind our shack, and people were always pulling crawfish out of it to eat. I couldn't face eating them myself and I often wonder how I ever developed the taste for lobster I had later in my life.

If fending for yourself carries its satisfactions, I had my share of satisfactions rich and plentiful in my childhood. But I've often heard that if you want someone to really enjoy the pleasures of heaven, then just pitch her into hell for a spell. Perhaps that's why I enjoyed my life to the brimful.

We were always a little hungry. My father and two brothers worked in the sawmills. Henry could never earn full pay because he had been born with a crippled foot. He'd stack slabs of wood for sixty cents a day. But Joe could earn as much as $1.00 a day when work was in full swing. And when my father was well enough, he went back to the saw too. Mama was always tired, upset, angry with the world and, especially, us. My sisters were no comfort to me.

Sawmill camps are all pretty much alike. The shacks surrounding that mill in the middle, the company store or the commissary; the doctor who patches up the living and takes care of the mill families for a standard wage deduction of fifty cents a month. The doctor is always busier in mill towns that feature two-sided band saws. Two-sided means twice the chance of being killed or maimed. Saws are always breaking apart or belts flying loose or splinters shooting off jagged wooden bullets. Snatches of nasty conversations and miserable tales fill my mind when I try to bring back those years. Black teeth and bad breath from all the tobacco chewing and the snuff. Those were smiles that made me cringe even as a child.

Men are paid in chips. We never see money. Chips can be used for the rental of a company-owned house or redeemed for food and clothing at the company commissary. On hungry days we walk back to the mill with Papa after the noon break to get our chips. Simply having him report back to the job at that point, and telling the foreman he is healthy enough to stay till dinner, can qualify us for enough chips for dinner. The foreman gives us a slip of paper. We take it to Chip Charlie, who is so fast at counting out those chips—each equals five cents—that even Mama, scowling and counting as best she can, can't keep up with him. But we'll have dinner that night. And that makes me happy.

The use of chips instead of money is an incredibly powerful way to keep workers enslaved to the mills. For the chips are good nowhere else but at the commissary. And being attached to a mill like this was actually worse than slavery because even slaves had some measure of security. We didn't.

As long as the logs are coming in, the saws keep turning. When they stop, we must move on. Sampson...Bagdad... Millville...Panama City...

As a child, I decided that these mills considered it their job to destroy beautiful forest land. The men would slash and sear the trees back to stumps, and then all the way down to the wasted sands on the forest floor in that part of Florida. It was a terrible way to conduct a business and an even more terrible way to live. When the logs stopped coming, my family would stay in a camp for as long as the food lasted or part-time work materialized—which wasn't very long. Then we had to move again, which was dreadful with no money for transportation. Sometimes, though, we were offered passage on the train for the family's labors, even mine.

I am in the caboose of a train traveling probably from Bagdad to Panama City. Every once in a while the train stops and we all get out to help the crew gather lighter knots, those knotty, unsawable parts of pine trees that are full of tar but fine for train engine furnaces. We get off and on so many times that I am exhausted. My feet ache and I wish I had shoes. I'm very conscious that I don't have any and other children do. We stop at a little town and some black people come on board the train, selling fried chicken and bread. It smells wonderful. Some passengers buy. We don't.

Now something else rivets my attention. Desperately, I watch as a man comes through our car selling glass pistols filled with small balls of candy. I want one more than anything before in my whole life. I know I can't have it and I don't cry. I lose myself in a fantasy of all the things I'll buy when I can buy *whatever* I want.

The train ride is about 100 miles long and we get off in Panama City. But we can't stop yet. Our destination is Millville, and Millville is a three-mile walk away through sand bogs. I trudge along and sink in deeper than the others. It covers my ankles—I remember that clearly—and my stomach is empty. I can still feel that exhaustion even now.

Finally, we arrive. But we are nowhere as far as I can see. In fact, we are at the edge of the camp, and our house is almost exactly like the one we just vacated. No windows. On stilts. Near a branch of nasty water. Awful. It's a second showing of the same horror movie and I knew it then as I do now.

I go out looking for food. A farmer lives nearby, and in back of a shed near his house I discover tubs of sweet potatoes boiling for livestock, probably pigs. I see some pigs. He won't know. I am hungry. So I "borrow" a couple of the potatoes and eat them right there. I can't wait. I won't hide. They are wonderful.

The next day I discover how delicious pine mass can be. I find them on the floor of the forest in back of our house after the men have gone on to the mill to start work, and Mama is busy. Pine mass are the small nuts that drop out of the pine cone in the fall. They are tasty, and later in life I learned they were also very nourishing. At the time it didn't matter how nourishing they were. They filled my empty stomach.

I'm at the waterfront in Millville two days later and I've met some children whose father has seined for mullet in the night to sell that day. I must look woebegone because they give me a panful of fish to take home. I'm ecstatic and on the way past the farmer's house I decide that what we need to make the fish into a really fine meal is a cup of lard to help cook them. What nerve I had. I stop and ask our next door neighbor—the farmer whose potatoes I've pinched—if he will loan me a little lard.

In those sawmill towns, people just didn't ask others for help like that. I must have surprised him. Or he must have taken a liking to me. All my life, others have been kind to me. Strangers used to take to me. I often thought they looked at me as if I were an unusual or striking-looking wild animal that wandered into camp needing to be fed and cared for. That farmer wasn't the first or the last to oblige me.

Hunger was a permanent way of feeling when I was growing up, common to all. And the pan of mullet cooked in lard was my family's first hot meal in a week's time. It helps explain my lifetime compulsion about food—preparing it, cooking it right, eating it with good friends alongside good conversation.

LOOKING BACK DOWN SAWDUST ROAD

It was a good thing I stopped when I stopped in that first Bendix race because when we looked at that engine in the light of day, the bearings were burned out and I wouldn't have lasted more than another 30 minutes in the air. Someone might still be looking for me in the wilds of the Rocky Mountains.

But I was glad that I took off and showed that a woman could take it along with the men. There had been a lot of talk the night before about whether or not I was qualified to fly by instruments alone, and I certainly proved I was fully capable of flying in fog. But I never really wanted to copy men or to do what men can or should do better. I only wanted to be myself. And for me that meant flying. I had to take that fast airplane whenever it became available to me and then make the best of it.

Aviators do a pile of campfire talking as a rule. It's known as "ground flying." Repartee has sometimes been defined as what you think of after you get home that you should have said snappy-like at the time. Well, most ground flying—including books about flying—belongs in the same compartment. Landings under trying conditions are made from the campstool in the hangar just as they should have been made according to all the rules but were not.

What happens, however, is that the real dangers and thrills are usually talked down. They didn't mean a thing to the pilot. "When I finally came out of the spin I found myself down in a steep canyon, so I just squashed her in on the river bed. No trouble at all." Aviators are like that.

Chuck Yeager used to say to me, "Aw, Jackie, they don't build airplanes that take superhumans to fly them. If they did, they wouldn't sell very many of them." Chuck is like that. But like Chuck Yeager, aviators have amazing life stories to tell, if the high spots are laid down end to end.

Every brush with death has left me with a great memory. I must have been about six years old in this one. I had been playing all afternoon down the road from our house—which was really not much more than a shack on stilts on the edge of Bagdad, Florida. My foster family—Mama, Papa, Joe, Henry, Mamie, and Myrtle—didn't worry too much about where I was or what I was up to in those days. I was the youngest and a regular little ragamuffin running wild, doing exactly what I pleased. Besides, they had too many other things to worry about.

Night came on and I had to pass a small cemetery on my way home. The children I had been playing with insisted that a ghost lived in the cemetery and it would certainly go after me. We'd call them haints back then. The kids dared me. They taunted me to try it. I couldn't make it home, they said. I'd get scared and come back to them.

There was a wooden walk past the cemetery and it was raised over a particularly low spot of ground. As I started tiptoeing ever so softly along the shaky slats in this raised section, something or someone rose up from the walk in front of me.

Two dark arms reaching for me—suddenly they kick up wildly. I jump back. And then a bleating sound beckons me to come closer. See what might happen, it says. The dark and the shadows play nasty tricks on six-year-olds. I stay back.

Still, I don't want to give up so easily. I never can and couldn't then either. If I've got to choose to lose to something or someone, it won't be to those "friends" back down the walkway jeering and insisting that I can't make it. I know I have to make it.

I always seem to choose to fight those "ghosts" of the unknown. And that night I retreat a little back down the walk to wait. And to watch. My heart beats fast. Gathering courage, I run forward, screaming out at the top of my lungs.

"Aaaaaaaaaaaaaa," I holler, and charge up as the ghost rises to grab me. I keep right on going to grapple with it.

Poor thing.

My haint is a calf with its hind legs caught between broken boards on the walkway. The sound and movement of my footsteps has frightened the struggling animal. Obviously, it's been trying to escape for some time. It was probably more afraid of me than I ever was of it.

I knew even then that I had won an important contest. Funny, but all ghosts in my life look a little like scared calves caught by their hind legs.

That reminds me of the time the nose of my Northrop Gamma caught fire when I was heading for New York and about 12,000 feet in the air above Indianapolis.

The gas tank is inches away but I don't jump...yet. Ten miles from the Indianapolis Airport, I radio the tower to have firefighting equipment ready. The cockpit is far back enough. I think I can make it.

I point the nose downward for my descent and the smoke just misses me. Fire has always frightened me. The field is cleared for one of the fastest landings I'll ever make in my life. I never even try to put my flaps down. They've been giving me trouble, and what I don't need is more trouble. The fire is enough.

The smoke is thick and the plane is hot, very hot. The airport's barely in my sight. I'm concentrating on the moment, not even the immediate future. Death wasn't something I feared. But I've always insisted that what would push me out of a plane in midair is a fire. Now it doesn't. As my wheels touch down, suddenly I can't even see as much as I had seen seconds before.

I'm level with the nose, the flames, and the smoke. The runway, I know, is short. I roll, unable to stop short of the field of dry grass at the end of the runway. The grass catches. Flames leap in every direction, but the plane doesn't explode.

I jump to the ground, and for once I leave everything behind, even my cosmetics case. That's when my story goes from bad to worse—not horrible, just worse in a what-else-could-possibly-happen-next fashion.

I broke my toe in the fall. Can you believe that I emerged unscathed by the fire, unharmed by the awful smoke, and then had the misfortune to break my toe? Oh, but it hurt. And I was so frustrated. Moral: Don't raise hay alongside air strips and don't jump from burning airplanes without knowing how to land properly, I guess.

I was probably born near Muscogee, Florida, but I'll never know the truth of it. A priest, a certain Father Sands, whom I tried to contact years ago to get to the bottom of my birth story, died in an insane asylum.

Mama told me when I had been born and I always took it for granted and presumed it was correct—in the month of May. They—my foster parents—were never sure about the date in May, so somehow or other, we all picked the eleventh. I don't think they accurately knew the year of my birth because I used to ask Mama in later years. And when I got my first passport to go to Europe about 1929, I calculated that I was about nineteen years old. I needed an affidavit of birth in lieu of the birth certificate no one had, so I went to Pensacola, Florida, to check dates as carefully as I could. No one knew anything. So on the affidavit I chose the oldest possible age and added four years to my life. That's one of the reasons why the year of my birth varied on official reports from 1905 to 1908. I tried to subtract those four years at one point but people accused me of being ashamed of my age.

Being an orphan never bothered me until 1936, when I was about to marry Floyd. I thought he should know as much about me as anyone could, so I went south again and got letters from the two people still living who might have more facts than I had. I gave those letters to Floyd in an envelope sealed with a quarter imbedded in wax. On the outside, in my own scrawly handwriting, I wrote, "This is for you Floyd. I have never read the contents. You can burn it or read it as you wish. I love you very much. Jackie." Floyd chose not to read them then or to burn them either but, instead, handed them back to me.

Truthfully, I didn't want to know what the letters said about me. As a young girl I used to ask myself: am I illegitimate? Who were my real parents? Why would a mother give away her child? But having gone through my childhood never knowing exactly what happened or why I was never officially adopted by anyone, not even my foster family, the letters didn't hold much sway over me. I didn't care what they said. I realize that might sound strange, but what could the knowledge have added to my life then? More important, what could it have taken away from me? But I thought Floyd had the right to know. The sealed envelope with those letters stayed sealed in our lock box for more years than I care to count at this point in my story. Call it a testament to will, if you want. Or perhaps it was more of a sign of the love and respect Floyd and I shared.

After we moved to Millville when I was a small child, my family started doing a little better. With chip money my father and brothers could earn, we ate fresh vegetables and occasionally some meat. I can remember bologna being cause for celebration. We moved up the ladder of so-called success and acquired furniture—if you could call it that. Broken-down chairs, cast-off, rickety tables, a mattress my foster parents had to stuff with excelsior, those fine, curled wood shavings.

Have you ever seen a mojo lamp? It's made by shoving a hollow corn stalk into a bottle with a little oil on the bottom. A piece of cloth, preferably wool if you've got it, is inserted through the stalk to act as a wick. Well, we got ourselves a mojo lamp.

In my ranch house living room in Indio, California, I had the biggest lamps you could ever imagine. They were beautiful and picked up the coloring in the house fireplaces. Whenever I turned on a light, I'd think of how my foster family had been able to sit back and sit around that goddamn mojo lamp. Not me.

Glennis Yeager

(GENERAL CHUCK YEAGER'S WIFE)

Small things would have been lost in Jackie's ranch house down in Indio, California. Lamps were ten times the size that you would normally dream a lamp needed to be. The furniture was in proportion. Huge. It was all beautiful and I learned a lot from Jackie about decorating. She had a rug, for instance, that she and Floyd built a room around. That thing was just huge. Beautiful too. The fireplace was made of uranium rock and they had this black light on it. There was all this color in the room. It was absolutely fabulous.

The men in my family worked fourteen hours a day in the summer. Winter hours were shorter because of the shorter daylight hours, of course. And the old men? Well, some of them were like Grandpa Whiskers. He'd sit out front of that company store and tell stories all day. Some of them weren't so nice.

There I am, not more than six or seven at the time. I have a belly button, he tells me, because an Indian shot me in the stomach with an arrow. In my excitement over being shot, Grandpa Whiskers says, I sat down too suddenly and right on the blade of an ax. All the girls would cringe at this point in the story. I'd try hard not to. In sitting on this ax, we became girls, not the boys we must have been at birth. Being a girl is a punishment for carelessness. It's a story that sticks with me, I know, even when I no longer believe in his "wisdom" or worry about what I could or should have been.

I'm proud of my sex but I've always preferred the company of men. Men liked me. I liked being with them. I was short-tempered with women friends and especially with women who couldn't seem to put their own lives in order. It was unfair, of course, but it's true.

It never dawned on me not to do something because I was a

woman. I just went in there and competed with men because I wanted to fly, and I had to keep on flying. I thought nothing of approaching men like Vincent Bendix, the airplane manufacturer for whom the transcontinental air race was named, to explain my position: "I can fly as well as any man entered in that race." I didn't see it as being boastful so much as speaking the truth. I learned through hard work and hard living that if I didn't speak the truth about myself, no one else would fill in the missing pieces.

I never let my insecurities stop me and I guess I'm lucky in that way. Or perhaps people like Grandpa Whiskers made my determination a quality based on more than luck.

During my early years of flying, just as now, the jobs as test pilots and airline pilots went to men, not women. The chances were that if a woman had been selected for this training, before she had returned a profit on the heavy investment in such training, she would have converted herself into a wife and mother and stopped working.

A woman in the air, therefore, had the choice of flying around in a light plane for pleasure or of obtaining for herself fast, new, and experimental equipment and determining the maximum that could be obtained from using it. I followed the second course. The objective in every one of my flights was to go faster or farther through the atmosphere or higher into it than anyone else and to bring back some new information about plane, engine, fuel, instruments, air, or pilot that would be helpful in the conquest of the atmosphere.

GETTING MY BEARINGS

When I was racing, there wasn't any thought of food. In a small box inside the cockpit I'd carry a half-filled cola bottle with a glass straw in it. Filled bottles would overflow with expansion at higher altitudes and the straw allowed me to take a sip without detaching my oxygen mask. The old-fashioned kind had tubes that went over your cheeks, under your chin. Your mouth was uncovered. I'd take a few small-sized all-day suckers to keep my mouth moist.

There was practically no time for anything in those Bendix races. Nothing but the necessities of flying. The cockpit was small and what little space was left over after I climbed in was filled with instruments. You're buckled in and buckled down. With a helmet on your head and your face partially covered with that mask and long tube leading away from it, you looked like a man from Mars. Or in my case, I've got to say *woman*.

There was no chance to move from that basic position. Feet were occupied with pedals. One hand was on the stick. The other was free to radio, change gas-tank feeding lines, or study the map. An extra gas tank was just back of my head. My maps were always arranged in a concertina'd folding book form and tied to my knee by a long string.

And that map had a lot of marks on it—some of them indicating when I'd be needing gas changes, what I could expect to see when I could catch sight of the earth. The maps helped me dead-reckon my way into the winners' circle on more than one occasion.

19

I always carried a small tank of helium because I had a bad ear and on descent the helium helped. That cockpit would get terribly hot near ground level, but I'd always be clothed for outside temperatures of many degrees below zero—which is exactly what the outside temperatures would reach up high. I could zip or unzip my flying suit to let in air or clothe myself tighter to keep warm. The zippers were like little vents. You see them on flying suits today too.

Now, just try sitting strapped to a chair in one position for several hours and you'll get a faint notion of what I'm talking about. And the sitting was the smallest part of it. I was a woman in a man's world. There were a few of us—but not many. I'm feminine but I can't say that I was ever a feminist. I remember when I crash-landed at Bucharest during that London race after hours of hard flying without having had any food or water and being nearly chilled to the marrow with cold. I refused to get out of the plane until I had removed my flying suit and used my cosmetic kit. That was feminine and it was natural for me. It gave me the pick-up I needed and I wasn't ashamed to do it. I didn't want to be a man. I just wanted to fly. This doesn't mean that I'm not extremely proud of what women have been able to do in aviation. Women are just as capable as men in the air. Sometimes they are more capable, in fact. But I do believe that women, especially women like me, are many-sided creatures. As the poets might say, we're diamonds with many facets.

OTHER VOICES:

Major General Fred Ascani
(RETIRED UNITED STATES AIR FORCE OFFICER AND AN ACCOMPLISHED TEST PILOT)

I was Director of Flight Test out at Edwards Air Force Base in the fifties, and I had seven prima donnas in my command: Chuck Yeager, Pete Everest, Wolfe, Nash were just a few of the test pilots there at the time. Jackie Cochran was the eighth. You better believe it. You've got to know how to handle prima donnas—don't cross them too often. They are like children of five, six, or seven. They have to know that you love them but they also have to know who's the boss because they are always testing you. Jackie, for instance, had to have things a certain way: precisely aligned. That's a Type A person: neat, orderly, driven by parallel lines; to achieve those records she had to be that way. She was always driven by one objective to the next, wasn't satisfied with what she had achieved, and even when it was painful, she'd push on.

Funny, though. I never asked myself the question: What the heck is this gal doing out here with all these men? That never came up in my mind. We all accepted Jackie. We didn't think of her as a woman when she was flying. But it wasn't because she wasn't feminine when she wanted to be. She could be very soft, very feminine. I danced with her once in Spain and she was as female as any other woman I've put my arms around.

Some women resented Jackie. Why? Because she was a man's woman. Where the men were talking war stories, that's where Jackie Cochran would be. She was an outstanding pilot. In fact, I'd say she was every bit as good as I was and I consider myself a pretty good pilot.

She never knew who her parents were and that always bothered her because we would talk about it. Floyd and Jackie had uncovered some kind of information and it was in this sealed envelope, she told me. Jackie told me that she debated for three days and nights about opening it but in the end decided not to unseal it. But the temptation would have been so strong, I wonder. I think if she were a man, she would have opened it.

There were two women in my childhood who turned me in my tracks. I met the first when I was sent off to school. Someone was worried about the authorities cracking down, and that's where I was supposed to be: in school.

Her name was Anna Thompson and I'll never forget her even though we were in each other's company for only three days. On that third day Miss Thompson whipped me with a ruler. Why, I don't remember. I was always a feisty, independent child. Perhaps that was it. But because of the child I was and the woman I would become, it wouldn't have been like me not to hit back under such circumstances. So, of course, I did. Then I ran out that door immediately, and a year passed before the subject of school became a serious issue again.

What I learned that year was probably just as valuable as what I might have picked up sitting in a classroom. I hunted, fished, crabbed, and "stooped to conquer" chickens, as they say. I perfected what became a locally notorious way of catching some local farmer's chickens. Using a piece of corn with a hole bored through it and a long string through the hole, I'd attach myself to the other end of the string. Coaxing the chicken to eat the corn, I'd draw it toward me and its untimely death. I know: the chicken didn't belong to me. But neither did the corn belong to the chicken.

I was always looking for a handout. One day I wandered over to a group of people preparing a pig at the other side of the camp. They were making "chitlins," I remember. You do that by cleaning the small intestines of a pig in running water, cutting them up, and then boiling them for days. After all that, chitlins can be fried, but in the meantime the odor is revolting. Tripe, made from the lining of a cow's stomach, is the aristocratic relative of "chitlins," but I've never been able to stomach either. Yuk.

October was always the best eating month. We'd have chicken and oyster roasts and my hands became tough and quick from killing, cooking, and shucking. I was better than the boys in my crowd. We'd pile oysters on live coals on the beach and add layer upon layer of chicken parts, oysters, late corn, squash, more oysters, and whatever else we could find in the nearby farmers' patches. What feasts they were! I can almost taste them now.

When I was flying planes like the unmerciful Gee Bee in the London-to-Australia race, other pilots (male) would wonder where I found such strength in my hands and arms. Believe me, oftentimes those early ships took more muscle than skill to stay in the air. And in looking back at my life, I suspect that I started my phys-ed program as a preschooler.

I can still see the other woman clearly: Miss Bostwick. She's the new schoolteacher in town and she's got to be the most beautifully dressed woman I've ever seen. She's from Cincinnati and speaks with a northern accent I've never heard before. She's tough, I can tell after a few days in her classroom, but she's fair. The children who misbehave expect to have their knuckles slapped, but it never happens to me. I've fallen in love.

"You live near here, don't you?" she asks.

"I don't know," I answer stupidly.

"If you'll bring firewood to my room in the afternoons, I'll pay you ten cents a week," she says.

I'm thrilled. Just thrilled. That afternoon I chop wood, break it up into little pieces, and carry it up into her room. She lives in a cozy little palace to my way of seeing back then. It's in a two-story rooming house and she just has a room there. But her little stove, the beautiful bed, and a pot of prunes simmering make a long-lasting impression on me. It is the first time I've ever seen a screen on a window. She gives me some prunes to eat and they taste so good.

Every afternoon after that I pile wood for her until her bedroom is in danger of becoming stacked solid. I don't want to stop. I want an excuse to return...to go every day. It's warm and wonderful and I look for every reason to be there, to be near this woman.

One day she gives me a little dress to wear. I think it is new. My first new dress. Probably from a Sears, Roebuck catalog and nothing special to look at, but it's never been worn by another. It's not a hand-me-down and it's not made from an old flour sack.

Later, Miss Bostwick would read to me in the afternoons. I realized then that her books were far beyond my comprehension, but word after word, I was learning to read. I can still hear *David Copperfield* in Miss Bostwick's voice. At the end of the school year she presented me with my first comb and brush set and a promise that she would return for the next school year. I wondered about that but I'd wait.

About that time I started going to Catholic Mass whenever the priest came to town, which was usually once a month. My family never came with me and it was obvious that it wasn't their faith which determined my going. They would send me alone and I liked it. Why was I there? I didn't know, but going made me feel good, and the priest knew my name.

"Do you hear anything about Jackie's family these days?" a friend of my foster mother's is asking. I'm within earshot but not sight.

"Not a word," my mother answers.

Silence. My heart beats faster.

My mother continues. "And I'm going to keep it that way. Jackie doesn't know she's any different from the others."

But I always knew I was different from the others.

MORE THAN ONE WAY TO ESCAPE

AROUND 1913

My heaven in those days was a very physical place with golden gates and streets paved with jewels. Even when I was older and piloting airplanes, I used to worry that our Heavenly Father might insist that I float around slowly like a crowned helicopter in a vacuum, which would have been hell for a restless soul like me. If not hellish, it would certainly be something less than heavenly. I saw heaven as an action-packed place.

I didn't know about airplanes then. So I couldn't foresee the kind of action I'd add to my fantastic picture of golden gates, jeweled streets, good food. It took the Roosevelt Flying School to complete my picture. But by age seven I knew instinctively that if I were to reach some measure of heaven on earth, it wouldn't be anywhere near Sawdust Road.

The only song I ever learned as a child, and the one I occasionally sang as an adult with all the gusto of my youth and the fine hillbilly accent few friends heard, goes like this:

I'm livin' on a mounting that's bountiful supplied, and
I'm drinkin' from a founting that never shall run dry, for
I'm dwellin' in Bueler Land.

"Bueler Land" bore no resemblance to the towns I grew up in and from where I was always planning escape. I tried running

25

away with gypsies, staying out in the woods all night with a neighbor boy and his older sister—no one looked for us—and once I decided to hitch my wagon to the stars in a local circus.

That bearded lady and few scrawny elephants camped at the edge of town were much better company than my foster mother. Though her life was never easy, Mama always seemed to be able to make it worse for herself and everyone around her. She'd take out a lot of her frustrations on me. Will-o'-the-wisp and outsider that I was, I probably made her angry because she couldn't seem to touch me with her foul moods, and when she tried to whip me for "bad conduct," I once found a chunk of firewood to help us "talk" things out. That day I raised my hand holding the stick to hit back, she took several steps away from my life forever.

But the day the circus came to town, the steps I needed to take to grow away from her became more tangible to me than ever before. I honestly saw that motley carnival crew as my future. When they leave, I leave, I said to myself. Their small-town Florida circuit looked like the big wide world to me. And while I don't remember telling a soul of my plan, I do know that the elephant trainer indulged my fantasies. The big slow beasts didn't frighten me, and that world I had only glimpsed on the sides of the passing train boxcars was going to be mine one way or another. The letters on the sides of the boxcars had offered me my first lessons in the alphabet as well as good clues to what adventures lay in wait for me out there.

Have you ever felt that giddiness that comes when you are on the verge of something good or even great? That energy seems to bounce off the roof of your mouth and want to break out in a nervous giggle, not a laugh but a giggle. Well, I had it when the circus came to town and it stayed with me, caught right there in my throat, drying my mouth.

I was going away.

I hung around for hours and hours, feeding and watering the elephants, making friends with the poor lady who earned her living by the hair on her chin. I finally fell asleep on a pile of straw, and in the morning I awoke all by myself. Tents, people, animals, everything was gone. Someone had put a sack over me. Funny, but I don't remember begrudging them for leaving me, but I do recall that taste of giddiness over the cupful of adventure I had almost had: the escape that had eluded me. It was still there. If not then, well, someday I'd go. And one day I'd even ride an elephant in Madison Square Garden, thanks to Floyd's respect for my childhood fantasies. His sense of adventure always found its outlet in me, and my dream of riding an elephant in the circus would one day come true.

In the meantime, I'll never fully understand why my Miss Bostwick came south that next year and took me in her arms. All I know is that she became the greatest positive influence on my early life. From her I learned how to take care of myself, to stay clean and neat in spite of the sneering I always received from my sisters. I learned love from Miss Bostwick when she touched me. But I learned how to turn my back to what others thought—to turn my back on them if that's what had to be done.

My first hair ribbon—that comb and brush set—those hours of reading together in the afternoons—the prunes. I wanted desperately to thank her many years later for showing me that the rest of the world was out there for me. I went to Cincinnati to find her, my very own Miss Bostwick, and called every Bostwick in the telephone directory with no luck. I wanted to see her lovely face again and put my arms around her in the same way she had hugged me. But she was never to be found.

When she stopped teaching after that second year of my schooling, my formal education stopped too.

Informally, I never stopped learning.

I like to tell others that I passed through the School of Hard Knocks of which there are no real graduates because you simply keep on learning until you die.

When the mill shut down again, we moved out of our company-owned house and into an abandoned shack not far from the black section of town. There was an empty attic— empty except for the bats and bedbugs—and I liked to sleep outside when the weather was warm. I could have had my own "St. George" bed if I wanted one but I didn't. A "St. George" bed is sort of a shelf of rough boards built out from a wall with legs under only the outer edge. Yes, there's a mattress of sorts. I chose to sleep outside rather than in an attic bedroom where I'd battle the bats and bugs or on a bed which hardly deserved sainthood.

Outside, I discovered what fun the blacks had on Saturday nights when they played boogie-woogie music and ate those awful chitlins. There was a tall tree just outside their two-story rooming house, and up in it I found a perfect perch near a second floor window. I would climb up into that tree—at least thirty feet into the air—and watch them dance and boogie into the night.

A one-eyed black man—his name is Fish-eye—plays the piano. Lilly, a black woman who everyone knows keeps company with the white banker in Panama City, leads off the dance. It's wonderful. They drink and dance and sing and no one at home misses me. They think I'm outside sleeping as usual.

I always leave home just as dusk is disappearing into night and I negotiate the distance to my tree quietly. Bare feet make climbing a cinch, no problem. I'm like a cat up there and so very comfortable.

One night I fall asleep and off my perch sometime before dawn. What a shocker. I still remember it but my body forgot very quickly. No bones were broken.

The horizon was something physical then, something to be gauged only by my eyes. Something I could fall out of, or into. Later I would find that my horizons were limited only by my imagination and knowledge. And after I learned how to get higher up into the air than those thirty feet up a tree, my horizons became nearly limitless.

Years after I had fallen from that branch, I thought of the crash and my perch as I was wobbling around at an altitude of 33,000 feet in an airplane. The year was 1939 and I was trying to get another foot or two out of my ship for an altitude record. I looked down over the left side of my cockpit almost into Mexico and over the right side into Los Angeles.

Thirty-three thousand feet doesn't sound very high by today's standards, but in a fabric-covered biplane without heating, without pressurization, and without an oxygen mask, I nearly froze to death. The pipestem between my teeth through which I tried to get an oxygen supply from a tank with a connecting tube was totally inadequate. I became so disoriented for lack of oxygen that it took me over an hour to get my bearings to make a landing. Perhaps that's why I dreamed I was up in the tree hearing boogie-woogie music. The difference between the pressure my body was accustomed to on the ground and the atmospheric pressure at 33,000 feet was so great that a blood vessel in my sinus ruptured. What a headache! But what a feeling of accomplishment. Besides establishing the record I wanted, my test flying led airplane manufacturers to insist on cabin pressurization as well as mandatory use of the oxygen mask above certain altitudes.

There has hardly been a race or a record flight I have flown in which I haven't tried out something new or experimental. Sometimes it was a new design of plane or wing, sometimes a new engine or a new fuel, an oxygen mask, a chicken in a cage. Once it was a pulsating seat to help maintain the body's circulation. I've tried new helmets, new masks, and new spark plugs. And the information I was able to gather about these gadgets gave me some of my greatest satisfactions.

But I wouldn't have been able to open my eyes, ears, and all my senses to that kind of test flying if I hadn't learned how to be ready for anything life handed me as a little girl. For instance, I remember seeing my situation at age seven as full of great promise and fortune. Fortunate, it wasn't.

Pregnant women at the mill began to come to me for help somewhere around my seventh birthday. They would pay me ten cents a day to stay with their families before and after their babies were born. I'd cook meals standing up on a box to reach the stove top and I'd take care of the house, wash diapers, and watch the other children. It was good money when I got it— which wasn't very often because most of the time they paid me in promises. But I never stopped believing in those promises and I learned how to cook, how to deliver a baby, and how not to live your life.

I remember one young girl, who must have been barely eighteen and expecting her first child. She asked me to be with her out in a cabin in the woods she shared with her husband. He was a logger and had gone into the forest to cut trees and wouldn't be home.

It's dark. Raining buckets and I'm scared because her labor pains have begun. I know I've bitten off more than even I can chew. Me, who made a lifetime habit of insisting I could do things I knew nothing about. (I think this attitude is the right one, however.)

She wants me to fetch a neighbor. I'm more worried about getting lost in the woods with the rain coming down in sheets. We wait. We work together. And the baby is born on that dark,

damp, rainy night. A seven-year-old midwife and an eighteen-
year-old mother. I was no fool even then and I knew that hers
wasn't the life for me.

Once just before Christmas in Millville, I worked really hard,
washing diapers, taking care of children, helping mothers do all
those miserable chores no one else clamors to take on. I earned
about $6.00 and I was supposed to have the money, but at
Christmastime people had even less money to pay me than at
other times of the year. No one came through with the cash, and
I wanted a little stove that was for sale in the commissary. I was
tired of standing on the box to cook and this little stove was real.

The stove brought me into the store, but what kept me coming back was a doll. For every twenty-five cents worth of toys
you bought at the commissary at that time of year, you received
a chance on the most beautiful doll I had ever seen. It sat in the
showcase.

I stood in front of that showcase until I had almost worn my
nose off. That doll was marvelous and I was sure it would go to
one of the wealthier children in town. I looked at the children of
the mill foremen as being wealthy then. They really weren't
much richer than anyone else in town but even that little bit
more was a lot to me then.

Anyway, I was determined to get more money somehow to
take a chance on this doll. I started thinking that I might win it.
To a small girl, all things seem possible.

For three weeks before Christmas I drew water from wells
for women until my hands were almost bleeding. Perhaps I
exaggerate here, but I really don't think so. I remember being so
short still that if I let too much water into the bucket and leaned
over to pull it up and out, my worries about falling over and in
were to be taken seriously. That meant I'd have to fill buckets
half full to lighten the load and carry twice as many to earn my
pay. But earn it I did: fifty cents.

Now, you didn't get very much for fifty cents, but I didn't
care what it bought. What was more important to me were those
two coupons that came with the purchase. I filled them out and
put them into the box.

On Christmas Eve you can just imagine my emotions.
Keyed up, holding my breath, the anticipation is killing. The

drawing is held and believe it or not, I win. I win the doll. I'm in heaven. She's mine. Curly blonde hair, brown eyes, painted cheeks, pearly skin, real doll clothes. She's a beauty.

Mama and Papa are looking at me strangely. What is it? What can the problem be now? It's my sister Mamie. No, it's not Mamie this time. It's Mamie's little girl, Willie Mae. Mamie was married then, had a baby already, and Willie Mae must have been about two at the time.

Doesn't little Willie Mae deserve the doll for Christmas, Jackie? Mama and Papa are asking me.

You're too old to play with dolls now, aren't you? they're telling me. Then they demand.

"Give the doll to Willie Mae," they insist.

"I won't," I answer. "It's mine. I won it."

"You will," they say. And they win—this time.

I have a memory like an elephant and a wrong is something to be righted. Years after I was made to relinquish my doll to Willie Mae, she called me. I was earning my own money at Saks Fifth Avenue in Antoine's beauty salon and living right there in New York City.

Willie Mae was grown-up, broke, and had a child of her own. She needed a fresh start for her life. I decided to offer her one—but on one condition.

I wanted my doll back.

Was I stubborn? Perhaps. But even as an adult I had gritted my teeth to think of what an injustice I had endured that Christmas Eve. It had broken my heart.

When Willie Mae and her daughter arrived in Manhattan, they returned my doll. And I gave all three—Willie, her child, as well as the doll—new clothes and new lives. In fact, the doll was refurbished and became part of a collection I am very proud of. I've collected dolls from all over the world. They were never simply toys in my eyes. Least of all, that very first one.

I wanted to keep it near me for a lot of very good and probably very complicated emotional reasons. The least of them being that it was one of the very first prizes of my life. And no one should have been able to take that away from me.

No one.

MONEY = INDEPENDENCE

1914–1915

You guess your speed in the air by the sound of the wind in the wire struts of the wings on your airplane. When you want to land, you put your nose down and get the speed up until those strut wires signal softly but clearly: we are ready. Then you pull the nose up just enough to stop this singing. You judge your letdown as you approach the airfield by the position of the engine with respect to the horizon. That makes your eyesight extra important. The only instruments you have are a little compass and the tachometer, which tells you whether or not your ship is level. You don't want to rotate too badly.

A pilot's own ears and eyes are crucial. In fact, when I first learned to fly, one eye was always on the lookout for a suitable pasture or beach for landing in case of engine trouble. Forced landings were the rule, not the exception.

Those early days were really pioneering times—and they were so interesting.

I once had a Travelair which had an engine that couldn't hold on to its own valves. They kept falling out and to have them re-seated was very expensive. Fifty-two forced landings in that plane in the span of a year kept me on my toes, but what good flying it gave me too. When a valve would drop, I'd just put down and hire a mechanic to go out to whatever field featured my stranded plane.

I stayed away from populated areas, looked for beaches or

farms, all the time learning how to handle my own steam. It's never a good idea to get too excited in a crisis. And I never did.

But from my vantage point here forty years later, I'm disappointed. That coolness I acquired was probably the cause of my missing all my own good opportunities to parachute-jump from a plane. That's something I never did. And something I would have liked to experience.

But those valve-dropping ships, dead-stick landings, and farm barnstorming days gave me the most wonderful training a pilot could have. Rough it might have been, but I loved it. I loved it for itself, for the *feelings* it gave me.

Pity the man or woman who doesn't have the chance to love the way I loved flying.

But earlier I loved my job in the cotton mill in Columbus, Georgia, too. It made me happy. I was pushing a four-wheeled cart up and down the aisles, delivering spools of bobbins to the weavers. These weavers worked by the piece, and in this particular mill, the pieces were pieces of cotton duck cloth. An expert could handle six looms. I wasn't an expert at the age of eight but decided I would be one day. The working conditions were despicable; the pay was delightful. That's why I was happy: money. The money made me happy because of the freedom I knew it could buy.

We were in Columbus because life in the shadow of a darkened Florida sawmill had become terribly bleak. At the point of near starvation, my foster parents had finally picked up the pieces, packed us up and onto a train for Georgia. We changed trains in Dothan, Alabama, where I remember sitting in the cold station for what seemed like an eternity. One blanket, cut into six or seven smaller strips, won't keep cold out, especially when you are barefooted and stockings are something you see only on other children's legs.

The word had spread through Northern Florida that good jobs were easy to be had in the Georgia cotton mills. And it was the truth, of sorts. "Good" is the critical adjective in this instance because "good" is a word that requires a real stretch of the imagination when you use it in the same breath with that southern cotton mill scene of 1914, 1915.

My whole family obtained these "good" jobs, but I think I

valued the pay, six cents an hour, twelve hours a night, more than anyone else. My money, unlike theirs, held the promise of hope. Hope for an honest-to-goodness better life was not something my foster family considered very often. They were all too exhausted trying to make the ends that existed meet while I was always scheming for something more.

I was supremely happy, if you can imagine that. The money and the independence were exhilarating. I would deliver spools to the weavers even though I wasn't as tall as the cart I pushed. It was the money that kept me moving. At the end of my first week, I had earned $4.50 for myself before Mama claimed it as her due. But I was no dummy, and while mathematics was never my strong suit, the next week I handed her $3.00 and kept the rest for myself.

I bought my first pair of shoes from a peddler. Of course, aged eight, I picked a pair of high heels. The adult in me was dying to be recognized, but the heels were hardly practical for my nightly runs behind the cart. Even bare feet were better than trying to balance myself in those heels. So, the next week, I added a pair of low shoes to my wardrobe. My love for shoes started there and then.

In two months time I earned the job of repairing the warp. The warp is in a huge roll at the back of the loom. In the weaving process, it's the yarn that extends lengthwise through the loom and it's got to be straightened out before a weaver can cross it with the woof. I'd run from loom to loom and weaver to weaver fiddling very fast with my fingers to keep the pace from slowing down. Weavers earned their pay by the piece, and the last thing they wanted to do was to have to stop to repair and ready their own warp. They liked me a lot because I hustled and the job paid a whole dollar more a week. My eyesight was exceptional, they insisted, and my fingers were fast. All our faces would be gray with cotton dust when we emerged from the mill in the morning. I can imagine what our lungs looked like.

Then, while I was still not ten years old, I was promoted to inspection room supervisor, where the cloth was sorted for flaws, folded into bolts, and readied for shipment. Fifteen other children reported and turned to me for help. Being the boss was a role I reveled in. It came naturally to me even when children older than I was were in my crew. I talked. They listened. But they'd question too. "What are you going to be when you grow up, Jackie?" they'd ask me. I never wavered in my response.

"I'm going to be rich," I'd say, knowing even then that they thought I was silly or crazed. "I'll wear fine clothes, own my own automobile, and have adventures all over the world."

They'd laugh. But the laughing wasn't very loud or harsh. I knew that they knew there was more than a small kernel of truth in my boasting. Because I was certain that's where I was going, I felt no embarrassment about my big dreams. No dreams, no future. They could laugh, but most of my mill friends wanted as little from life as they were destined to get.

On Sundays I'd walk down Broad Street, the main drag of Columbus, window-shopping, never spending. Then I'd go back to the peddler to buy. A georgette blouse. A colored corset to go over. A black wool skirt and always those high heels when I was out for my stroll. I must have looked like a midget clown parading along in my costume. But it wasn't Halloween candy I was looking for. It was a life lived well.

The "good" money didn't last long. Whole families of children worked all night along with me. The lighting was poor. The ventilation, bad. And the sanitary conditions, just terrible. There was no rest room and no place to sit down from six o'clock in the evening to six o'clock in the morning. You were given a half hour break at midnight for a bite to eat, but I used my time for sleep, which was probably a mistake.

Off your guard in that place could put you in an awfully dangerous position. And one night it happened. I didn't see him coming, but a foreman was suddenly over me and pinching in a way that no little girl should ever be pinched. My reaction was immediate and not surprising. What surprised me was his reaction.

My fist flew up and I hit him squarely on the nose. Hard.

He jumped back and then backed away, shocked. He never touched me again. What I don't quite understand is why he didn't have me fired.

Labor unions were really needed in the cotton mills when I was a child. The management in those southern operations had a lot to learn, so when the time came, I paid my dollar for a union membership card. A strike was called and all hell broke loose when twenty-seven mills were shut down. I confess, I was one of those kids who threw the bricks and added to the general mayhem.

For three months I spent my days roaming the streets, trying to collect enough bottles to buy my way into "Skeeter Flats," the local movie theater, which ran lots of high-action, serial adventures. Twelve Coca-Cola bottles found and returned to the store brought me one nickle and bought me one admission to the nickelodeon.

Proper people didn't go to "Skeeter Flats," though. Later, when I was fourteen, I found out that a "skeeter" to a proper northern "damyankee" was a mosquito. But then, I didn't mind the mosquitos in "Skeeter Flats." The adventures on screen for a girl hell-bent on seeking such adventure in life always outweighed any disadvantages, bug bites, or anything else that might come along.

When those old-fashioned, high-action serial movies played, nickelodeons like the one in Columbus would pack people in. At the end of each episode, when the heroine was left lying on that edge, tied to those tracks, that tree, that cliff, on the stake, I could put myself on that point along with her. To feel what she was feeling became a real goal for me.

PUSHING IT

1916–17–18

Mrs. Richler was no heroine, but she had something I wanted. She was a small dark-haired woman who ran three beauty shops in Columbus, and I landed on her doorstep one morning because the beans and fatback offered at union headquarters had become disgusting and tiresome. I wanted my old job back because I missed the money, but in lieu of that, I wanted the shot at a future I just couldn't see anywhere in the mill. Mrs. Richler had it within her power to give me such a chance.

"I'm quick with my hands," I boast. Oh, and her house looks so nice. I can see through the open door behind her. "I'm an excellent cook. I've been cooking for years. I'll clean, care for children, and do just anything you need to have done. You really need me, Mrs. Richler."

My way had been prepared by one of the female foremen at the mill, and there was probably little need for me to embellish the way I embellished that day. The list of accomplishments I reeled off as real on my resume must have been laughable to her. I added and subtracted information at will, as it suited me. I didn't see it as lying so much as surviving. She hired me.

I moved in with the Richlers—wife, husband, and six children—when I was about ten or eleven. Their house was lovely and they were orthodox Jews, so on their Sabbath, when they were forbidden to work or cook, I'd prepare the kosher meals. I became quite good at it as friends of mine from later in

37

life will attest. On weekdays, I was up at 5 A.M., helping with breakfast, cleaning, and then we would be off to one of their shops, where I'd spend days sweeping out beauty booths, mixing shampoos, making hennas, learning how to permanent-wave hair, to make what we called transformations, or small hairpieces, and to color hair. I actually became a dye specialist. Permanents were so new. They'd take twelve to fourteen hours to complete. For this I received my room and board plus $1.50 a week. Much less than the mill had paid, but the Richlers' life held much more for me in the long run. I worked hard at it—*how* I worked!—because I figured I was learning a trade that would get me away from mill life.

"Fancy ladies" were regular customers at the Richlers' salons. We called them "fancy" and fancy they were when we finished with their hair dye or permanent wave, but they made their livings in less than fancy fashion. These "fancy" ladies were actually the prostitutes who always walked in the front door of the shop while "good" women would sneak in the back for an appointment. I really think that the women in Columbus, Georgia, had to be among the last in America to try short haircuts. The local prison for women was called "The Rockpile," and on release from there, a woman always had her hair shorn almost absolutely off her head. That's why if your hair was short, or bobbed, and you lived in Columbus, invariably it meant "The Rockpile" had been in your recent past. Not something to shout about.

One of our regular "fancy" customers was the madam of a "house" of prostitutes in Columbus, but she was so well-spoken and well-read that I was fascinated. I think she became worried about me and what I might want to do with my own life. She didn't want me to have hers.

"It would be easy for a pretty girl like you to earn a living without mixing shampoos or waving hair, Jackie," she told me one day. "But don't do it. You'll lose your self-respect. Work for a living. Get where you are going in life the hard way."

She had done a lot of traveling and would tell me stories about beautiful cities and lovely clothes. Men were a species she understood only too well, and she made sure I listened when she talked about them. I was always spellbound, though. She didn't have to coax my attention.

Mrs. Richler's operators worked on commission and could earn as much as forty percent of their take. I'd help them speed up the beauty process, and they'd tip me out of their commissions. Sometimes at the end of a week I'd be able to count as much as eight or ten dollars pay. So besides learning a business, I was able to earn enough to send some home. Meanwhile, the mill strike was continuing to wreak its misery in people's lives, and my foster family needed every cent I could send.

Two years passed. I wore my hair up to look older than my thirteen going on fifteen years and one day I overheard Mrs. Richler telling a child labor investigator there in the shop that she employed no children under sixteen. She even told this man that she was my legal guardian and she signed something attesting to these facts. A shrewd woman she was, but I was shrewder still. God, did I have guts.

The man from the child welfare board is hardly out the door and the little light bulb in my head is blinking crazily. It's a plan, an outrageous plan. The next thing poor Mrs. Richler knows is that I'm demanding full pay as a beauty operator or I will tell the investigator the truth.

"You know as well as I do that I'm no sixteen years of age," I say. "You've got a child labor problem here, don't you? And when did you sign papers becoming my legal guardian? I know my foster family would never relinquish their rights to me. I mean too much to them in terms of money."

She couldn't believe how ungrateful I was. The poor woman had certainly taken a chance on me, but I had paid back her investment in spades. And I didn't intend to work from early morning to late at night for a meager $1.50 a week—the tips weren't from her—if there was even a sliver of a chance to better my lot. And a lot more it was: as an operator, I knew I could bring in more than $30.00 a week. In 1921 dollars that'd be worth something like $300 now and $30 sure *felt* that way to me. She hesitated, flinched, and wanted to be rid of me, but I had her caught. What devils we both were.

"I know all your clients and they like me. If I have to, I'll take them with me to another shop," I warn. The "fancy" ladies would definitely take my side, I knew.

No answer from her. It all comes tumbling out of me.

"I want regular working hours like the other girls. And I'm not going to mix those dyes or make those transformations in that back room anymore. I can't breathe there and the smells make me sick."

"You're under age, Jackie. No one else will hire you," she says.

"But you've certified that I am over sixteen and that you are my guardian. I'll go back to the investigator if I must. You lied."

Quiet.

"I don't want to do all your cooking and housework anymore," I say. "I want to live my own life."

Perhaps it was mutual respect for each other's power that kept us—the Richlers and me—going for another year. Anyway, at the end of that time, I had saved several hundred real dollars, when a traveling salesman arrived in the shop one morning. He was selling permanent wave machines and was complaining to Mrs. Richler that not enough operators understood the damn process. Why, he had one machine practically sold to a big store in Montgomery, Alabama, when they realized they needed the operator to go along with the machine and backed down on the contract.

Quick. No chance for any mid-sentence pause. Not a second for Mrs. Richler to consider the possibilities inherent for anyone else in her shops, let alone her. There I am. The person he needs to make that sale in Montgomery. A permanent wave expert at (maybe) fifteen.

To get the best performance, to do better than anyone has ever done before, you've got to take chances. Every speed flight which tests something to its extreme has its dangers.

Over the mantel in my New York apartment an oil painting by Orlando Rouland used to hang. It was Rouland's conception of the fabled flight of Icarus from one of the Mediterranean islands to the mainland. Icarus and his father had fashioned wings of feathers and wax.

In the painting Icarus is standing nude and alone on the cliff with a beach below. His wings are outstretched for takeoff. According to the fable, he flew too high, contrary to his father's warnings; the sun's heat melted the wax, the wings disintegrated, and then he fell into the sea.

My husband, Floyd, gave me the picture partly because it was pretty. It was a true symphony in greens, blues, and grays. But the aviation motif of the painting was supposed to serve as a gentle warning to me. Don't try too much, Jackie. Be careful. Make sure your wings of wax and feathers will hold together before you go.

But I like Icarus's attitude better. And I see it so clearly in the attempts at "flight" I made as a very young woman. You can't let fear steal your nerve.

This story about Icarus makes me think about the time I landed on the aircraft carrier *Independence* sitting there in the North Atlantic about fifty or seventy-five miles off the Long Island shore. God, it looked small from where I was up in an A3D two-motored plane built by Douglas. It was a fast plane, not supersonic but fast, and had tremendous range. Commander King was the pilot. I was just along for the ride. Jeez, it was violent.

I was the first woman to land on a carrier like that. We took off from Floyd Bennett Field in the worst fog. Visibility was only about an eighth of a mile and the ceiling was 200 feet. No more. I couldn't believe King would try it, but we got off okay and the weather was clear up above. Then the carrier came into view. So damn small. Sitting out there on the surface of the blue-gray ocean. Made me feel like Icarus. I wasn't worried about the sun melting the wax on those wings. I was worried about all the planes stacking up there in the air, waiting for the green light to land. There were at least 75 planes—hot little fighters, medium-sized bombers, all of us trying to get in and on this flat-topped dot. An intricate mirror system helps. Rubber hooks catch you, but sitting up there, you wonder if the hooks ever miss and what happens when that happens.

It's so violent. A controlled crash. That's what landing on an aircraft carrier feels like. It made me wonder why there weren't more medical reports on broken necks, insides being catapulted apart. Taking off is bad too. You've got to keep your head against the headrest or else. You'd snap your neck otherwise. Now, there's a real jolt. You black out for an instant—others besides me said this was true—but it's not sustained. So fast.

I stood on the deck after we had landed, watching the planes coming in across that flat deck, thinking that airplanes had come so far, so fast.

I was near sixty at the time and someone asked me what I was going to do next. "Drive a hook and ladder fire truck in New York City," I answered, joking. I didn't know wrestling with a Lockheed Starfighter was still in my future.

BLOODY DECISIONS TO MAKE

I was probably fifteen to sixteen when I walked every street in Montgomery, Alabama, until I found the nicest neighborhood in the city. Then I knocked on the door at 12 South Anne Street and asked the startled woman if I could rent room and board. At first she was horrified. But I was determined. I had never lived in a house as elegant as her house was, and I pleaded my case to the limit of my persuasive power.

I lived at 12 South Anne Street for years.

At the store I worked on commission, giving more Nestle permanent waves than Montgomery society could believe and earning more money than even the store manager could feel comfortable about. My taste in clothing had improved since the days of my eight-year-old extravaganza and, what's more, I could afford good things. So Montgomery, Alabama, began to offer me glimpses of other sides of society. I bought a car and through my landlady I made friends with people my own age who could no more imagine life inside a mill or on Sawdust Road than I could imagine the sight of my real mother. I often wonder what she looked like.

I went to college fraternity parties, met men who were educated and interesting and some who were interested in me. But I never lost my compulsion to be totally self-sufficient. In fact, I even learned how to repair the engine on my car. That Model T Ford was such an asset. I absolutely loved traveling, always

42

have and always will. I made sure I understood what it took to keep that car going smoothly. I personally ground the valves on that engine and the engine paid me back for my labors.

One of my customers in the salon at the store was a woman whose name was Mrs. Lerton. She had been the first female to hold public office in the state of Alabama and I was truly impressed, so I always tried to impress her. Mrs. Lerton, whose first name escapes me now, was a judge in the juvenile court and a real power in the community. When she came in for a permanent, I made sure it took me all day. And she didn't seem to mind my dawdling. We would talk and talk.

"Why do you want to be a beautician, Jackie?" she'd ask.

"Oh, I don't know. I guess I just fell into it. I like it."

"You could and you should do more with your life. You're a smart girl and you're so good with your hands," she'd say. Mrs. Lerton taught me how to crochet and do needlepoint, which were both skills I've kept up throughout my life.

"But what else can I do with my background? I never even finished third grade."

"I can get you admitted to the nursing program over there at the Montgomery hospital," she assured me. "You could become a nurse and you'd be a good one," she said, insisting that being a nurse would be much more rewarding than being a beautician. I wondered. But because Mrs. Lerton believed in me and what I could be, I believed in her.

OTHER VOICES:

Ann Wood

(A CLOSE PERSONAL FRIEND AND AN AIR TRANSPORT AUXILIARY
PILOT IN GREAT BRITAIN DURING WORLD WAR II)

Jackie Cochran was very quick to make dramatic decisions. She could walk into a room, survey the situation immediately, and know what to do. Suppose you had a little child who had the sniffles, for instance. Jackie might decide on almost a glance that your child had more than the sniffles and she was in danger of developing pneumonia. It had to be flown to Minnesota right then, right there. You might balk, but nine times out of ten she was right. It takes a special clairvoyance to be able to do that, and she had it. She also had a need to be in charge, to take over, to do something. Her threshold for boredom was very low indeed.

I went to nursing school for three years and the nuns in that Catholic hospital were marvelous. The rituals and discipline couldn't have been better training for me. And spending that concentrated time with good practicing Catholics was especially important. I always suspected that my Catholicism was one of the few links to my real past, so to strengthen this link could only be good for me. The formal academic requirements for entry had been waived for me, as promised. I'm certain that hospital had never admitted a second-grade dropout to the program before. My grades were always terrible but my performance on the job was consistently excellent. I remember being one of the few nurses who had two tours of duty in the operating room because the chief surgeon requested it. Once I assisted at a cesarean section on a midget from the Miller Brothers Carnival. And I can remember teaching some hotshot intern a funny lesson. This guy kept drinking all the milk I set aside for patients, so one night I substituted some mother's breast milk, and when it disappeared, I quietly asked him what had become of that breast milk. He didn't get mad. He just got sick.

I was at ease in the hospital but never comfortable with the sight of blood. It always frightened me, but I'd fight the urge to quit, telling myself that a nurse's life was more valuable to society than a beautician's.

Was it really, though?

On my day off I'd wander through the wards, giving haircuts, manicures, applying a little makeup to the women, and shaving the men with one of those old-fashioned broad-sized razors. They loved it and there were smiles when I showed up with my tools in hand.

When I completed the formal training, I decided not to take the State Board examinations. I just didn't dare attempt that test. I knew I'd fail. My handwriting alone, not to mention my rudimentary arithmetic, would never have allowed me to pass. I suppose I couldn't bear the thought of flunking, losing this race Mrs. Lerton had so invested in. So I used the excuse of an immediate position with a country doctor in Bonifay, Florida. I didn't need to be licensed by anyone to become the Florence Nightingale to the same Sawdust Road people I had grown up with. They needed me, I told myself as well as Mrs. Lerton as I piled my belongings into the Model T.

But the real question was: Did I need Sawdust Road again? Or, could I survive another stint in the hell I had left behind?

The place stinks. The filth is a shocking contrast to what I've learned is right and proper for a man of medicine and his dutiful helpmate, the nurse. That's me. God, the dusty cabinets full of vials and bottles of medicines gone bad, filmed over because no one took the trouble to put caps back on. And those instruments undoubtedly purchased by someone with high hopes for changing the way things were in sawmill towns—instruments and hopes alike were rusted, bent, and broken by a doctor who couldn't do enough and decided that too little was just that, too little. I worried about the prime rule of medicine: "First, do no harm!" I worried about the harm we must be doing to these people by practicing the kind of medicine we seemed to be practicing—and then I'd worry about not practicing any medicine for them at all. It was like the proverbial daisy-petal picking: they need us, they don't need us. There was no way to win.

Then, two incidents in a row helped me pack my suitcase and head out.

The doctor paid me $3.00 a day. One day we were alerted to a mean situation in a logging camp fifteen miles from the office. We get on a logging train and get going. We find a man with a badly crushed leg in great pain, which wasn't really eased by the sight of us with our saw.

Quickly, I build a fire under an old tub and boil water for sterilizing that saw and for cleaning what will soon be a fresh wound. Me, who had never gotten used to seeing someone else's blood, whose stomach still did flip-flops in anticipation of it.

That man lived, though I'll never know why. I stayed with him for four days in the camp, sleeping four-hour stretches in a chair. The woodsmen, who kept vigil by their friend's side, would wake me then to change his dressings and cleanse the wound.

The second encounter which put me to packing was the delivery of a baby to a mother lying on a "St. George" bed. Three children sleeping on pallets in the same room. The only light from a mojo lamp. There I was with neither the strength nor the money to do the smallest fraction of what needed to be done to make those lives any better. That was that.

Mrs. Lerton wasn't wrong about trusting that I could do something serious with my life, but nursing wasn't that something. It wasn't for me. But I never forgot what I learned in nurses' training, and one day it would help me save the life of a future president of the United States.

In Bonifay, I wrestled with my decision to quit but not for too long. That sinking, I'm-in-over-my-head-with-no-chance-of-winning feeling we've all experienced at one time or another was so strong. How I hated that. I felt I was in an emotional quicksand and the physical weight of it all pushed me toward Pensacola, the nearest biggest city, where I knew that beauty shops were bound to be abundant.

In a beauty shop the customers always came in looking for a lift. And unless I really screwed up, they left with that lift.

I could give them that. I could give them hope along with a new hairdo.

THE COURAGE TO SCREAM

Happiness is such a relative thing. A mangy cur with fleas in his fur will be happy and contented when the fleas are removed. But a Fido the Great may sulk until he gets his homogenized milk and ground porterhouse steak. Then he's happy too. But who's happier? The flea-free mutt or the well-fed Fido?

You almost had to have been there to know what such a range of existences did for me. Because of where I came from and then where I went, I ended up understanding intimately one very sustaining line of life: *I could never have so little that I hadn't had less.* It took away my fear. It pushed me harder than I might ever have pushed myself otherwise. The poverty provided me with a kind of cocky confidence and made me relatively happy with what I had—at any given moment. I just couldn't sit still for very many moments.

God helps those who help themselves, I'd say to friends. But does he protect the stupid? they would ask. Jeepers, how else could I have survived all those years of rushing in where even angels feared to tread?

The hitchhikers, for instance, that I had in my Model T Ford are enough to make your skin crawl. On that two-lane road, in the sunshine I found after leaving Bonifay, Florida, I lost all the anxiety it had taken years to accumulate in nurses' training. And one by-product of my mood was: I simply could not pass by a hitchhiker.

47

Once, when traveling between Miami and New York, I let a hiker drive when I was sleepy. He drove until he drove off the road, over the embankment on the side, and rolled us and the car over. We walked away, but not together. I was so angry I wanted to do what the accident hadn't—kill him.

It didn't change my attitude toward hitchhikers, however. And they were all over the southern roads, it seemed.

I'd always pull over to the side of the road in a flash, not bothering to make accurate assessments of these strays, my potential passengers. I think that's what almost got me into trouble on one occasion.

He ran up to the passenger side of my Ford before I could catch a glimpse of him in my rearview mirror. When he hunched down to look over at me behind the wheel, I knew it was a bad idea immediately.

What a face. It was straight off a U.S. Post Office "Most Wanted List" cavalcade of mug shots. He just didn't look safe at all. But I wouldn't give him a hint of my anxiety.

"Hop in," I say.

He says? Nothing. But he opens the door and slides in.

This is bad, I think, as I get the car back into first and out onto the highway again. I start scanning road and town signs for what's next. I move my maps, which are still on the seat, closer to my leg. There's no need for him to see where I'm really heading.

"Sorry I'm not going very far," I explain. "Where're you headed?" I ask.

"Down the road a piece," he answers without much of a glance.

That's it—that's about the sum total of my conversation with the infamous Dutch Shultz, an escaped convict whose face was plastered all over the front page of the newspapers the next morning.

Dutch and I parted company as soon as the Ford pulled us into the next town. He never questioned me about what I was doing there and I never asked him what his plans for the future were.

I don't like to think what complications he could have caused, but the experience didn't stop me from seeing hitchhikers for what they really—and usually—are: people in need of a lift. I once drove a man all the way from Wyoming to Los

Angeles. I guess I simply loved having people around and I'd always talk my head off with anyone about anything.

In Pensacola, I did something I had been considering for a long time. I went to the first phone book I could find, ran my finger down a list of names, and decided on *Cochran*. It had the right ring to it. It sounded like me. My foster family's name wasn't really mine anyway. I continued to support them with money whenever I could send it because they never really moved very far from Sawdust Road. But I wanted to break from them in name. I had my own life, a new one. What better way to begin than with my own name. *Cochran*. Why the hell not?

OTHER VOICES:

Yvonne Smith
(A PERSONAL FRIEND AND
CO-EXECUTOR OF THE COCHRAN ESTATE)

Cochran was the name she chose. That's the story she told me. She created it herself, and earlier in her life I even saw a typed-up account of the story. First versions of *Stars at Noon* carried it. In edited copy it was omitted.

She believed that she was someone's illegitimate child and didn't want to know her background. Her foster family's name wasn't hers, however, so she decided to create her own name. It took a lot of strength to do that as a young girl, but she made no bones about it. I think it adds to the uniqueness of my good friend, Jackie Cochran.

She used to say, "Yvonne, I've pretty much figured out my age." Then every once in a while she'd question herself, "I could have been tall for my age or perhaps it's the other way around, maybe I was short?"

I blame my blindingly good mood for pushing me into a partnership too quickly in a beauty shop in Pensacola. I hadn't made a clear-headed assessment of my new partner's moodiness and how it would affect our clientele, not to mention me. God, she was so sullen. Mrs. Stickley's morose temperament matched the backwoods scene I had so recently escaped. So, the first chance I got, I put my alliance with her on hold and took a job selling dress patterns for a firm that would reimburse me for my mileage in the Model T. I can still see me in that car, on those roads, trying my darnedest to sell patterns—maps at my side and a dictionary on the seat too. The number of new words I learned probably amounted to more than the number of patterns I sold, but I did get a feetfirst course in salesmanship that came in quite handy much later.

For me, a passion for facts, some important and some not, has had to substitute for that formal education. I never lived a day I didn't regret my lack of schooling, worrying about what other people thought, whether they could tell outright, or if someone would catch me counting on my fingers. But as I told my friend Yvonne Smith later in life, "If I had had that decent education and a fine family behind me, I probably wouldn't have accomplished half of what I did in my life. I would have been a teacher, Yvonne. A good teacher but nonetheless, just a teacher."

I can't punctuate or spell to save my life and when I see a semicolon, it might as well be a small intestine for all the use it ever afforded me personally. But I did acquire one habit worth mentioning here: I'd "prospect" for new words constantly. And finding them was just like looking for diamonds in the rough. When I would be driving along, reading at night, or talking to just anyone at all, I was all ears for new gems. Those new jewels would turn up in my speech regularly. Even though the most fundamental rules of grammar confused me endlessly and my handwriting looked like chicken-scratching across a page, I never failed to put my new, four-bit words into the right context. Floyd used to say that my vocabulary was amazing.

Margaret Boylan
(A WOMEN'S AIRFORCE SERVICE PILOT)

Jackie Cochran was very childlike even though she was a grown woman when I knew her. Sometimes she chopped up the language. One day, after she had been repeatedly mispronouncing a word, I can't remember what it was, I said to her, "What's with this word?" She answers me, "Floyd likes me to pronounce it that way. I like to pronounce it that way and, Margaret, I'm going to keep on saying it that way."

I moved from Pensacola to Biloxi, Mississippi, where for a time I operated the beauty salon at the Edgewater Beach Hotel. Then a hurricane sent me back to Mrs. Stickley, because we still shared the beauty shop business. Her mood was a little improved. Being in Pensacola wasn't such a bad deal for me either. Though flying was the farthest thing from my mind then, I took at least one step in the direction of my later life when I began going to dances at the Pensacola Naval Flying School. Names of men I danced with and dated then turned up later with captain and even admiral affixed. They talked flying. I listened.

My rented room was on the ground floor of a private home in a nice residential area. It was midsummer and hot. I arrived home late because I had given a young working woman a permanent after dinner. A taxi trip with a surly driver left me feeling unsettled, so in spite of my exhaustion, I slipped into bed and read for at least an hour. It was so pleasant. I can remember the window being open and finally a break in the still heat that night when the breeze picked up, blowing the curtain at my window.

The door to my room opened onto a combination back porch and dinette, but the window gave me the backyard at a glance. Lovely and wild and way, way back there, nothing but a grove of trees...leaves and branches rustling in the wind. I was exhausted but kept at my book until I collapsed into a deep, deep, dead-limb kind of sleep.

Suddenly, I was awake. Someone was standing over me. His breath was coming hard and fast and I could see his features in the moonlight. He was black and burly and he held what looked like a knife.

I open my eyes wide.

"Don't scream," he says. "I'll kill you if you make a move."

What did I do?

Well, I screamed at the top of my lungs. He hesitated an instant, then dropped the knife and fled out through the window he had obviously used to come in by.

When I stopped shaking and turned on the light, I could see that the knife was an ice pick he had picked up on the back porch. There were cigarette stubs and footprints all over the ground beneath my window. I never did find out whether or not he was the taxi driver who had brought me home, but whoever he was, he had apparently waited for some time for me to go to sleep. I moved into a room upstairs the next day.

A formula for success has many components. It's never precisely the same mixture. And a drop of luck can substitute for a dash of opportunity. But in every well-blended recipe for success, you'll probably find honesty, determination, some skill and experience, as well as a lot of courage.

I screamed partly out of reflex, maybe stupidity, I suppose. But I like to think that part of my scream came from courage.

FORCING DREAMS TO COME TRUE

OTHER VOICES:

Adela Rogers St. John

(A PROMINENT JOURNALIST
WHO INTERVIEWED JACKIE IN 1938)

Jackie Cochran was one of the prettiest women I ever saw. I doubt if her pictures ever did her justice, because pictures couldn't reproduce the big, soft brown eyes and the shimmering golden hair or the lovely clear skin.

When you first see her, you literally gasp with amazement because she looks so little and almost frail and so very, very feminine. Then, as you talk to her, you notice the square jaw, and the fire in the brown eyes, and the steel poise of her body. Shining steel in a jeweled case.

Amelia Earhart, who was her idol, always looked like Lindbergh's younger brother when she wore flying togs, or even street clothes. She looked like a pilot; Jackie Cochran doesn't. But when you get a clear, cold blast of the Cochran personality, you begin to realize why she became one.

When we met, she wore a simple white blouse pinned at the throat with a bright clasp and a gray wool skirt, and blonde curls were caught up high on her head. She talked carefully. I think I

53

have never interviewed anyone who went over each word so thoughtfully, who seemed to feel that the spoken word was, after all, a thing to be respected, not tossed about.

The trade magazines which arrived in the Pensacola shop each day were all talking about a course in the latest hairstyles offered up in Philadelphia. A refresher course, they called it. I called it time to make another break. It was probably about 1928 and I was hungry for the hot styles and "in" scenes I imagined in the Northeast. I promised Mrs. Stickley I'd be back with the latest at my fingertips. We'd wow them in Pensacola.

In Philadelphia, I signed up for the marcel-waving curriculum only because the entire course was too expensive. I plunked down my $60 and discovered that the operation was being run very unprofessionally. No one would show up until 10 A.M. or after, and I knew more about hairdressing than my instructors. So much more that they offered me a job teaching. I taught for nine months and always felt a little guilty about the school's philosophy. They'd high-pressure people who had little chance of becoming skilled beauty operators into buying the course, high-pressure customers into making appointments, and then ask these ill-equipped students to work on unsuspecting clients who assumed they were getting the latest from the greatest. People were charged for these big beauty treatments and then students were charged to work on the customers. And I never did get my $60 back as promised. They were crooks.

I had something else on my mind. And Philadelphia had brought me several steps closer. So, I went back to Pensacola, arranged to sell my share of the shop to Mrs. Stickley, and set out to seek my fortune in the biggest city of all: New York, New York.

Walking down Broadway brought back Broad Street in Columbus, Georgia, especially at night, when all the lights were bright. I had seen my first streetcar in Columbus, but there I was in New York City, where the streets in 1929 featured more than open-air cars: people everywhere going places, making lots of money and doing things—things I wanted to be doing. Though others may look back on '29 as the year of the great crash, it was a year of great growth for me.

I rented a room on the corner of Broadway and 79th Street because it had two big windows looking out onto a park and I didn't have to share bathroom facilities with anyone. It was only $3.00 a week, which was a bargain. The hitch was that I entered and left through a busy kitchen. But it really wasn't so bad. I glued felt to the rim of my door and doorjamb to keep the cooking odors to a minimum and the truth was I liked to cook, so a kitchen at my disposal was a credit not a debit.

Start at the top, Jackie, I say to myself one morning out job-hunting: Charles of the Ritz. But what an irritating snob of a man Mr. Charles was. I made the interview worse by insisting outright that I was an expert at everything. He didn't believe me. I didn't look old enough to be expert at anything, he said.

We were two big egos out to prove who is bigger, better. In fact, I told Charles of the Ritz that not only was I good, I was probably better than he was. That amused him for a minute, but he was not so amused when I wanted fifty percent commission on every customer I had in his salon. I was sure my outrageous demand would end the interview right there when he said, "You'll have to cut your hair."

"Wait a minute. I wouldn't cut my hair for you even if you promised to turn your whole business over to me," I answer.

The next morning he called me at my rooming house. Changed his mind, he said. I wouldn't have to cut my hair. I could have the fifty percent commission. Anything I wanted. Did I want the job or didn't I?

I didn't. I was so stubborn. Still am.

It makes me smile now to think that the cosmetics company I would found several years later, Jacqueline Cochran Cosmetics, still competes with Charles of the Ritz. Charles himself is long dead, of course.

I went to work for Antoine, who was all the rage in New York and whose salon in Saks Fifth Avenue was always packed with customers—customers who liked me, asked for me, and preferred that I follow them to Miami or Europe when the season or a reason demanded that I swing that way. I never hesi-

tated and bought a little Chevrolet to get me to Antoine's salon
in Miami Beach, where I'd often spend months in the winter.
Those trips back and forth were a whiz with me trying to make
record time, breaking my own speed of the year before. I hated
to waste the time traveling, but I also loved to speed. I'd drive
all night, pushing that poor Chevrolet, a good machine, to its
limit. One day, not too far in my future in fact, I'd break even
more important records for a New York-to-Miami trip. But in
another kind of machine.

1932

We were gathering for cocktails and I was standing in the lobby
of a Miami hotel waiting for friends, Cliff and Molly Hemphill,
when I saw him. He was thin, clean-cut, and looked so sure of
himself as he took quick steps toward the coat checkroom. I
looked over at Cliff, who was beside me then, and said, "Why
can't you ever introduce me to men like that one? He looks as
though he does something with his life besides gambling."

"Oh, Jackie, you're incredible," Cliff said, evading my question. The Hemphills always liked to entertain, and they would
invite me to their dinner parties whenever they needed an extra
woman for that extra man. I had met Molly in the salon. I also
liked to gamble and Cliff knew how much I enjoyed returning
the advance of $20 he would give me in a casino. When I lost, I
lost his $20, but when I won, everything above the twenty was
mine to keep. We were all going to a dinner party given by Stanton Griffis. Stanton had been ambassador to Spain and was in
the same New York brokerage firm as Cliff Hemphill.

I looked for my blond, freckle-faced stranger during the
cocktail hour because I couldn't put him out of my mind. And I
went to find him: Floyd Odlum. He could have been a small-
town lawyer on a winter vacation in Miami for all I cared. I felt
sure I had met up with my destiny.

The story goes that while I was beating Cliff's ear about
Floyd on one side of the room, Floyd was being insistent with
Stanton Griffis about wanting to sit next to "a woman who
works for a living." He had no time or energy for mindless chitchat. What he got from me was hardly that.

We talked solidly through drinks and then at dinner, when we were together again. Floyd was staying in the cabana next to Stanton Griffis and told me he almost hadn't come. Stanton had insisted because there was a young woman who worked as a beautician in a local hotel he said Floyd just had to meet. Was I really a beautician? Yes, did he want to make something out of it? My skills as a beautician had bought me a one-way ticket out of poverty, and I'd never forgotten it. I was always proud of my profession. "You'll never have to force a conversation with Jackie," Stanton had told Floyd. And he didn't. Floyd wouldn't let the evening end with dinner, so he invited me into the casino for a bit of gambling. Cliff Hemphill had gotten a bargain with me compared to poor Floyd that night. I lost $100 in chips almost immediately and I wondered whether my luck had gone bad—or good.

Every orphan dreams of marrying a millionaire, but I had no idea at first that Floyd Odlum was worth so much money. I really did not know that this son of a midwestern Methodist minister had parlayed a small sum of his own hard-earned lawyer's money into a million dollars long before he hit forty. His clothes never hinted at the money he had to his credit. He was funny and kind and quite fascinating. We had a lot in common. He had a wife and two sons back in New York. But I kept my confusion to myself and let him do the thinking, the planning. Floyd Odlum was a good man.

"I've been thinking about leaving Antoine's to go on the road selling cosmetics for a manufacturer," I told Floyd that night. "The shop can be so confining and the customers so frustrating and what I really love to do is travel. I want to be out in the air," I said.

"There's a depression on, Jackie," he said. Floyd knew about all that only too well. Part of the reason he was in Miami was to rest from all the buying and selling projects his company, the Atlas Corporation, had been immersed in. "If you're going to cover the territory you need to cover in order to make money in this kind of economic climate, you'll need wings. Get your pilot's license."

Floyd had a way of turning negatives into positives. I liked that. It was not the first time I had ever considered learning how to fly, but this time it made sense, practical sense. The thought

of having my pilot's license hadn't bowled me over before or hit
me like a flash of lightning or anything like that. After talking to
Floyd that night, it just sat there, fermenting, bubbling around in
my subconscious. Flying? Me?

I saw Floyd only twice more in Miami. Then the winter
Florida season was over. I went back to New York in my little
Chevrolet, wondering if we'd ever meet again.

Beauty operators weren't allowed personal phone calls at
Antoine's in New York. But an exception is an exception and I
explained to the office when I was back in New York that if a
Mr. Floyd Odlum ever called to please make that exception.

Two months passed. Then, on May 11, 1932, the receptionist sends for me. There's a call waiting. The call I've been waiting for.

Floyd and I went to dinner that night, my birthday, and
when I told him so, he reached into his pocket and pulled out a
$20 gold piece I kept in my lockbox for a lifetime.

OTHER VOICES:

Mike Rosen

(HIS LIFELONG PERSONAL FRIENDSHIP WITH JACKIE
BEGAN ON A ROMANTIC NOTE WHEN BOTH
WERE BEGINNING CAREERS IN NEW YORK CITY)

I went to dinner one night with an old college friend and we
decided on a restaurant at Broadway and 79th Street. They were
all jammed up and the manager of the place, a fellow I knew,
asked if we wanted to sit with a young woman who was there by
herself. I said, "Sure, it's okay with me."

Jackie Cochran was high on New York then. In fact, she
hadn't been in New York City very long that first time we met
and she was talking about getting a job at Saks. I didn't talk too
much. She talked for all three of us, but I wanted to be sure I

heard every single word. She was fascinating. I had never heard a woman talk the way she could talk. What a storyteller.

"How often do you come here?" I asked her as our dinner was ending.

"Well, maybe two or three times a week, but I'm irregular because of my working hours," she explained.

I kept coming back and one night I ran into her again, when I was alone. She could have sold me the Brooklyn Bridge. She was so emphatic and so sincere. I lived about ten blocks away then, but I had a job that took me around to theaters all over Manhattan. I went over to Saks Fifth Avenue one day to see her and she introduced me all around. She was only just a beginner then—that's why her hours were so odd. When I asked her for another date, she told me she couldn't predict when she would be free. I thought she was brushing me off. But she called me later. I took her to meet my mother. Then she'd be off to Florida and we wouldn't see each other for months. Once on her return she had flying on her mind.

"Mike," she said, "I think I'd like to learn how to fly."

"Why do you want to go and do that?" I asked her.

"A lot of women are flying now, and I think it could be a very good thing for me. Will you help me pass my test?"

Sure, I'd help her. I didn't think she could pass an examination because I knew how limited her schooling had been. She couldn't write at all. "How are you going to do this?" I asked her later. "I'm going to take the test verbally," she insisted. Just like that, she kept saying, "I'm going to take a verbal."

Every spare moment we had together we spent practicing for her exam. I was almost a flyer myself by the time she got through. I'd say, "Jackie, tell me what this is." And she'd answer aloud. Or she'd say, "Read that to me again, Mike."

A month before she began her real flying lessons out on Long Island, she moved downtown, farther away from the restaurant where we'd met, to an apartment on Tenth Street in Greenwich Village. But we still saw each other a lot. In fact, we bought a car together, a little Chevrolet. She had found a deal and called me. "Mike," she said, "I want to buy this car I saw and I want you to split the cost with me fifty–fifty. But I also want you to promise me that we will let the local priest down here use it during the day. He needs it."

"Okay Jackie," I said, "it's a deal, and don't worry about the priest."

I knew she was seeing other men. In fact, I consider Jackie one of my best friends. But I was surprised when Floyd came along. I hadn't realized how serious they were. And for all of our talking, Jackie was a very private person. She kept her life with Floyd private.

FLOYD

Floyd was fourteen years older than me. He didn't look it, though. When we first met, he still had a house in Forest Hills, Queens, where he never played tennis but kept up his membership in the West Side Tennis Club anyway. He preferred modeling clay figures in the evenings when he wasn't working, and he once told me that he had fashioned enough figures to fill a room but he always smashed them back into worthless lumps before going to bed.

He was rare. He was unique. With his horn-rimmed spectacles and that mind which wouldn't quit. He'd lie there on our couch, planning strategy for my races, mapping routes, measuring engine possibilities against fuel-consumption tests. He wanted me to be more than even I dreamed I could be. And he helped make my dreams come true.

People saw him as a "tycoon," and I knew that side of Floyd too. But he was also the gentlest, kindest, and most generous human being I ever met. There were scores of individuals who depended on Floyd for profitable investments—until he was well into his eighties. He was never too tired or, in later years, too sick to do something for someone else.

He didn't want me to talk about him. With the money he had amassed and the notoriety neither of us needed, I saw no reason to put our relationship before the public's eye. It had begun quietly, privately, because he didn't want to hurt his sons, Stanley or Bruce. He had two boys by his first marriage. He was a kind man—always kind—kinder than I could ever hope to be. His first marriage to Hortense McQuarrie was over except on paper when we met.

There was a *Time* magazine article about Floyd that appeared in the August 19, 1935, issue. It referred back to his 1912 class graduation picture at the University of Colorado and the caption beneath read: "...manages to get his hands on everything that makes money." That was Floyd for sure.

Floyd had worked hard to become successful. We talked about his life and mine and how they contrasted but how they compared too. He had earned his first pay picking berries, spraying vegetables, digging ditches, and selling clothes in Union City, Michigan, where his father was a Methodist minister. He was one of five children. One summer he even jockeyed an ostrich in a race against a horse. He had done everything. I wanted to do everything. I envied him his education, always. Floyd's family had moved to Boulder, Colorado, after he graduated from high school and he badly wanted to go to college even though there was no money for that kind of expenditure. So he told me that he appeared in front of the University of Colorado registrar and offered his personal guarantee that one day he would pay back his tuition money—if they would only let him enter and graduate. They accepted his offer and jeepers, he paid back that note many times over—with all the contributions he made to them over the years. In college he reminded me of myself as he reeled off the jobs he held, the hopes he had. He ran the school newspaper, the laundry, the dramatic society, worked as an assistant librarian in his spare time and even sold maps from door to door for a spell. We'd laugh at each other when I described my stint in direct sales down south, pitching dress patterns. Floyd had the highest grades in the state bar examination when it was given in 1915 after he graduated from the University of Colorado Law School. He married Hortense, the daughter of a local Mormon elder, when he was living in Salt Lake City and earning $75.00 a month working for Utah Power and Light. That company was bought out by Electric Bond and Share, and when that happened, Floyd got his chance to come to New York as an apprentice in their law offices on Wall Street.

That same *Time* article claimed that Floyd Odlum must have *smelled* the Depression and the great Wall Street market crash coming in 1929, and I don't think the writer was far from wrong.

Floyd did have an extraordinary sense about money. He probably did *sense,* or you might even say, *smell* success early in life
and set out to achieve it. But so did I.

OTHER VOICES:

Aldine Tarter

(AN EMPLOYEE AT THE COCHRAN-ODLUM RANCH IN CALI-
FORNIA, AN EXECUTOR OF JACKIE COCHRAN'S ESTATE,
AND CO-EXECUTOR OF FLOYD ODLUM'S ESTATE)

Mr. Odlum was an incredible man. He hired me to run the
accounting side of the ranch, and when I toyed with the idea of
going back to school to become a certified public accountant, he
hired a CPA to teach me. "You can learn more here, Aldine," he
said to me, "than you'll pick up in a classroom. Give it some
thought. I want you to get the facts, but the experience is right
here." And it was. That ranch business life was out of this
world. I did learn more than I ever could have gotten in any
classroom.

Mr. Odlum was the founder of Atlas Corporation and its
chief executive officer from its beginnings in 1923—he was only
thirty-one at the time and managed to keep a full-time job at the
law firm, Simpson, Thacher and Bartlett at the same time he
parlayed his and other people's money into millions, literally
millions of dollars. For years he burned both those candles. He
was still running Atlas when I came to work for him, and he
didn't retire until 1960.

Mr. Odlum was just a giant in business and finance. God, he
used to say, "I never made an illegal dollar in my life, Aldine."
He was so straight-laced about his businesses. Back in 1927, the
backers of a newly formed investment firm offered Mr. Odlum
the incredible salary of $200,000 for his help. And he helped get
them up off the ground. But he never cashed a one of his pay-
checks. The money wasn't why he did it. "I was the fellow who

set the salaries at Atlas," he told me, "so the biggest draw I ever made was $100,000." It sounds like a lot, but when you consider the money he could have been making, it's not. Before the stock market crashed in 1929, Mr. Odlum had converted his investments into a cash value of about $14 million. Can you imagine having that much money when no one else had any?

He told me that it all started when he convinced a couple of friends to let him play the stock market with their money. It began with about $40,000 and they stuck with utility stocks. This was the beginning of the Atlas Corporation. Before the stock market crashed in 1929, Mr. Odlum liquidated his company's holdings into cash and, after the crash, he began to reinvest it. It wasn't magic that made him do it. "Aldine," he'd say to me, "stock prices had reached an unreal level in the twenties. They couldn't go much higher. There was only one direction a major move could take, and that was down. Stocks were selling for much more than the real value of the companies they represented." Mr. Odlum always did his homework.

Floyd Odlum

The Depression hit the market hard, but the investment trusts took the worst beating of all. They were companies that issued stocks of their own and then used the money to invest in producing corporations. During the boom the public had put more than $6 billion into them and had lost all their faith. They felt the investment trusts had helped bring on the crash.

I saw a strange situation. The public's confidence had dropped so much that the investment trusts were priced lower than the value of the stocks they owned. For $5 you could buy a share of Trust X that owned securities of railroads and factories that were selling for $10 a share.

It was a wonderful spot for someone with nerve and cash. But the only way to take advantage of it was to buy control of these investment trusts and then sell the companies they owned. I decided to try it. I told my colleagues at Atlas, "I think we can do better now than ever before."

Aldine Tarter

During the Depression and afterward, Mr. Odlum controlled or managed or reorganized companies in almost every kind of industry, including banking, public utilities, motion pictures, department stores, railroads, aircraft, oil, and mining. At one time or another he obtained control of or was involved in the management of things like the Greyhound Bus Company; RKO Pictures Corporation and Paramount Pictures; Bonwit Teller, Inc.; Franklin Simon & Company, Inc.; the New York Plaza, Ambassador, and Sherry Netherland Hotels and Hilton Hotels Corporation; Consolidated Vultee Aircraft Corporation (producer of the Convair airplane and the B-36 bomber); Utilities Power & Light Corporation, which later became Ogden Corporation. Gosh, there were others. He'd get into these deals and out as fast as he could, staying only long enough to make back his money plus lots more...at least forty or fifty percent. A friend of his, Sidney Weinberg of Goldman Sachs, used to call him "Fifty Percent Odlum." They weren't friends at first because Mr. Odlum had taken full advantage when Goldman Sachs went bottoms up in '29. Some of the companies came under his control because they had been funded by those investment trusts. That's where Bonwit Teller came from.

I remember him telling me about the time he tried to buy something from J. Paul Getty. It was a West Coast oil company that was priced in the stock market for at least $40 million and Mr. Odlum called Mr. Getty and offered him $60 million. Getty told Odlum no. But he made him a strange offer.

"I'll sell you five percent of the company for thirty percent less than the market and actually less than its real worth," Getty said to Mr. Odlum. So when Mr. Odlum asked how come he wanted to make that kind of deal, Getty told him he needed some cash for personal matters. We always wondered which wife it was.

Another billionaire who was always short of cash was Howard Hughes. Mr. Hughes was a regular figure around the ranch but Mr. Odlum always described him as a suspicious recluse who often needed a dime to make a phone call and thirty cents to buy some gas. "He never has any money," Mr. Odlum told me.

Mr. Odlum even went to work for the government for only $1.00 a year during World War II. He helped out Hoover, Roosevelt, and Truman as a consultant for the War Production Board. But he didn't like politics personally very much. He liked to dabble from behind the scenes. He used to say that Johnson was a blabbermouth when Jackie and Lyndon were doing all their meeting. And Eisenhower...well, he liked President Eisenhower a lot. The Eisenhowers spent many a Christmas holiday out at the ranch with Jackie and Mr. Odlum. Kennedy? He wasn't so crazy about Kennedy. I think that was partially because he had once hired Joe Kennedy, John's father, to help him on a Paramount Pictures takeover. Mr. Odlum became convinced that the elder Mr. Kennedy was trying to do him out of the deal and he fired him. He even told *The New York Times* in an interview that he didn't mind being remembered as the man who fired Joe Kennedy.

Patriotic—that's how you'd have to describe that man. He and Miss Cochran were two of the most democratic people I've ever known.

Uranium was a hot issue around the sides of their ranch pool. There he'd be in his cap and swimming trunks with that phone cord strung across the lawn. He was on it constantly. He didn't like to fly very much when airplanes first became the way to go, but when they invented the telephone, they gave him the key to his fortune. He didn't believe in desks. "A storehouse for junk, bad for posture, and a setting for cold conversation" is how he described them. Mr. Odlum always conducted his affairs from the big pool because his arthritis just killed him. It was so painful. He'd put the board of directors of one company at one end of the 100-foot pool, feet dangling in the water on occasion, and a different group on a different side. It was up to Vi Strauss to make sure the twain didn't meet undiplomatically. Poor Vi. Jumping between Mr. Odlum and Jackie sure kept her hopping on those weekends.

During one month's time back in the heydays of the Cochran-Odlum ranch, we had General Hoyt Vandenberg, his wife, and son; Sol Schwartz, head of RKO Theatres; Admiral Kirk, former ambassador to Russia; Senator Stuart Symington of Missouri; General Tooey Spaatz; test pilot Chuck Yeager and Glennis; Bob Stearns, president of the University of Colorado; Henry and Edgar Kaiser; Jay Hopkins, president of General

Dynamics; Sam Goldwyn; Dr. Menzel, a Harvard astronomer; General Rosy O'Donnell; Baroness de la Grange; one of the Du Pont ladies; the widow of Robert Patterson, former Secretary of War; and Jackie's good friends, Mike and Louise Rosen.

Mr. Odlum could be funny. His sense of humor could be cute and he could laugh at himself. He used to tell us about his first day in New York City, carrying his one and only battered straw bag and wearing his only pair of shoes, which were laced high above the ankle and bright yellow. Going to dinner with some big-time lawyers at his new firm a couple of weeks later, he couldn't afford another pair of shoes yet, so he simply blackened them up. But they smelled to high heaven during the dinner. He never said a word.

He was always playing tricks on his friend Harry Bruno. Harry had purchased some desert land right next to the ranch and always intended to build something on it one day, someday. Floyd would smile about his one day, someday postponing. So one day he hired my husband and a couple of fellas to dress up in pith helmets and carry prospecting equipment around the property. Harry could just barely see what was happening from Floyd and Jackie's windows and he couldn't believe his eyes. What a stunt. Harry thought something big was about to happen on his land. And he didn't know what. I don't believe Floyd ever told him the truth. And I remember the time he constructed a grave marker, a big monument, and put it right out front of Harry Bruno's property. Ranch hands put up this big thing which said: "Here lies Harry's house." Or something like that. Harry just howled.

Helen Lemay

(WIFE OF AIR FORCE GENERAL CURTIS LEMAY, HEAD OF THE JOINT CHIEFS OF STAFF, AND A PERSONAL FRIEND)

Floyd was one of the ten richest men in the world, and he and Jackie were married in 1936. They met in 1932, when she was still running between beauty shops, and the relationship just grew. Jackie wasn't like other women and certainly not like

Floyd's first wife. But that first marriage must have been over for a long time, I know that. After the divorce Floyd gave his first wife the Bonwit Teller department store to run. He made her president. He owned it and he could and would do things like that. Can you imagine?

Jackie always did things on her own. She needed Floyd but she didn't need Floyd. Do you know what I mean? A person in her circumstances didn't have to keep pushing herself all the time the way she would but she did. She was never just Mrs. Floyd Odlum. You would never say Mrs. Odlum to Jackie. It was always Miss Jacqueline Cochran and Mr. Floyd Odlum, even on invitations for the two of them. It had always been that way, she told me. She was very proud of Floyd, but she wanted to be herself. Her name was her name. It meant a lot to her.

When Floyd met Jackie at that dinner party in Florida, he must have been immediately attracted. She had the most beautiful skin I've ever seen. It was like the loveliest whipped cream, and her big brown eyes were wonderful. She had pretty hair and was always giving herself permanents, always asking me if she could do my hair.

Floyd always encouraged Jackie and was so proud of her records, her accomplishments, where she had come from, and all that. Jackie would talk about her childhood and loved the idea that she was a foundling, that she didn't know who her parents were or what ever happened to them. She and Floyd had investigated and came up with some information in a letter that was sealed. She was to open that letter whenever she wanted to, she told me. And she claims she never opened it, but I don't know about that. She was a rascal.

We had a lot in common because we both knew a lot of military people and we were involved in projects together. My husband is retired Air Force General Curtis Lemay and because Jackie was a lieutenant colonel in the Air Force Reserve, we were involved in projects together. She was a very close friend of mine and that means a lot to me because Jackie wasn't a woman who had very many close women friends.

I remember how she used to drive like the wind and insist on doing it. We really had a lot of fun together even when she was creating a crisis a minute, which was something she'd do all the time. In the center of attention—that's where she wanted to be. Once when we were in Egypt, leaving Cairo and trying to go to

Aswan, she wanted to drive so we could see all those little towns along the way.

"Jackie, you are not going to drive," I insist. "If you do, I'm not going with you. It's too dangerous. I don't want to do it."

We had been at a party in Cairo the night before, and everyone said it wasn't safe for two women on the road to Aswan. It was really the boondocks we'd be crossing and the roads weren't all that safe or good. A couple of weeks before that a tourist had rented a car and driver to make the same trip. As the driver was coming through one of those little towns, a child ran out in the road, right in front of the car, and was killed. It couldn't have been avoided.

The people in that town came out, saw the dead child, and took up machetes to chop that driver into pieces. Right in front of the tourist.

"They didn't do that, Helen," Jackie says. "I don't believe those silly stories. They are trying to scare us."

"And they've succeeded," I say. "I won't go."

She was so frustrated with me, but as her friend she stuck by me. Nothing like machete attacks ever frightened Jackie. We took the train.

I remember how she insisted on taking a watermelon along with us on the train because those Egyptian lines didn't have dining cars. When the porters saw us coming with the melon, they descended on us and took it. She had a fit, a royal fit. We got the watermelon back, though.

———————————

There weren't night and day differences between Floyd Odlum and me. Temperamentally we may have been miles apart, but when it came to knowing what we wanted out of life—security, power, and a certain kind of fame—we were very much alike. And work. Hard work was always a tie that bound us together. When it came to schemes and dreams, Floyd had as many as I did.

FLYING

It was inevitable. I'd been working on the idea for months. The book by my bedside in the apartment on West Tenth Street was *How to Learn to Fly in Three Easy Lessons*, (or some such ridiculous title). The magazines that arrived in my mail belonged to an aviator. The conversations being held in my head were about flying—both the replays I had heard from the Pensacola Naval Flying School guys and the ones I had been having with my friend Mike and with Floyd. That's where I was going: flying.

My first day in the air began on a train. It was a Saturday and the start of a six-week vacation I had coming to me from Antoine. The free time had built up from three years' efforts and would build no further. Take it or lose it. So take it I would. And I'd choose nothing from an ordinary vein. I wanted to do something extraordinary with my time off, something that would prove that I had a mind, because I had been engaged in such mindless activity for so long in the salon. To be a good beautician you've got to be artistic but you certainly don't have to be smart.

There are none of those Long Island commuters on the early train to Westbury. It's an August kind of hot and I wait, station by station, for the conductor with the deep, singsongy drawl to call it out.

I knew that the Roosevelt Flying School would be only a

short distance from the Westbury station. In fact, the school had quite an advertising program in 1932. The first lesson was offered as kind of a teaser and lasted 30 minutes. They charged $495 for 20 hours and they would not guarantee that you would get a license or even solo. I remember a Chinese boy named Frank whom I saw there. He had 50 hours already and had never soloed. I met him again in Formosa about twenty years later.

Floyd bet me the $495 that I couldn't get my license in six weeks' time. I said I'd do it in three because I didn't want to spend my entire vacation in the air over Long Island. I denied the bet for years because I thought it made my desire to fly look silly. But it was for real. And so was my desire to fly.

Husky Lewelleyn is really husky. Huge. He's to be my instructor. When I look over at the airplane, a little machine, and then back at Husky, I seriously question whether or not it will take the two of us up. No way, I think. But I say nothing.

Without a single explanation we climb into the plane, Husky opens the throttle and off we go. The sun is high by now. August—why have I waited so long? I can't believe that I have put this off—a reason for living—for so long. Why? For some queer and unknown reason, I catch the feel of the plane right away. I had just scratched the surface, but I was less beautician and more flyer already.

"How many hours do you have to fly to get a license?" I ask when we're back on the ground. Husky's let me bring us both back to earth there after only one circuit of the airfield. I'm thinking that he must have as much confidence in me as I've got in myself to let me land. On the other hand, he could be interminably bored with these teasers he's been orchestrating since the beginning of the big ad campaign. I'm just another wide-eyed woman to him...at least for the moment.

"You've got to fly 20 hours and then pass a test," he explains. "It'll take two or three months if you're lucky."

"I have to do it in three weeks because I don't intend to spend my entire vacation out here," I say. He just laughs.

"That'll be tough," he says.

"I don't think so," I say. And I plunk down the $495 for the course. We started putting in the hours that afternoon.

The next day was Sunday and I arrived out at the airport by train again and by seven A.M. No one was there until nine and I spent two glorious hours watching the sky, which had suddenly taken on a new aspect for me. I intended to conquer it. I browsed around the hangar, looking over the airplanes and studying a mural on the wall painted by a woman pilot, Aline Rhonie. All the "greats" in aviation as well as their exploits were there in Aline's painting.

I'll never forget when Husky took me up for an acrobatic lesson with every intention of making me sick. Loops, spins, rolls, and other maneuvers in dizzying repetition. Finally, I touched him on the shoulder and pointed to the landing field. He smiled, thinking he had done his job, and we came down. When we climbed out of the plane, I invited him over to the small field restaurant, where I ordered a hot dog and bottle of pop.

By three o'clock Monday afternoon, just 48 hours after I first climbed into a cockpit, Husky climbed out of "our" trainer and said, "Okay, it's all yours."

I wanted to be the world's greatest pilot and I didn't think twice about soloing after so little time in the air. Up in the air, I was at ease, so at ease and inexperienced that I didn't worry when the motor quit. I assumed Husky had fixed it to stop so I would come down. And come down I did, with no problem. The Roosevelt people—Husky included—were amazed and quite impressed. At any rate, fifteen years later Husky told a *New York Post* reporter that I was "a born flyer, one of the smartest gals in the air I ever saw." Just another wide-eyed woman out for a teaser I wasn't.

I think pilots depend on their engines too much these days. That isn't always such a good idea when you have only one to hold you up there in the air. Learning how to land a plane with a stalled motor, or, as they say, to dead-stick it in, is something all pilots ought to learn.

On the following Wednesday I was having dinner with friends. I was still training every day out at Roosevelt and still high as a kite from the feeling that soloing offered me. It was exhilarating. They said: "What kind of plane did you fly?"

I said, "I don't know." I hadn't asked Husky the name.

They said, "Was it a biplane or a monoplane?"

"It had four wings," I said. I knew that the wings were not a solid formation but had been broken in two by the fuselage.

"What kind of engine did it have?" they asked.

"I don't know," I answered.

"Did you fly that plane?" they wondered, smiling all the time.

"I certainly did and I didn't need to know the name to do that."

Later, I found out that I had taken my lessons in what was called a Fleet trainer, with a sixty horsepower engine.

The speed of an airplane is the result of a compromise—a compromise between the physical drag of the plane through the air and the thrust its engine is providing. One side or the other in this tug-of-war is aided or abetted by the pull of gravity back toward the earth.

The plane the Wright brothers flew, which looked like a box kite, had things physically sticking out of it in every direction, so it had lots of drag. And its engine had just a little more than enough power to overcome such drag. What designers and airplane makers have done over the years is reduce the drag and increase the thrust. To do that, they have streamlined the plane's body and swept back the angle of the wings, besides changing their shape. They've built more powerful engines and come up with better fuels.

About forty years ago Dr. Theodore Von Karman, the Einstein of aviation, held up an Indian arrow for me to see and said that planes should be built according to the same configuration. Today we see such shapes in our Delta wing planes and in our guided missiles. The Indian's arrow receives its thrust from the snap of the bowstring. A jet engine does the same thing for a plane in a greatly magnified way by squirting power out through the tail. This thrust is measured in pounds. And a pound of thrust in a plane going 275 miles per hour is the equivalent of one horsepower. Double the speed and that one pound of thrust becomes the equivalent of two horsepower.

On my jet flights, the equivalent of 15,000 horsepower was

created in a power plant which started just back of my seat and was hardly longer than a coffin. And in missiles the packaging is much smaller. What a long way that is from the first Fleet trainer I took up over Long Island.

Dead-sticking, or gliding, in on my first solo flight that day gave me even more confidence than it probably should have. It was a confidence that was badly shaken but then reinforced by two horrible accidents in the two days following my first solo. The next morning as I was about to take off, a plane spun in across the field and my flight was delayed while fragments of a man and his airplane were being collected. It was definitely an incident designed to dampen beginners' nerve. But at the same time, it made me more aware of how much I had to learn and how crucial it was to get it right. I wouldn't let it stop me. Not even a nasty sight over at North Beach Airport, now LaGuardia, the very next day, could diminish the feeling that I would be a survivor.

George Gardner, a government flight inspector, needed to get over to North Beach in a hurry and I volunteered to fly him there. Any excuse would do for me. I wanted to be up in the air as much as I could. But I didn't know what kind of lesson I was in for that day.

A plane had landed several feet short of the runway and they were dragging bodies out of the marsh at the edge of the field. It was eerie. It was ugly and I wondered if George, whom I knew later as president of Northeast Airlines, had something more in mind when he asked me for a ride.

But you never see yourself like that—a body in a marsh at the edge of a field. You just can't. I never knew how I would die and even when I thought about dying, a fast plane seemed a better alternative to anything else I could imagine. A great pilot— and remember, I thought of myself as on the way to becoming one—ought to have the right to go fast, to die as he or she lived. Years later, I used to argue with Frank Hawks, a fearless racing pilot I knew in the early days, about the best way to land a plane. Frank insisted that if I did not stop bringing in my overpowered Beechcraft so fast, I'd kill myself. I didn't think so. Finally, in exasperation, I told him that I'd be the one sending the roses to his funeral and not vice versa. It was a joke. But a bad one. He hit a power line while taking off from a friend's front yard in a new midget private plane not too long after. I ordered the roses.

OTHER VOICES:

Mike Rosen

Jackie called me one morning and said, "Mike, I've got to see you today. Don't go golfing. Okay?"

"Okay," I said. "What's up?" She had "our" car and said that she'd pick me up because she wanted to take me out to the airfield—Roosevelt Air Field. "I want to show you something," she said.

We got out there and she says to me, "Climb in this plane, Mike. Sit down." So I sit down, thinking she is going to show me the instruments, let me know what it feels like. All of a sudden she takes off. We take off into the air and I am shocked. That's when I realized she had passed her test, gotten her pilot's license. She flew me all the way to Philadelphia that day. She was so happy.

Jacqueline Cochran received her pilot's license in 1932 after three weeks of instruction at Roosevelt Field on Long Island. She piloted a Fleet trainer.

    —National Air and Space Museum, Smithsonian Institution, 1981

THE CRAZY TRIP TO CANADA

I won that bet with Floyd and got my private pilot's license before my vacation from Saks was up. The timing couldn't have been better—or worse. I saw it as great timing—then—but in retrospect I did what could have been a very stupid thing.

There was to be a sports pilots' meet up in Montreal and the Canadians had invited American flyers. Everyone at the airfield was talking about it. If I got hold of a plane, I was determined to go it...alone. I went up to a man, practically a stranger to me, whom I had met at the airfield. I knew he owned a Fairchild 22.

M. E. Grevenberg asked me how much experience I had and when I admitted that my license was only two days old, he wanted to know if I had done any cross-country flying to back up the license.

"None," I say.

"You're not going to go to Canada alone, are you?" he asks.

"Yes, I am," I answer.

"This is stupid," he says. "I'll go with you."

"No, I'm flying to Canada alone. I want to."

"You're crazy," Grevenberg says. He pauses. "But if you're serious, I'll give you my plane on one condition."

"What's that?" I ask.

"Come up with the full price of it—when it was new. I'll take that as a security bond," he says.

Grevenberg—everyone called him Grevy—was really a gypsy of the air and I'm sure he thought that either I wouldn't be able to come up with the money in cash, or even if I did, he couldn't lose. His plane was second-hand and hardly worth the $2,000 he was asking. But I got the money. And he gave me the plane.

Then I bought some air maps and I hung around Roosevelt until I found an old-timer who would explain them to me. He wasted no energy or explanation on instruments, however. In looking back at myself then, I might as well have asked the old codger how to get to the emerald city of Oz, for his directions were almost as simplistic as "Follow the Yellow Brick Road." And like Dorothy, I took them at the face value so offered.

"The best thing for you to do is follow the Hudson River until you get to Lake Champlain. Then take the lake around until you come to a town. That'll be Burlington, Vermont. You'll find an airport there, where you should land. You've got to clear customs and you can ask them how to get from there to Montreal. It shouldn't take you very long then."

I didn't know anything. I didn't even know what I didn't know...which was probably better than realizing how little I knew for what I was undertaking. A compass? Who knew what that could do? When it said 30, it meant 30 to me, not 300. North, south, east, and west? Directions on a map, of course, but for navigating? Nothing.

This is a funny story.

There I am, buzzing up the Hudson on a beautiful clear day. Unlimited visibility. My feet feel the buzz and movement of an engine at work. My right hand rests on the control stick easily. I know what I'm doing, I think. The exhaust is steady. The plane flies with me, for me, with no problem even though I've had no practice with it. This plane and I had barely met by the time the security money was in hand and Grevy agreed to part company with it. Now I'm sitting in the rear cockpit, happy that no one else is along for this ride, and I'm looking down on the Hudson Valley, the sweeps of green and brown and blue-gray of the river. I'll never be happier, I think.

The Fairchild has an airspeed indicator but I don't remember how fast I was going. The Fleet trainer Husky and I flew had nothing but a compass and a tachometer. I just want to keep flying forever.

All of a sudden I notice something. The Hudson River has turned into a canal, and directly in front of me? A mountain.

I did know how to turn that plane around and I wasted no

time doing it. Then I retraced my steps, and put a lid on the apprehension that wanted to build inside me. I couldn't afford to lose my cool then. I had a long way to go.

The river returned and I chased it on up to Lake Champlain, where I went around the rim of that lake until I finally spotted the town, found the airport, and landed. Clearing customs was a miserable nightmare, though, because of all the papers I had to fill out and how difficult it was for me to write, let alone spell anything right. Finally, though, I was finished.

Sitting back in the plane, I yelled over to the airport attendant, "Which way to Montreal?"

He thought I was kidding. "Don't you know the way to Montreal?"

"No, I really don't. I wouldn't be asking you for directions if I already knew."

He still didn't believe me.

"How did you get here?" he asks.

"Well, I came up the Hudson River and then followed the lake shoreline until I found the airport. I landed and here I am."

He was stunned. Then he started to explain the way to Montreal by way of compass degrees and mileage. He even calculated what difference the wind conditions that day would make on my flying time. He really wasn't such a bad guy at all, and everything he said should have made sense to someone flying solo from New York to Canada. The only problem was, I had no idea what he was talking about.

"I don't know how to read a compass," I admit.

This he really didn't believe. He turns and walks away, leaving me to my wondering.

I'm sitting in the airplane when the customs official comes back out with some men who start pushing that plane around right there on the field. I'm still inside.

"Watch that compass," he orders me.

As the plane moves, so does the compass needle. That was my introductory lesson in navigation. I learned what all the different compass markings were doing there and how long I ought to be in the air before Montreal came into sight. And someone's outstretched arm pointed me in the right direction.

I was still worried. "Suppose I'm not good at reading this compass. Suppose I wander off. I don't think I fly that straight. What will I see on the way?"

Here was a man with patience. But I was wearing it thin by now. "Well," this poor customs official says, "there aren't any highways or railroads you can follow. They just don't go that way. You'd better just head in the general direction."

Then he remembered something. "When you are about half-way there, you'll see two big silos. You'll know you're on course when you spot them. If the visibility stays as clear as it is now, you should start seeing some airplanes at that point. Just go where the other airplanes go and that's where the airport will be. If you get lost, or never see the silos, turn around and come back. Maybe someone here will go with you or you could follow another ship."

Back in the air I became fascinated studying my compass. And when the silos were in my sight, I tested my understanding of compass readings a little more by flying circles around them while keeping one eye on how that compass needle changed. I thought it was a marvelous tool. Any farmer watching must have wondered what fool was up there making circles in the sky.

After the silos, finding Montreal was no problem. What was a problem after I landed at the airport was trying to convince everyone at the meet that I had so little flying time. Then, when they finally believed me, I think they thought I was foolish or darn lucky. A trip of that distance had been an invitation to disaster.

Nevertheless, I was something of a heroine and spent several wonderful days reinforcing my feeling that flying was something I'd never get out of my blood. Even good old Grevy showed up, probably surprised to see me safe as well as his plane still sound, and this time when he asked for a ride home, I said okay. But I insisted on taking the control stick out of that second cockpit. I wanted a passenger, not a copilot. Off we went.

A wall of haze hits us almost immediately. And I know I can't bluff my way through. What I don't know about flying is beginning to dawn on me. I look back at Grevy and he's waving to me frantically. Down, he points. Get down. Land. Is he kidding? Where? Finally, I pull the throttle back and I can hear him yell, "The weather is getting bad. You'll kill us if you don't put this down somewhere."

We found Syracuse in the fog, circled, and landed on an airstrip, where we were stranded in unflyable weather for two days.

On the ground Grevy and I had a lot of time to talk. I asked him about the miserable weather front we had hit so suddenly and which could have been so lethal. It struck me then how much flying depended on something as undependable as the weather.

"Sure it does," he explained. "You don't know what you're liable to hit up there. Now," he said slowly, probably knowing how the thought would implant itself in a mind like mine, "you can always learn how to fly blind."

"How do I do that?" I ask. To mix terms like "blind" and "flying" was shocking. How could anyone fly blind?

"You use instruments only," he answers. "I don't know how to do it, but some mail pilots do. And that's the only way you're ever going to get through storms like the one we saw. Either that or move to a place where it's sunny all the time."

I'd do both.

Most of us call it just plain air but I began to learn that there was much more there, in that air, than ever meets the eyes—my eyes, anyway. Oh, sure, I had stood out there on Sawdust Road as a child, watching the stars. Wishing with their help for that something more—wondering what else was out there. But it wasn't until I hit that storm on the way back from Montreal that I could understand even remotely why aviation people were always talking about the conquest of the air. It *was* a conquest. Pilots had to fight all kinds of unpredictable and occasionally invisible enemies up there in the air. Imagine, for instance, battling a tornado or a hailstorm.

I learned a lot about our whimsical weather in the years after. Do you realize that meteorologists know that approximately 4,000 storms will hit our earth every hour? And that the sun is the master of ceremonies in this destructive play? Cold air has greater pressure than warm air. One rises, the other descends. They fight it out for pressure equalization, each trying in a given area to occupy the same space at the same time. They fight it out on "fronts." Rain, hail, snow, lightning, hurricanes, and tornados are the battles which always end in a draw. Sides are drawn and conflicts go on. Airplanes get caught in the middle. And sometimes they lose.

Because of pilots like myself, scientists were able to learn about the giant rivers of air that sweep across the country at an altitude above 30,000 feet and below 50,000. They are called jet streams and I made the acquaintance of one unexpectedly one day while climbing in a Sabrejet for the start of a dive through the sound barrier.

I was out at Edwards Air Force Base and it was a Sunday morning. Chuck Yeager and I were up there. He was behind me, flying wing in the back. All of a sudden, I hit something like the side of a wall in the middle of nowhere. And so help me, you don't fight an airplane if it's turned around suddenly, almost 180 degrees from the direction it was going. The edges of a jet stream are not as swift as the center funnel or channel, where speeds can be up to 300 miles per hour, but we started doing some balloon tests on that one. It was not very wide or deep, but it was a stream of air estimated to be going around 200 miles per hour.

But in 1932 trying to get myself up into the air when the weather had nearly drowned my dreams in rain, fog, and sleet, I couldn't even begin to believe in the existence of jet streams. All I wanted was more sun. Aviation magazines were all talking about a Ryan Flying School in San Diego, California, where the skies were always blue. And the idea wouldn't let go. I couldn't shake the notion that in flying I could find a career—if I could only learn how to fly better.

GO WEST, YOUNG WOMAN

1933

The wind sock is there. The field is there. Everything looks fine from up here. The air maps say there is an airport here. So this must be it.

But I'm still guessing.

Down close it's not an airfield. It's a *plowed* field and I'm too low to turn. Trees at one end. Hills to the side. There's only one thing to do.

I cut the ignition switch to avoid a fire. And I do the best I can. I crash.

The soft dirt packs between the wheels and the wheel "pants" of the plane and the ship somersaults onto its back. Cars on the neighboring road screech to a halt and people rush over to find the body. But there's no body. Just me. A live young woman who walks away from what the local newspapers later described as a plane that had to be picked up with spoons.

I think those onlookers were disappointed—and, as someone once said, "Reports of my death were greatly exaggerated."

But I'm not exaggerating when I say that "Sunday afternoon controlled crashes into plowed fields"—that one was in upper New York State—became part of the process. I was becoming a professional pilot and that's the way I learned back then. In fact, some of this experience-gathering was gotten on trips for Floyd. We were seeing more of each other and Floyd—being Floyd— was always looking for what he called "special situations," or business opportunities. They weren't always on the beaten track, and he relied on me to take him off it at times.

I believe I had myself analyzed pretty carefully—my natural abilities as well as my disabilities. My education was of the self-help variety, which doesn't equip you for very much except the hard knocks. But I was mechanically inclined. I could do everything with my hands well, and my brain and body were also well coordinated. I drove well and I was satisfied with my endurance at it. More than once I had driven a car for about seventeen hours without stops except for meals. In emergencies I handled cars the right way, instinctively, and I never experienced fear in a crisis. I decided there was a real place for women like myself in aviation and I'd take it up as a profession. I'd do more than just play at it. I'd make it pay and I'd learn everything I could possibly learn about flying. It was a cinch.

In fact, I still think that most of the time playing the piano was more difficult for me than keeping a stable ship properly trimmed. In quiet air she flew herself.

The leaves were still on the trees in the Wasatch Mountains when I reached Salt Lake City on my way to California. They had turned into a riot of red, gold, yellows, and browns and then, too, the first snow had fallen lightly. It was breathtakingly beautiful.

I put myself back up in the air there by renting an old Curtiss Wright pusher plane with an engine in the rear. I had become nervous about losing my nerve after five or six days on the road in the Chevy. Would I forget what I had learned about airplanes? I vowed that it would be my last trip cross-country in a car—and it would. The owner of this pusher plane agreed to give me an hour in the air, never even bothering to check my flying hours. He simply started me off. But as I tried to pull up off the field, I knew something was drastically wrong.

It was the balance. The nose wouldn't stay down no matter what I tried. Simply getting it around and back onto the airfield was tricky. But I landed, found the owner, and we discovered the problem.

The sandbag was missing.

In order to keep this ship of ancient lineage in line, you had to take a bag of sand along for company in the first cockpit.

In went the sandbag and out I went for a second try.

Skimming the mountains, I fly across the Great Salt Lake to an island in the middle when I spot them: a herd of buffalo quietly grazing for the moment—but not for long. I just had to buzz them, so I flew low and chased them into a stampede. They went wild. Flying offered me the most stupendous sensations.

In 1933 Jackie enrolled in the Ryan Flying School in San Diego. There she took further instruction from Bob Kerlinger in a Great Lakes Sport.
—National Air and Space Museum, Smithsonian Institution, 1981

I was terrible in a classroom, and one night I described my predicament to a friend, Ted Marshall. I wanted to be up in the air more than I was and, in truth, I was such a poor student, I probably needed that one-on-one relationship with a teacher. Ted was an air officer in the Navy and here's what he proposed: if I'd buy my own plane, he and a group of Navy pilots we both knew would teach me the Navy way. Their ship, the *West Virginia,* was then stationed in San Diego. Later, when it moved up the coast to Long Beach, I would follow suit. I begged, borrowed, and pulled the money together for the used Travelair I mentioned before. It was a good plane. It just needed a valve job I couldn't afford.

It took me six months. But I experienced ten years' worth of trial-and-error flying. In fact, that crazy Travelair cracked up the very first time I flew it, and I'm sure I landed on a substantial number of all the beaches and open spots of Southern California. Ted and my Navy trainers made me practice spot landings, figure eights, 80's, 190's, and other turns and spins by the hour. I got so I could almost land on a silver dollar. It was monotonous at times but well worth it and I barely left the airport. On the ground I hired a regular tutor for mathematics and studied the course given to the Navy students at Pensacola. I could tell what was wrong with a motor by its hum long before I could plot a proper compass course. Instinct always raced past education. I'd cringe when asked to tell which course a plane should take to arrive at a given point, with a given speed, and an assumed wind-drift from a particular angle. God, I hated that study.

I passed the exam for my commercial pilot's license, the highest rating I could get then. There were five licenses:

student's, private, limited commercial, commercial, and airline pilot's. I even got an instructor's rating.

Not, however, without embarrassing moments, of which there were hundreds eventually. One forced landing took me through a fence out onto the road and into a parked car. It was a Sunday afternoon and I had my instructor with me. We had just taken off from Grand Central Airport in Los Angeles and risen to a height of about 75 feet when the engine failed. To turn under such circumstances is sure disaster. We just weren't high enough. And the only vacant lot was on the other side of a road, on the other side of a fence.

I nose the ship down, hoping she'll stop before reaching the road. And it almost works—but not quite. She barrels on through that metal fence, crashing, banging, turning onto her nose just over the curbing on the highway—while I curse nonstop all the way. And damned if there isn't an automobile parked there, against regulations. Its occupant has been watching the planes taking off and landing—which we proceed to do right into his car.

We crash to a stop and no one is hurt, not even the disgruntled car owner. I'm not feeling too bad about the car because it looks like it is ready for a junk heap anyway.

That's when I find out that the car belongs to a traffic judge. I ended up with a $25 fine for unlawful parking. Tough luck, you might say. But the accident brought me a bit of good luck too.

With the plane sitting out there getting parking tickets, I found someone at the airport who offered to come over to advise me whether or not it was worth fixing. And who should arrive on the scene but Jack Northrop himself. The Jack Northrop who had left the Lockheed brothers, gone into airplane building for himself, and had been making the most beautifully streamlined planes the United States had ever seen!

He must have thought I was crazy. "Someday I'll be flying Northrop planes," I said to him as he studied the Travelair.

"Of course you will," he answered absently. Then he suggested I contact one of his test pilots for some flying lessons. It looked like I needed all the help I could get.

I remember the time I flew an old Tri-Motor Ford into the Grand Canyon. I had taken Floyd, an Indian chief, a tribal pottery maker, and the tribe's painter down into the Grand Canyon below the rim after picking everyone up in the wonderfully

colorful area known as the Painted Desert. We were all going to
Indian celebrations in the canyon. Almost too late I realized it
wasn't going to be easy.

There is no real airport in the Grand Canyon. It's just a flat
spot in the sand and it was only on approaching this flat spot that
I could see the field was dotted with hundreds of wild horses.
There was no getting back up and I could just picture us plowing
into these poor horses. What a way to go!

We are nearly down and I spy a dog. He starts chasing the
horses out of our oncoming path like the pro he is. I can't
believe our good luck and only later do I discover that this dog
has been trained by the airport officials to listen for the sound of
airplane engines. That's his cue, a cue that comes mighty late as
far as I could see. Until your plane's wheels are so close that
you can almost feel the sand between your toes, you don't know
whether you will be making horse meat or not.

When we climbed out of the plane, that dog was cool as a
cucumber. I was sweating like one of his scattered horses.

I had fallen in love with the desert in Southern California when
Ted Marshall's brother George invited me to visit his ranch in
the Coachella Valley. I flew there from San Diego and became
convinced that I had found *home*. The soil in that desert lies
below sea level, having been diked off from the Gulf of Southern
California through the centuries by silt from the Colorado River.
Look at a map and you'll see what I mean. In time, the water
behind this natural dike evaporated...all except for the Salton
Sea, which has its surface about 300 feet below sea level and
salty water to boot. Coyotes, bobcats, pack rats, lizards, and
rattlesnakes are all there. And summer heat can see you in 130
degrees Fahrenheit. But it can be so beautiful. And so peaceful.
Under the sun's glare, deep colors shrink into pastels and the
limitless white of the sands merges into the grays, greens, and
purples of the sage, the desert holly, the yucca and the ocotillo,
the mesquite and smoke trees.

George Marshall could see what happened to me immediately. That uptight, "can't-sit-still" buzz I always had on around
his brother when we talked flying disappeared in the desert. So,
when George called me several weeks after my first visit to tell
me about land for sale, I lost no time buying twenty acres. And I

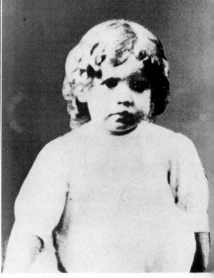

Expensive man-tailored suits were a trademark for Jackie in the 1930's but the dress she wore at age four was a hand-me-down.

1938 in a Seversky fighter: leather flying hats might flatten her hair but lipstick was always a must after a big Bendix Air Race.

Amelia Earhart and Jackie on the diving board at the Cochran-Odlum
Ranch, Indio, California.

Jackie's marriage to Wall Street wizard Floyd Odlum lasted 40 years.

One dream come true: riding an elephant at Madison Square Garden.

Flying a pursuit plane designed by Major Alexander P. de Seversky (above right), Jackie captured the #1 spot in the 1938 Bendix Air Race and got a handshake from Vincent Bendix himself.

Hugging a propeller that had forced her further and faster.

picked what I thought would be the perfect spot for a house—a house I'd build myself on what seemed to be the biggest hill around those flat parts. I became a part-time bricklayer, carpenter, and plumber, and Floyd would laugh at me when he came to visit from New York City. "The House That Jackie Built" was how he'd describe our place in later years. Eventually, Floyd would buy close to 900 acres and we called our property "Cochran-Odlum Ranches." We shared equal billing, alphabetically ordered, but mine was such a paltry share at twenty acres—a rabbit compared to Floyd's horse.

We leveled, enlarged, landscaped, and in the beginning, it was all on $6.00-a-day laborers—no architects at all. I laid tile down on hands and knees. I worked like a dog on it and it took me a year and a half to finish. The house was a mongrel. It grew topsy-turvy-like and had no claim to architectural beauty but became quite lovely in spite of itself. All the buildings were the most beautiful shade of green. It's soft on the eyes, you know. When we moved from it, Floyd and I wanted to paint our new home green, too, but it was an old Spanish house and green just didn't fit. God, there was a lot of my own sweat and blood in that ranch house. Grapefruits, tangerines, dates—we had the most delicious dates you could imagine—my flowers, my vegetables, and more. I built a home. I remember fighting with the damn mason about the fireplaces. I wanted a certain look and he couldn't give it to me.

Floyd used to order western cowboy shirts for good friends and regular guests who came out to get away from it all. And from the very beginning, Floyd Odlum, the wizard of Wall Street, turned into a more relaxed person away from the pace as well as the weather of New York. He never stopped working. But he sure slowed down. Slept better too.

People were amazed by what we were able to do in the desert. If I were flying high up there on an April day, I only had to close my eyes and sniff to tell when I was above the ranch. The fragrance of those fruit blossoms in bloom would rise at least a mile high. A nine-hole golf course eventually—which we opened for free to the young kids in the area—a big pool—those beautiful date palms and citrus bordering along the ranch driveway—it all rose right out of the desert. It was magic for me. And for Floyd Odlum too.

The ranch would save Floyd's life at a time when almost

everyone—bigwigs at the Mayo Clinic, medical men at Johns Hopkins in Baltimore, and everyone up at Columbia-Presbyterian Hospital—told my husband to go back to bed and live from there.

OTHER VOICES:

Vi Strauss Pistell

(MANAGER OF THE COCHRAN-ODLUM RANCH HOUSEHOLD FOR NEARLY THIRTY YEARS)

I didn't agree with Jackie about that desert. But there was no disagreeing with Jackie.

Nobody was like her. She was an amazing, intelligent—naturally intelligent—woman and I used to wonder, Well, where is all this coming from? Then I'd think, Well, she's psychic, that's how she does it. It comes from somewhere else. Yes, that's what it was. To me—and I worked for her for more than twenty-five years from the early days at the ranch until 1960—she was just great. There were so many things that she could do—and do well. Take that ranch house, for instance. There was nothing out there when I first saw it. It was so darn hot.

My parents insisted that I meet her when I was living in Los Angeles. They knew her and knew that she was looking for someone to take care of the property when she was off flying or in New York. I wanted no part of it, but I was free at the time, so I said I'd talk to her. It was a funny meeting. She, of course, did all the talking and thought it would be a great job for me, running her ranch household from October to May. Then we'd close the place for the hot summer months. Hot? It was almost always hot there. I wasn't sure I wanted the job and I told her that. I didn't want to leave Los Angeles. But she wouldn't take no for an answer and said, "I'll see you on October first." This conversation took place months before. Then I never heard a word, not another word from her. I thought it had all blown over.

September thirtieth I get a call from her. "Are you ready to go?" she asks. "I'm in town."

The very next day I went to the ranch with her. Yes, I went. I couldn't say no.

Hot sand and dry desert wind. I really wasn't sure I was going to stay. I stayed more than twenty-five years. Jackie made me.

One day she said to me, "I want you to furnish the big living room." It was still empty then.

"Oh, no, I'm not going to do that, Jackie," I say. "It's going to be very expensive and I'm not going to be responsible for that. What if you don't like it?"

She let the subject drop for a while. Then she came back to it. "Vi, go check out furniture for that room," she asks. "You can do it."

I knew her well enough to say no again, but she persisted. "I don't want to do it because my taste may not be your taste in furniture," I say.

"I always like what you do," she answers. "I like your taste. It's just like mine. I'll tell you what. If you go and furnish that room for me, I'll write you a letter saying that even if I don't like it, I will not say a word. Not one word."

"Can I hold you to the letter?" I ask.

"Yes, you can," she agrees. And the next day she wrote the letter just as she promised. I went to Sloan's, met a nice fellow in the furniture department, and I furnished the big room myself. Everybody liked it, including Jackie. She never said a word to the contrary either.

A lot of people who didn't know her felt that she had to be masculine to do what she was doing. But she wasn't masculine at all. I do think she could fly as well as any man. Chuck said that too. She was as good as any of them. Better than most.

I'm prejudiced, I guess. But it's the truth.

She always loved clothes and had beautiful outfits. You know, she'd come in from breaking one of those records, wash her own hair, and be ready to go again in record time. People always said she had a hairdresser, but she usually did her own hair. And her eyes...why, they'd be all red from the strain of flying when she'd come in from a race and tell us she was going out right away. I'd be thinking, "You must be kidding, Jackie.

You've got to be exhausted." But she'd put something in her eyes to take the redness out, dress up, and look like a princess.

She always forced herself to keep going even when she was sick, so sick I thought she was dying. What a determined woman.

I was in New York one of the first times it happened. The pain was excruciating and I couldn't imagine what was wrong. My tummy was on fire from the inside out and the cramping was like nothing I experienced before. Floyd was wonderful. I landed in a hospital and he came to my rescue both during and after my surgery.

When I was fifteen years old I had suffered acute appendicitis and a local doctor, someone the Richlers knew, had done me the honor of removing it. Years later I would learn that he had also done me no good because talcum powder from his surgical gloves remained behind after my appendix was long gone. I may have been one of the first warm bodies this guy operated on because his blunder put me into a hospital operating room at least seven different times. Sometimes I put myself there for other stupid reasons, but many times, my abdominal adhesions were his fault. Little adhesions—I used to call them barnacles—would form around those pockets of talc and scar tissue would build up. The scars would tear or my intestines would become blocked and jeepers, I'd be in pain.

Elephants—Floyd knew exactly what to do to help me recover from that first health battle we fought together. Floyd Odlum, who had bought a piece of Madison Square Garden by then, offered me a ride on an elephant around the center ring at the Garden as a lead performer for Ringling Brothers. The picture he had taken for my memory box still makes me smile as I smiled that night remembering how I had planned my escape along with the elephants in the little circus in that backwater Florida slum.

DEATH COMES CLOSE

AUTUMN 1933

Willie Mae and her daughter had been staying with me in New York then. And I had been feeling so strong about myself and my life. It wasn't just the fact that something I'd lost—my doll—had been finally returned. I think it had more to do with the belief that my life was coming together. Floyd and I had talked seriously about our relationship, where it was going. And having a little girl in my apartment had added a special dimension. I used to tell myself, "Someday you'll have your own children."

Then came the devastating news of Ted Marshall's death in a crash somewhere off the Hawaiian coast. I was going to miss him terribly. Ted and his seven Navy flying buddies had really given me the best training a pilot could ask for, before he was transferred to Hawaii. He hadn't wanted to go. Something told him it wasn't a good idea, but he honestly was a duty-bound individual. He and I had been building big plans together for the London-to-Australia race, the race that was on every pilot's mind at the time.

I had decided to fly west by the northern route and to take Willie Mae's daughter along with me for company. We had cut across the country through Memphis and St. Louis to Omaha. And my poor niece had experienced airsickness for days. Then it passed and we were enjoying ourselves. It was fairly late in the afternoon when we reached Rock Springs and started to push on to cross the Rocky Mountain divide. I turned on the radio, which turned out to be our undoing. For some reason, when the radio was on, it pulled the compass about 20 degrees off true course. I didn't know this, of course, and kept following the compass, not my nose. I did have some strip maps of the area, but in following the compass, I had even flown us off the map. Instead of flying across the range on a tangent, I had been trying to cross the mountains nearly 100 miles south of where I should have been. That's when I encountered that down draft of wind. I had never experienced such a nerve-racking sensation. You're caught there. It was stupid of me to get caught like that....

I'm in a down draft of air in a cup in the mountains and I can't rise above the crest. I'm desperate. The compass is badly off true, and all I know is that I'm somewhere between Rock Springs, Wyoming, and Salt Lake City, Utah, on my first attempt to fly across the United States. I was in my new Waco at the time, a four-place plane with a cabin, and it cost me $3,200. But there was no lucky 13 on the side as yet.

I had traded in both my car and the Travelair to buy the Waco, and it would have been devastating to lose it so soon—not to mention my four-year-old niece.

Wind, after rising over a mountain range, sometimes turns sharply down again, and if it's strong enough, it will make the unlucky plane that happens to get caught in that draft lose altitude—very rapidly. *Woosh!* Did we go fast!

Try as I might, I couldn't get sufficient altitude to fight it. I put the nose up at almost stalling angle and open the throttle, wide. It looks like I'm about to smack into the mountain. Can I turn back? The mountains behind us are just as bad. High and dangerous. I criss-cross back and forth between those ranges, trying like crazy to get higher. I'm not sure of my position and I've given up on the compass.

Then I spot the green. A little green spot below us that's got to be a farm up here. I head for it. My landing speed is 60 miles an hour and it turns out that the field is a patch of alfalfa, but a patch of alfalfa with an irrigation ditch running right through the middle. To hit that ditch at that speed is absolutely not a good idea.

Bang. Bump. I throw the plane into what is known as a ground loop, which means I tip it sideways so one wing will hit the ground and spin me. If you do this, you're sure to damage a wing but you may be able to stay upright. We stop, look at each other, and we're fine, my niece and me. The left wing isn't fine. It's been torn off.

When we crashed, my thoughts jumbled for an instant. Where to go? What to do? Don't panic. The thoughts dance between poles for mothers I know. And I was playing at mother there. You can panic alone if you'd like, but when you have a child who needs to be calmed, you do what you must. And in the doing, you calm yourself as well.

All wasn't lost. I borrowed a car, a Ford, from the farmer and we drove 110 miles to Salt Lake City, where I rented a hotel room for my niece and me. I left her there in the charge of a hotel manager and located a mechanic with a sense of adventure. Then the mechanic and I drove back that night to the farmer and the plane in his field, appraised the damage, and returned to the city, where he put in an order for a new left wing.

My niece and I pressed on for California by regular airline for the funeral, but we made arrangements to return to the alfalfa field on our way back east. And we took off from that very same field, having lost no appetite for flying. In fact, I'd venture to guess mine had become even more voracious.

I hadn't wanted to miss Ted's funeral in Long Beach because his family had begun to mean so much to me. His mother, in fact, had been wonderful to me. And I made it though it hurt to think about what an important link in my life was missing with Ted gone.

Ted and I had been talking about entering the MacRobertson London-to-Australia race to be held in the fall of 1934. The prize money added up to $75,000, and though we didn't expect to win it all, I'd have the chance to see more of the world.

Sir MacPherson Robertson was a seventy-four-year-old Australian who had amassed a fortune making Old Gold candy and was always looking for promotional opportunities. He had financed the first automobile circuit of the Australian continent in 1927 and a year later footed the bill for an Antarctic expedition on the condition that a piece of that ice be called "MacRobertson's Land." The London-to-Melbourne air race was going to be in celebration of the 100th anniversary of the founding of Melbourne. Those races in the early days of aviation were more than simply races for prize money. They were often the only way airplane designers and manufacturers could show their stuff. Winners might walk away with some cash, of course, but the airplane maker wanted to walk away with orders for more planes.

The MacRobertson race was the first flying project in which manufacturers took an interest in my doings. I approached them on my own initiative then, but later they'd come to me.

The proposed route stretched over 11,300 miles and followed a course that had taken two brothers 4 weeks and 2 days to complete in 1919. The record in 1934 stood at 6 days, 17 hours. You'd be crossing deserts, mountains, tropical rain forests, water of all kind and distance. In fact, the news had pointed out that sharks infested the Timor Sea over which you'd be flying for 2,084 miles without sight of land. Pilots all over the world were crazy with anticipation. What an adventure Ted and I had cut out for ourselves.

I just couldn't consider quitting without giving it my best shot. I went to see Mabel Willebrandt, who was a successful woman lawyer with a real "bug" about aviation. She was a pilot herself and I knew she'd take an interest in another woman trying to enter a big race. Mabel became crucial when plans and planes began to fall apart, and she shared the burden of the incredible financial costs as well.

I also started thinking about what else I'd need along with the money and support of someone like Mabel. To get to London and from there to Australia I'd need to know more about flying. Gone was the girl who pretended to know what she didn't. I knew that if I wanted to win, I had to know flying upside down and from the inside out.

Back in New York, I joined Johnny Livingstone's Air Circus. It wasn't unusual in those days for good pilots to work in air circuses. You've got to remember that the Air Force didn't even exist and the few planes the Army Air Corps had or the Navy could boast about were really nothing. Hot pilots and good planes were to be seen and flown in circuses. But not everyone is cut out for circus life. I had been left behind by a circus once before in my life, and flying airplanes in one was not to be compared with riding an elephant.

It's called the Immelmann turn. It's a maneuver that allows a pilot to quickly reverse the course of his ship and I couldn't seem to do it, try as I might. Twice in one day doing a show with the circus in Buffalo, New York, I went into a terrible power spin trying to execute the Immelmann turn. I wouldn't recover from it until I was less than 500 feet off the ground and I know that stubborn insistence on righting that plane could have spun me right into the ground. I never considered my parachute until it was too late. I'd keep trying until it was almost too late for either: the chute or the dead end of the spin.

I now know enough aerial acrobatics to keep out of trouble in the air and I can certainly bring a plane out of a spin. I learned that the hard way. Understanding a spin is crucial to every pilot because practically everything that goes wrong with a plane puts it into a spin.

I quit the circus after that and entered some air races that year, considered a couple more, but the big one was really on my mind. I had to be ready.

FLYING HIGH AND BLIND

WINTER 1934

Floyd had come down with a dreadful cold and we were in New York together, so I decided to fly him south for a weekend of sunbathing. We would take the Waco. No problem.

In the Carolinas, I hit murky, terrible weather and I was honestly scared. It was all I could do to stay right side up while flying straight and level, so we plowed on for forty minutes like that, hoping that nothing was in our path. Floyd never spoke a word of his worry but when he saw me cross myself, he knew we were in big trouble.

What did he do? It was just like Floyd to tell me he needed a nap. Later the truth came out: he kept one eye open the entire time, pretending to be relaxed enough to sleep so I'd feel more confident. But nothing could make me confident in that weather, knowing what I didn't know.

Forty minutes of dark gray and no way to turn. I kept my foot on the rudder and my hand on the stick and I didn't dare let go.

When we finally got into the clear, Floyd could hardly talk, his mouth was so dry from being tense. We landed in a cow pasture near a house and asked a startled farmer for a drink of water. Then we took off for Orlando with absolutely nothing on our minds but two days of sun and sand. We had earned it.

But first a small problem. No sooner had the plane rolled to a stop on the hard-packed sand of a deserted beach, than two federal revenue officers pounced on us. Floyd Odlum, one of the most important men in American business, was about to be bounced into jail for smuggling drugs from Cuba. Can you believe it?

We convinced the officers we were up to nothing of the kind and they left us in peace. But I'd have no peace of mind until I understood blind flying. In fact, I made up my mind that I'd never take a passenger up again until I had mastered this new skill.

OTHER VOICES:

Floyd Odlum

Jackie didn't dare turn back. Yet she couldn't see a foot ahead. I could see she was worried, so to ease the tension I said casually that I'd take a nap. But I watched her out of one eye, saw her cross herself repeatedly, knew she was praying hard. We got through. But when we came down, her first words were, "I'll never take a passenger up again until I learn how to fly by instruments."

Wesley Smith was one of the best all-around aviators to be found in '34. He had been a transport mail flyer almost from the time air mail existed and his reputation for staying alive had been made because he could fly in all kinds of weather. Neither rain nor snow, sleet nor dark of night could kill Smith. Not even fog—and I still consider fog the great menace to aviation. I prayed for fog when I was learning to fly blind, but I don't like it one bit. There has been some historical controversy about who flew first on instruments. Some say it was Wesley Smith; some say Jimmy Doolittle; and I often wonder about Wiley Post. I knew Post couldn't have flown around the world without having been on instruments and I even tried to hire him. But he wouldn't do it. And Smith was a crackerjack.

Before I hired Smith, I had tried to teach myself by putting a hood up over my cockpit and using another student to warn me of other airplanes. I had already taught myself to stay straight, level, and how to hold a course on instruments. But I needed lessons.

Then Smith's bad fortune turned into my good luck when the U.S. Army bungled its way into the air mail contract business and put flyers like Smith out of commission. It was a bad idea for the Army and it didn't last long—but long enough for me to make my move. I convinced Wesley to teach me everything he knew and he agreed to train me. I knew he didn't agree to like me, but for a time there, I really thought he hated me.

Flying on the beam, the radio beam. That's what we did together back and forth across the United States continent time after time. So many times I've lost count. At one point I calculated that Wesley and I had spent 500 hours together in the air. He was ever so patient with me.

The beam is what an airplane pilot in the thirties used to guide herself when she couldn't see any landmarks visually. It was a sound sent over a certain course through the air by a radio station. The signal stayed on a specific course, almost as if it were a wire strung in the air, let's say, between Newark and Detroit. The message was continual and you'd hear it as "right" if you were north of the wire, "left" when you were south of it, and "on course" when you were right along that imaginary wire. This beam message wouldn't arrive in your airplane unless your radio receiver was tuned into the proper frequency of the station you were nearing. Think of it like a road between two cities— one you are leaving and one you are moving toward. It extended as high as you needed. Altitude didn't affect it.

About every 200 miles along each of our air ways, there would be one of these sending stations either at, or quite near, an airport, and you could hear that signal for up to 100 miles away. Just as you left one signal, you could pick up another. The signals were sent in Morse code, dashes and dots, and the stations were operated by the Department of Commerce (DOC) back then. I learned—and it was the hard way for sure. Those maps the DOC put out looked like cobwebs in pie shapes covering the whole of the United States, and Smith insisted that I know all the ins and outs of those webs. I could hear those irritating dots and dashes in my sleep sometimes. Dash dot was Morse code for N and dot dash was the signal for A. N, of course, would mean you were at true north while A would be heard south of the station. If you heard one continuous sound, it was Morse code for T, and that meant you were on course, where the beams met.

The signals became louder as you went toward a station and weaker as you headed away. It was a bit more complicated than this simple explanation. But you've got the idea here.

There were rules of the air just like rules of the road and I had to know them. For example, planes flying westerly must fly at an altitude based in the even thousands of feet, let's say between 2,000 and 3,000 or between 4,000 and 5,000. And planes flying easterly based in odd thousands. Every so many times an hour, the beam signal would be turned off for three minutes and the weather report was broadcast so you'd know if the airport was clear. And a pilot would have to report her own position every so often over a transmitter. You'd stay to one side or the other of the beam depending on which direction you were flying, east or west.

In the beginning of beam flying, snow, rain, or bad weather would cause static on the line. That was a problem. But radio attendants didn't have the trouble air traffic controllers have today. There weren't as many planes up there.

Where's the blind part? Well, part of it came in when you wanted to come in for a landing. Right over the sending station there are no signals to be heard. It's a zone of silence and pilots would call it a cone of silence because the higher the altitude, the bigger the silent zone became. If the zone were visible, it would have been shaped like a cone. When you got to that silent zone, you'd descend to an altitude where you hit clear sky. When you reached that "ceiling," you would let down so many feet per minute with a given air speed in order to bring you out at a certain point. Then the runway would be right in front of you, you hoped, and under normal conditions, you could make a normal landing.

You do the same thing today flying by instruments alone but with much simpler procedures. There is nothing to it and some of the monitoring we've got is really something.

The artificial horizon today is just exactly like the artificial
horizon we had when I started learning to fly instruments so
many years ago. The turn and bank indicator is just the same
now, save that it is electric. The one Wesley and I had then was
by vacuum. All of your instruments today aren't really new but
are merely takeoffs from the old ones.

Nothing was ever good enough for Wesley unless it was perfect. He'd growl at me all the time about beams, signals, maps,
and how I didn't double-check enough. "It's awfully simple to
double-check everything before landing but it's simply awful to
take it for granted." He'd hover over me until I'd growl back,
begging for compliments. "Jackie," he once told me, "you sure
can read a map even if you do hold it upside down."

I was so proud of myself the first time I flew all the way from
Albuquerque to Chicago, nonstop, eating my lunch and having
my smokes, flying completely on the beam and by instruments
only.

"If you keep it up," he admitted, "you may even be able to
fly straight someday." He was the best in the business and I
loved it.

I know it sounds preposterous, but I wanted to win the
London-to-Australia race and I realized I'd need more than
Wesley's know-how to do it. Women pilots in the thirties were a
very special breed. I hadn't been born to such surroundings, but
if I had to push my way in, push my way to the top, I knew I'd
do it. Winning such a race would offer me an entry. And I'd
need Wesley himself as one of two copilots. He kept saying,
"No thanks." In the meantime, I looked for a third pilot for my
adventure and came up with Royal Leonard, an airline regular
who had made celestial navigation a hobby. I wanted Royal to
take the second leg of the distance with me. And I still hoped
Wesley would reconsider flying the first half.

Smith knew how much I wanted to be in that race and to be a
serious contender. He had even heard me making arrangements
with Jack Northrop and TWA for one of a litter of eight new airplanes. Northrop had built these Gammas for the airline when it
still had a mail contract with the Postmaster General. They were
bullet-shaped, had only one cockpit but were long range and
speedy. Just before the eight planes were wheeled out of the factory, the government canceled all mail contracts with airlines

like TWA. I figured they might be stuck and contacted Jack Northrop. He was open to my suggestions. And when TWA released claims to the plane, Wesley stopped saying no to me. I felt like I had finally received my diploma when he got an official leave of absence from TWA and agreed to the adventure. Had I convinced him of my ability? Or was it the stamina he saw in me every time he had said, "No"?

In late June, Wesley and I were flying west on one more training trip, when I put myself back into a hospital with another abdominal obstruction. I blamed it on overwork, quick lunches, odd hours, and Albuquerque, New Mexico, which had been our base. We were staying over for the night. I'd live it down, I said. But, as my pain worsened, I knew I wanted to get into the air and back to Los Angeles, where I knew people who knew my medical history.

I thought I'd die on the way. Wesley had the controls and the fog had Los Angeles. We struck out for Long Beach and just over that city a small hole in the clouds offered us a glimpse of a large gas tank I recognized even in my pain-crazy state. I knew Long Beach so well because I had trained there. We landed and I immediately called a doctor, who met me at a hotel and insisted I get to a hospital. The surgery would throw my whole racing plan out of whack, but I knew what I was up against.

The doctors' arguments in favor of immediate intervention were irrefutable. They told me I'd be dead before morning if they didn't open me up.

I survived that night, but three days later I thought it was all over again. Something I had eaten, they said. I don't know what it was, but things looked black. I felt miserable and felt even worse when the surgeon warned me away from flying for weeks.

But I was never one to take advice second-hand. Any hypotheses deserved a test. Mabel Willebrandt had asked to borrow my Waco for her work, and I had promised to get it to Los Angeles for her. It was over in Long Beach, so a few days after my operation, even before the stitches had been removed, I slipped out of bed, went to Long Beach by car, and flew the plane over to the L.A. airport.

It was the longest short trip I've ever made. Mrs. Willebrandt never suspected, and that's the way I wanted it to stay. She had stuck her neck out for me—another woman in a man's field—and I couldn't begin to repay her in kind for her gratitude.

Jack Northrop's factory cut up one cockpit in a Gamma and squeezed in a second. Then they refitted the mail compartment so that it could be filled with gasoline—enough gas to go 3,000 miles without stopping. And with a little help from the wind, the speedometer might see 220 mph. One of the reasons it was going to be so fast for its day was that GE had just built the first turbo supercharger and I planned to put one on my engine. It was the first time a private airplane ever had one and my liquid-cooled engine with the supercharger never did function right. It was like any new mechanical thing. It kept blowing up.

BLOWUPS IN THE NIGHT

SUMMER 1934

The first time my souped-up Northrop Gamma blew up was in the factory, on the test block, two days before the start of the 1934 Bendix transcontinental race I had negotiated to enter. I figured an extra $7,000 in winnings would help finance my way across the European continent and I had to take the ship east anyway.

Four mechanics taking a course in engines were training in the factory at the time and saw it go up in smoke on a final test. There went my plans for the Bendix.

We all knew that this first blowup was in the turbo supercharger. The engine was a Conqueror liquid-cooled engine Curtiss Wright was very hot to promote. There was a lot of competition then between the air-cooled engine manufacturers and the liquid-cooled proponents. Guy Vaughan, president of Curtiss Wright, wanted me to test the Conqueror with a supercharger they themselves had recently designed. General Electric had also been working on a supercharger at the time. If I had been able to win the race with the Curtiss Wright design, it might have set off a worldwide demand for more. But it wasn't to be.

That first blowup wasn't to be the last.

Curtiss offered me another experimental supercharger to replace the one that had blown. And they'd make good their promise in a hurry. They'd simply take an engine that had been built to make government tests and put it into my plane. What a mistake.

I was in California when I heard the news of the second blowup. It had occurred in the factory again and something was radically wrong. The manufacturer agreed. The engine couldn't take the super high speed, and the bearings would blow. But what a mish-mash at that point. They insisted they would make good my loss, but the loss of time was almost irreplaceable. We had only days to get a completely rebuilt plane to New York, from where it would be shipped to London for the start of the race.

And rebuilt was no exaggeration. Because of accommodations made for the supercharger, there were 600 pounds of extra weight in the nose, the power plant assembly, and the propeller. The propeller had been designed to rotate in the direction opposite from the usual. Now, with 600 extra pounds and no supercharged engine, my cruising range would have been cut by 30 miles per hour. Northrop offered to make all the necessary changes in 48 hours. I wondered. But I cabled the racing committee in London just the same.

I was shocked when my answer arrived. They wouldn't let me enter the race with an engine different from the one on my application. God, I was angry. I tried everything. Even Mabel Willebrandt went to bat for me, and in the end they relented on the condition that I add standardized features. In the meantime, the standardized parts Jack Northrop needed were east and the plane was still in the West.

Finally, four days before the boat was to sail from New York, the plane was ready, the changes complete, and the license procured.

Now, get ready for the third blowup.

I had to get that plane east as fast as I could and decided to fly along an airline route with Royal Leonard as copilot. We would meet Wesley Smith in Kansas City, where he'd take Royal's controls. It would be a practice run for the three of us working as a team.

Three mechanics stood watching as we warmed up the engine. It was two o'clock in the morning, but we didn't dare waste the hours till morning light.

"I've got no faith in this one either," I holler to them. "It won't last five hours in the air."

"Want to bet?" one yells over. They were laughing at my pessimism.

"Jackie you're just letting your fears show," one of them says. "That engine won't stop."

I was too optimistic in guessing five hours.

Royal and I had gone high to clear the mountains and were flying at 15,000 feet. We'd been up for about two hours and the heater had stopped working. It was perishingly cold. At least that's what I blamed my numbness on.

"Can you take the controls?" I ask Royal, telling him how cold I am. I want him to take us down lower. I'm thinking that might help me. As he starts to descend, the engine sputters and slows down. Then there's a ping and the cockpits are covered in oil.

"Take the stick, Jackie," he yells.

I can't. I can't even raise my arms an inch.

I wasn't numb with cold. I had been breathing carbon monoxide gas that had obviously been leaking into my cockpit, slowly asphyxiating me. Leonard wanted to fuss with the instruments, but when he saw what was happening to me, he tried to get me to adjust my parachute, to get ready to jump. He pulled open the hood to let cold air rush in, and that revived me enough to buckle up my chute.

It's funny what thoughts go through your head at times like that. I thought of the splash I'd make if the chute didn't open, and it made me laugh. How sick was my humor. I thought of the matches I had stuck behind me in the cockpit which I wanted to take with me when I jumped. I'd need to build a fire to warm myself and signal Royal if we were separated. I scolded myself for not having a flare or two attached to my suit. And, if you can imagine me back then and how tight I was with the money I had, I gave myself a mental pat on the back for having the airplane insured.

I wasn't afraid.

I also knew I wasn't going to be able to jump. Dead weight—that's how I felt. How could I have gotten myself up and out with no strength? If Royal had been able to see my face in the light, even he would have realized how far gone I was. Green—I knew I was green going on ashen gray. A real zombie.

Royal kept us up there for as long as he could. About three minutes. It was long enough because we spotted an emergency field as that engine coughed its last. The landing was perfect there in Arizona in the middle of the night, and I literally fell out of the cockpit, gasping for breath. My face was—you guessed it—greenish.

It took me about an hour to recuperate in the clear night air, and after we found a hotel room and a telephone, I roused those mechanics from their beds in Los Angeles. Spare parts were on the way as I got going by regular airline to New York. I hadn't given up yet.

The fourth time that Northrop Gamma engine blew up, Royal was alone and he wasn't so lucky. There was no emergency landing strip in sight. He threw down a flare, spotted what looked like a country road, and took the limping plane down. Closer to the ground he threw a second flare, thought the field at the side of the road looked better than the road, but ended up in an irrigation ditch. He was banged up but the plane was worse: it had broken its back.

We were out of the race, he thought out loud when he called me in New York. I had just gone to bed, hoping against hope that I'd see Royal and the plane soon, very soon. I had even hired mechanics to be ready to dismantle it for shipping.

"Give up, Jackie," Royal said to me. He was obviously exhausted. "It's over."

"I don't think so," I told him. And my mind started racing.

I'm not sure I like being referred to as a pioneer of aviation because it connotes age and no place in particular to go in the future except sideways. But I guess I'm a pioneer, if you measure by the usual standards.

My flying takes me back sixty percent of the way to the first powered flights by men, the Wright brothers. In fact, I met Wilbur Wright. There is really no one thing that marks a pioneer from the follow-uppers in aviation. If a pioneer is one who explores or opens the way for others to follow, then the Wright brothers were certainly pioneers, and so was Chuck Yeager, who broke the speed of sound. But aviation moves so fast and has so far to go that most of yesterday's pioneers are soon forgotten.

While attending a dinner of the Experimental Test Pilots Association, I saw a program about the first aviation meet in America held in Los Angeles in 1910, and of all the contestants listed, I had heard of only one: Glenn Curtiss. Curtiss had won the previous day's event by going ten laps around the course in 24 minutes, 54 seconds.

I've gone 40 times that fast. But Glenn Curtiss was a pioneer, and every pilot who leads the way in something that has not been done before is a pioneer.

I was the only American woman entered in that London-to-Australia race, and I wasn't going to let the fact that I didn't have an airplane keep me from trying.

GEE BEES

Gee Bee stands for Granville
Brothers, a Springfield, Massachusetts, airplane company
which made fast, unstable, dangerous planes in the thirties. The
nearly cute nickname is a sham. They were killers. There were
few pilots who flew Gee Bees and then lived to talk about it.
Jimmy Doolittle was one. I was another.

Thank God there were only about eleven Gee Bees built.
That plane didn't belong in the air. It would stall all the time,
regardless of its airspeed. I once asked Jack Northrop if he
could figure it out.

"This is just crazy," I said to Jack. "It doesn't have any indicated speed of stalling. Every airplane with a given load factor
has a speed considerably less than full speed at which it will
stall. This one doesn't. It does it anywhere, anytime."

Jack couldn't help me.

Later, after I had met Dr. Theodore Von Karman, the
world's greatest aerodynamicist, I even asked him about that
crazy Gee Bee. How had I been able to stay alive when others
were dead? And what was with the stalling?

"Jackie," he told me, "the reason it stalls like that is because
of the angle of attack, the angle at which you blanket out the
effect of your tail surfaces." I didn't quite understand what he
was saying at the time, but I made it a point to remember every
single one of his words and then ask the right questions. The
fault lay in the design of the plane, in effect. Dr. Von Karman

added, "You are lucky to be alive because you are quick enough to pull the plane back to flight position before it drops off on you. That's how you are getting away with it."

Sarabia, a famous Mexican pilot, was killed in my Gee Bee, taking off from the Washington, D.C., airport for an attempted record, nonstop flight to Mexico City. He was dead in an instant, right on takeoff. Others ended up the same.

I tell you all this as a prelude to my story about the London-to-Australia race.

I flew a Gee Bee, the Q.E.D. Gee Bee, but a Gee Bee nonetheless. The Q.E.D. was Latin for "Quod Erat Demonstrandum" and came from the designers who translated that as "Quite Easily Done." It was not easily done, however. The crazy Q.E.D. violated basic rules of aerodynamics.

Clyde Pangborn had entered his name in the race, hoping to find himself in a Gee Bee but because of problems at the factory as well as an offer from Roscoe Turner, who had never flown over oceans before and knew that Clyde had, the Q.E.D. was still sitting in the hangar, almost ready to go. Clyde had joined Roscoe's team but was still the registered owner of an entry. He had the official right to name an alternate crew, and I knew it.

Sitting in New York, after my conversation with Royal, searching for a way to stay in the race, I remembered Clyde's Q.E.D. and made all the right calls. Granville Brothers knew me because I myself had approached them earlier in the game but had changed my mind when I compared it with the chance to be in a Northrop. Jack's planes were so streamlined and beautifully fast for their day.

But any plane was better than no plane. I bought the Gee Bee with a little help from my friend Mabel Willebrandt. Granville Brothers were pleased because they were anxious to make a name for themselves in such a prestigious international contest. They even offered to send mechanics along to complete the plane en route to London on the ship. In the meantime, I had Wesley Smith and Royal Leonard take some of the sophisticated equipment out of the Northrop Gamma so we could install it in our Gee Bee.

We had four hours to make the official arrangements with the London officials. I needed what was called an airworthiness certificate, numerous permissions to fly over all those countries, not in a Gamma but a Gee Bee, and Mabel turned on the steam. Mabel even convinced a Department of Commerce official to go along on the boat to do the necessary testing. Landing lights, flares, radio equipment—we planned to install as much as we could as we crossed the Atlantic, in spite of storms and seasickness. Not much would get done as it turned out.

All this was done by telephone. I never set eyes on that Gee Bee until I arrived at the airport near Southampton, England, and tried to fly it to the field where the race would commence, twenty-four hours later. It was a disaster and still incomplete. The other disastrous aspect was the tremendous publicity surrounding the contestants. I had never experienced anything like it. I never sought publicity like that in my life because mostly it's a waste of your time. And I didn't like the scene there in London one bit.

The press kept rumoring about the mysterious American woman entry, but there was nothing mysterious about my whereabouts or doings. I had a tricky, incomplete plane to contend with.

Wesley flew the Gee Bee between Southampton and London while I sat in the back pilot's compartment on a vegetable box. The first time we landed, the bump was so violent, we thought we had damaged the plane, and to save our faces, we simply left it out there on the runway, heading for the pilots' quarters.

In the meantime, Clyde Pangborn was giving me trouble and demanding that I pay him for the transfer of his entry. After all the anguish that Gee Bee had caused me—at that point I had no idea my troubles were just beginning—he had some nerve asking for money. I was furious. And I told him so. If I had been a man, we would have gone out behind the hangar to fight it out.

Back on the runway, we could see that the Gee Bee was fine. It hadn't been damaged on the bumpy landing because its landings were normally bumpy. It always came down with a thud. The landing wheels were too close together, which made it impossible to taxi straight. We'd land with that thud and then wobble all over the field.

The starting point the next morning was a nearly completed Royal Air Force base at Mildenhall, sixty miles north of London. The lord mayor of London was there promptly at 6:30 A.M. to drop the official white flags. Planes took off at 45-second intervals, and the famous team of Mollisons—Amy was a wonderful pilot and flew with her husband—were first. Wesley and I were fourth in line and had been warming up the engine, but as soon as we were airborne, the plane sort of staggered, dipped slightly, and I knew we were in for a real ride. Neither of us knew that Gee Bee well enough. We recovered speed, however, and we were serious about sticking with it. The haze was horrible and I was happy Wesley had been such a nag about my instrument training and Morse code lessons. This race, however, was actually the first and last time I relied on Morse code.

After all the hullabaloo in America about this contest, only three American-crewed entries remained: Roscoe Turner, the United States speed king at the time; Jack Wright, a stunt pilot from Utica, New York; and me. When you compared the elaborate preparations I had made for the flight—sending specialists ahead on the route with automatic refueling devices, flares, spare parts, personal items, extra instruments—as well as the whole debacle with my Northrop Gamma—to Jack Wright's simplistic attitude, I really wondered. All Jack wanted to do en route was to "fly this plane while it's still mine." It was a tiny Lambert Monocoupe with a single 90 horsepower that hummed along. Who had more sense: him or me? I had even sent clothes along to Melbourne so I'd have something to wear to the festivities.

But I wasn't alone with my big thinking. Roscoe Turner had gone into hock to buy a Boeing transport plane he called the "Nip and Tuck." Then because of rough weather he hadn't been able to get it off the ship at Plymouth. They had to take it over to France, to Le Havre, where the French tried to make him pay import duty of $20,000. He got around that but had to unload the plane, assemble it, and fly it back to England in time. What was funny about all of our best-laid plans was that the Europeans had been sullen and some of them openly angry about what they believed to be a Yankee conspiracy to walk away with all the prize money. Little did they realize.

My Gee Bee was the fastest plane in the race, I believe, but right from the start I realized that it wouldn't be speed that would win. The prize would go to the plane and crew who could stick it out for 12,000 miles.

Noise. God, that plane was noisy. Wesley and I couldn't talk to each other and expect to be heard. There was no insulation to hold down the racket or keep out the cold. We were freezing and flying at 14,000 feet with no oxygen. But we stuck with it for hours and hours.

Somewhere over the Carpathian Mountains the weather cleared a little, and because the fuel in one tank was getting low, Wesley switched to a second tank. That's when our troubles mounted.

The engine sputters and dies. I turn back to the first, nearly empty tank and the motor starts again. But I know we can't last long on an empty tank. I try the tank switch again. We lose a little altitude but not much. I flip the switch up to On and we stall again. Wesley is worried.

He yells back to me and points down. "We may have to bail out," I know he's suggesting though I can't hear a word. He starts to open his canopy.

I look down at the snow-covered mountains and I wonder. I can see Wesley move toward the latch on his canopy. That's when I push up on mine to find that it's jammed. Even if I was serious about jumping, serious about trying to survive in those mountains, I can't get out of the plane. Wesley looks back and sees me pointing to the jammed latch. Will he jump alone?

A minute passes. I'm fiddling with the gasoline switches. Then, I pass him a note: "*On* means *Off*?"

I turn that switch down to its Off position and it catches. The gas is feeding. God, something as simple as a mismarked switch has nearly killed us. I had turned off the gasoline when I intended to turn on a new tank. In the meantime, we push on to Bucharest in the cold and the noise. I am freezing.

Nothing could be worse. As we approached the airfield in Bucharest, I know it can. Wesley and I make a horrifying discovery.

Here's what happened.

As we started to come in—I was at the controls—I went through the routine of letting my wing flaps down to slow down. No way. One was up and one down. You can't land an airplane like that. One flap was stuck up while the other one moved only a little. The stubborn flap wouldn't be budged, and it made the plane terribly out of balance. We climbed, went around, and tried again. Similar results. With one flap up and one down, landing would be almost impossible. Could we stop? Was the runway long enough?

Wesley passes me a note saying that we should break open

my canopy latch and jump if our third attempt is thwarted. By this time I had loosened my canopy.

Tricky flying is tricky flying. I knew what dead-stick landings, controlled crashes into farmers' fields, slamming through fences into cars, and doing ground loops meant, but I wasn't sure I could get that Gee Bee down. Maybe he was right. Q.E.D. never meant easily understood or flown. But we couldn't give up without trying. At least I couldn't.

I made the first attempt to land and couldn't hack it with the flaps up and down. I wrote a note to Wesley: "Do you want to make a pass at the field? You can bail out if you want to, but this is my airplane and I am going to get it to the ground."

"I won't go if you won't," he writes.

We really kept writing those notes back and forth. It would have been quite comical except that we were in a deadly serious spot. He writes: "You're a fool."

I knew I was a fool. I write: "It is my life. You can do what you please with yours. You can open the canopy and use your parachute, but I'm going to land this plane."

Third pass. The flaps go down. I'm going to land. We're coming in fast, very fast. We hit hard. That same dumb thud. And we keep right on going down the field—a restricted military airport—until there is no more runway. Cold, tired, dirty, and noise still ringing in my ears, I strip off the coverall flying suit and try to put on some lipstick. I've got to make conversation with the Rumanian Air Minister, Radu Irimescu, an old friend of Floyd's. And I've got to find words to say.

We used every inch of runway to bring that Q.E.D. to a stop in Bucharest, but I did it without any damage. Even as I was trying to comb my hair and pull my act together to meet Mr. Irimescu, I knew the race was over, though. And when mechanics estimated several hours of work to fix the flaps, they only confirmed my hunch. Even with flaps that worked together and went both up as well as down, that Gee Bee had outgrown the fields on our route. None were as long as that one in Rumania and I could only imagine where we might end up.

My race ended right there.

I am on the Orient Express to Paris a night and a day later. I'm exhausted, nearly asleep in a small compartment. A handbag, the same flying clothes I've been wearing for days, and a coat I picked up in Bucharest. That's all I've got with me. And all I want is sleep.

Wesley had agreed to wait with the plane in Bucharest until the repairs have been made, to fly it back to London and to arrange for delivery to the United States.

It must be midnight. We're at the Hungarian border and suddenly there is a loud, a very loud knocking at my door. I jump up quickly and when I open the door, a flashlight is thrust into my face. God, what next, I want to say out loud. But I don't. I can't understand what the officials—there are more than one—are asking me. Something about a passport?

"I'll get my passport," I answer. "No problem." That's when I recall that I never did have my passport stamped for legal entry into Rumania. I had been too preoccupied with everything else and I hadn't planned to be in Rumania for more than an airport stop.

"Here it is," I say, offering it over. I know I'm in for it now.

They rumble and grumble and someone goes to fetch an Englishman on the train who can speak French. It seems we'll be needing a translator. This isn't going to be easy.

"Where's my luggage?" they want to know.

"I don't have any," I answer. They can't believe me or they don't want to.

An hour and a half passes. We argue and I explain over and over again why I am there. No one believes such a story.

They want me off the train. Someone catches me by the arms and I back into the far corner of the compartment and get ready to swing with the water bottle I grab. I'll fight my way out of this mess. I will not leave the train.

Suddenly I remember something important. It's in my handbag.

"Can I have my bag?" I ask. "It will prove my story."

They soften. I pull out a copy of the Bucharest evening newspaper with a front page picture of me and Minister of Air Irimescu. I point to my flying suit, the same clothes I'm wearing in the photo.

"Now do you see?" I ask.

They back out of the compartment and I go back to my sleep.

The next morning the full story emerges from the conductor. The authorities had been looking for a jewel smuggler. And their description fit me to a T.

Who collected MacRobertson's cash in Melbourne, Australia? First place went to C.W.A. Scott and T. Campbell Black, Englishmen in a deHavilland Comet 2. Second place to K. D. Parmentier and J. J. Moll, from Holland, and flying a Douglas Transport. Third place was taken by good old Roscoe Turner and Clyde Pangborn in their Boeing 247. Twenty years later I got to Australia on a United States Air Force inspection trip and I even stopped on some of those intervening points I had so wanted to see in 1934.

Flying the Granville Brothers Q.E.D., Jacqueline Cochran entered her first major air race, the 1934 MacRobertson Race to Australia. However, she and her co-pilot Wesley Smith were forced down by engine trouble in Rumania.

—National Air and Space Museum, Smithsonian Institution, 1981

THE BEAUTY BUSINESS

1935

I had been itching to try my hand creating my own beauty products for years, beating Floyd's ear about it from the first time we met, but in looking back, I've got to say: if you are planning to start a cosmetics company, don't try to mix it with the demands of air racing.

OTHER VOICES:

Scott Kale
(VICE-PRESIDENT OF TRAINING AT JACQUELINE COCHRAN COSMETICS, INC., 1985)

"Scott, who do you work for?" people ask me.

I like to say "Jacqueline Cochran."

So they ask again: "Who?"

Then I tell them what I've dug up since coming to work here a couple of years ago. Jackie Cochran has become a pet project of mine around here.

116

I'm director of corporate training programs for Jacqueline Cochran Cosmetics and yes, it still exists right here with our corporate offices still at 630 Fifth Avenue, in the same building we had when Jackie had a desk and office.

Today not many people know very much about Jacqueline Cochran and who the woman was, but customers nearly go hysterical every year when we bring out a product called Flowing Velvet, a moisturizer created by Jackie back in the very early days of this company. She started the company in 1935 as a personally owned, unincorporated business and that moisturizer came about because of the problems she had with her own skin when flying at high altitudes and over long distances. We still bring out this Flowing Velvet—an odd piece of business for us actually because we are primarily a fragrance company now— once a year in a price special of $10.00 and it sells out immediately. It's lemon-yellow in color and very soothing. To this day, it is one of the finest products on the market and that's because Jackie Cochran was truly an innovator.

We ship it directly to Arlene Dahl, for instance.

In looking back through the early records, I discovered that Jacqueline Cochran Cosmetics was one of the first companies to make and sell moisturizers with the ingredients of Flowing Velvet. And she was out there on other fronts too: custom-blended cream bases for makeups, antiperspirants, hair dyes you could mix yourself, and the colors—well, they were so modern and ahead of their times: chestnut brown, topaz blonde. Those were our colors. There were a lot of formula breakthroughs for which Jackie Cochran was responsible. But she never seemed to want to be known as a cosmetics queen. She wouldn't join up with women like Dorothy Gray or Helena Rubenstein, from what I can gather. Not many people know this, but Rubenstein and Jackie spoke often, frequently. They weren't seen in public together, but they were friendly. Arden and Jackie were bitter rivals, however. And Jackie was a friend of Dorothy Gray's.

Dorothy Gray, Helena Rubenstein, Elizabeth Arden, Jacqueline Cochran—they were the women who founded our cosmetics industry back then in the thirties. Estée Lauder was a little later. The industry was paved for Lauder by the time she entered it in the fifties.

These women were all pioneers in many ways. Formulas,

for instance, were nonexistent. Researchers had to work from nothing to create a new makeup, a fragrance, a hair color. Today you simply go out and buy five or six different prototypes and say, "Well, let's make it this way—or that way." They had to make it from zero. They worked up those products from nothing. Jackie accomplished many of those firsts, especially in hair dyes. Nobody else was mixing peroxide and analine dyes to come up with chestnut, topaz, blonde. Nobody. We were among the first to have it. And we were the first company to manufacture transparent powder; liquid foundation; custom-blended, powdered rouge.

Jackie was very sexy in her thinking about selling and marketing. "We're not selling cars," she'd say to the models, "we're selling beauty."

We've always had offices in this building, near Rockefeller Center, but the laboratory used to be in Roselle, New Jersey. I'll tell you something. I think her spirit is right here in this building still. Jackie dedicated her business life to making busy women more beautiful and making it easier for them to feel good about themselves. The aviation accomplishments were for herself and for her country, but the beauty business...that's what she did for other women. Did you know that Jackie designed Marilyn Monroe's lipstick and gloss for the movie *Gentlemen Prefer Blondes*? That luscious look that wouldn't wear off came from some new ingredient she came up with to keep Marilyn's lips juicy and wet-looking on the set.

When I was in New York in 1929, still working for Antoine's, I had invested in several small beauty shops downtown which would offer cheap services. For every $40.00 hair dye I did up in Saks Fifth Avenue, one of these shops elsewhere in New York City would offer some of the same services for $1.00. I made some money and on paper it looked good but in reality, what headaches.

After working my day at Antoine's, I'd go to one of my shops—I was part-owner—to supervise the operators, most of whom were recent graduates of beauty school. Shampoos, hair waving, permanents, coloring—we offered our customers a lot for their money and I always thought it was money well spent. It's a woman's duty to be as presentable as her circumstances of time and purse permit. Fifteen minutes a day—sometimes that's all it takes—but looking good is so emotionally satisfying that you shouldn't ever take it lightly. I didn't.

By 1934, after I had my commercial pilot's license under my belt, I told Floyd that I wanted my own beauty business so I could end up at the top. I had started at the bottom and supervising shampoos and permanents was not for me anymore. I wanted no part of other people's products either because I was crazy enough then to think I could do better. Sometimes you can and sometimes you can't. But the profit margin in a cosmetics company can be so narrow that it is eternally frustrating. In the beginning years, however, I was high on possibilities. I hired a cosmetic chemist away from a subsidiary of a major oil company, found a consultant who understood perfumes, located the space for a small laboratory in Roselle, New Jersey, and rented the offices in Manhattan.

When I first set about to develop a greaseless night cream, I was told that a greaseless lubricant was clearly impossible. I knew they were wrong and I never recognized the word *impossible*. My most successful cream, Flowing Velvet, is the result of my stubbornness. I was also proud of what we used to call the Jacqueline Cochran "Perk-Up" cylinder. I would take one on all my trips, on all my races. It was a three-and-a-half-inch stick that came apart into six separate compartments for weekends or trips. It would fit anywhere and it had everything: a cleansing cream, special foundation cream, eye shadow pockets, clear red rouge, a solid stick of perfume, and a little sifter you could fill with your own face powder.

I also opened a salon in Chicago, where I'd test my products for customer reaction. Peter Rivoli ran that end of the operation right there on North Michigan Avenue. We'd put our formulas in plain bottles with typed labels and try them out. Then I'd go on the road and in the air, to sell. The combination of my flying career and the cosmetics worked. In fact, my first two department store accounts—Pogue's in Cincinnati and Halle Brothers in Cleveland—ordered precisely because of the flying angle. I knew several flying enthusiasts in those stores, and they honestly wanted to help start me off. We had a little newsletter which went to salespeople involved with Jacqueline Cochran products, called the *Merry-Go-Round*. My employees were a little like the Avon ladies of today, selling products to stores across the country.

How did my days go? Mixed, very mixed. I'd put in my time up front on Fifth Avenue, on the road selling, and I would putter in the lab trying to refine a product. The consistency and the moist, imperceptible but dewy residue Flowing Velvet leaves on your skin makes me proud of it even now. I used to get plenty of compliments from competitors who wanted a Flowing Velvet in their own product line.

Twice in my life, I was named Businesswoman of the Year, in '53 and '54. I was running my business because I liked doing it, not because I think all women should necessarily be doing such a thing. I honestly think that women have the right to stay in their own homes raising children or playing bridge if they'd prefer that.

I owe Floyd's chapped lips for one of my most successful business ventures: Lipsaver. He used to be troubled by dry, cracked lips which would only get worse when he'd visit the California ranch. He tried everything and nothing worked. One day I asked my laboratory to make up several lipsticks minus their color pigments. *Voilà!* They made his lips so moist that Floyd would offer them to other men friends with the same problem. Several test pilots we knew started using them for high-altitude work, and I had golfing friends who wanted them for dry, sunny days on the course. Finally, I changed the ingredients a little, put them into a line of men's cosmetics I was developing, and called it Lipsaver.

In those days I wanted to be quintuplets. If I had been quintuplets, one of me could have spent her time entirely on the domestic side, another could have been flying, another a full-time cosmetiste, another a rancher, and another ought to have been able to bring down the golf score. I would have had more time to play. But I wasn't quints. I just juggled.

Margaret Ann Currlin Clark
(JACKIE'S SECRETARY)

I forgot all about nine-to-five routines when I started working for Jackie in 1959. I'd report to her ranch in the mornings, where she would be in bed or getting dressed. She spent a lot of time getting dressed, doing her hair, putting on makeup. So I took my instructions or dictation from her sitting in bed just as though she were sitting across from me at a desk. It was pretty untraditional and surprised me at first. Whenever she was in California, I was her secretary. In New York, Florence Walsh took over.

Her mind was always clicking. Oh my, it was a hard job. Just one sentence from her might mean hours of work for me. She was so particular about so many things. I traveled with her occasionally. Once we went to Dallas to meet with her sales representatives and on another occasion I was in Los Angeles with her. Her employees were a little in awe of her and had a lot of respect for what she could do. She'd walk into the room and immediately, she'd be the dominant figure. People used to call her the Golden Girl because she was always sort of golden. Her skin was tanned, her hair was blonde, and she just kind of shone wherever she went. She was proud of everything about herself except her hands, and they were very masculine. For this reason, she never put polish on her fingernails. I can still see them right now. Jackie was once voted one of the ten best-dressed women in America.

Her address books alone told the story of her business and personal life. There were two six-by-eight notebooks filled with two inches of onion skin pages and there were about six names and addresses on every page. One book was the United States version. The other was devoted to contacts in foreign countries. Those books were important to her, and as her secretary I'd carry them wherever and whenever we went anywhere. And everybody on those pages was as important to Jackie as your best friends are to you.

She always expected me to know more than I did—from my very first day on the job. And the correspondence was incredible. I could never toss anything out. She saved everything. I remember that she saved all of her Christmas cards and was planning to paper a room with the Madonnas. Seriously. She was a Catholic so she would hear from nuns and priests all over the world. Jackie used to correspond with Amelia Earhart's mother and sister up in Massachusetts, and every month some money was sent to poor people she knew from her very early days. We didn't talk about that much though. I never delved into it.

When I stopped working for her, she thought it was the biggest mistake of my life. She sold her beauty company after I moved to Tucson. And in looking back now, I can say, "That really was some job." I traveled to Russia with her and Chuck Yeager. I remember how the hotel rooms were bugged. The only time she ever got rather cross with me was there in Russia when I neglected to take down Gromyko's comments about her in shorthand. He said some nice things about her in a speech at a dinner party, but I thought I was one of the guests at that point. She was upset with me. She was a very vain woman.

What I am left with now is a feeling of great admiration for her. Nothing ever stopped Jackie from doing what she wanted to do. She was a terrific American and felt so strongly about her country. She helped so many people—all kinds of people, even presidents of the United States.

More than $20,000 had gone down the drain as a result of my preoccupation with the London-to-Australia race. Mabel Willebrandt helped, but I was pleased when Curtiss Wright reimbursed me for the expenses I incurred on their engine's account. That company was wonderful. They added the cost of my race entry fee, the trip to England, refueling equipment, and more, so I emerged after all the chits came in without the deep financial scar I expected to have to nurse back to health.

In fact, I almost came out of that rat race smelling even sweeter profits. The Chilean government was interested in buying my Gee Bee for military purposes, and Granville Brothers assured me that if this happened, I'd get a royalty on every airplane Chile purchased thereafter.

Wesley Smith arranged to meet a representative of their government out at Newark Airport, but I wanted to be there too.

Ten minutes was all it took. I arrived ten minutes too late and in time to see my big plans come to a crash ending. The deal with Chile as well as Granville Brothers fell through right there as the plane with poor Wesley and the government rep fell onto the airfield. No one was hurt, but I knew then that there would be no future orders for Q.E.D.'s.

OTHER VOICES:

Mike and Louise Rosen

(NEW YORK FRIENDS WHO VISITED THE COCHRAN-ODLUM RANCH EVERY YEAR)

Mike: "I lost touch with Jackie when she went out to the West Coast in the early thirties. She never wrote letters back then. Her writing was just terrible."

Louise: "Mike and Jackie were sweethearts."

Mike: "What makes you say that?"

Louise: "Because you were, Mike. Admit it. That's why her marriage to Floyd in 1936 came as such a surprise to you."

Mike: "I'll tell you how I found out about it. She always called me when she was in New York. And she had insisted that she pay me back for that half of the Chevy. I didn't want it, but she insisted. We weren't out of touch. We just weren't in touch all the time in those years. I found out that Jackie was married by reading it in the newspapers, that's how. She had been flying with Floyd somewhere upstate in New York, to see about one of his business deals I think she told me, but they crashed. When the newsmen got ahold of the story—the two of them flying together—Jackie and Floyd insisted they had been married quietly in a ceremony out in Kingman, Arizona, because of some property deal there.

"It was only because of the plane accident that I found out. And the reason no one heard about the marriage was because Jackie and Floyd didn't want anyone to know about it. Nobody knew. Nobody I know was there...and we had a lot of mutual friends. Floyd was very publicity-shy. He was a very prestigious guy.

"The telephone in my apartment rings about two days after this story of the crash and the marriage is in the newspapers. 'Mike,' Jackie says to me, 'did you read about me in the papers?' I answer, 'Yes. Why'd you keep it a secret, Jackie?' She says, 'I wanted to tell you, but I had to be cautious. Floyd wanted to keep it quiet for a while. Can you come over to dinner?' So I went and I liked Floyd. He was okay for a millionaire. A charming couple. Jackie gave me a picture of the two of them and said, 'When you get tired of looking at us, give it back.' But I never gave it back. It's a great photo."

Louise: "Jackie always felt that there was nobody better than she was. She was equal to anybody and had as much confidence as anybody. That's why she was able to accomplish so much. If somebody else can do it, so can I. That was her theory, her motto. And once she was your friend, she was your friend forever. She would do anything for you. Of course, she'd expect you to drop everything for her too. But that's the least Mike and I could do. She made our lives so much richer because of our friendship. We'd visit her every year or so and she didn't have to like me, as Mike's wife. But she did.

"I was working in a man's world, too, just like her, as a general manager for MGM in New York City. Women had to prove themselves back then. You couldn't be a flag-waver, you had to fit in, prove that you could be trusted. When I took over a theater in New York, the man before me had been robbing the place blind. There was a man at the top who felt, 'Well, let's see what Louise can do. She can't do any worse.' And in fact, I did better than any man before me. You just couldn't be a hell-raiser as a woman or you wouldn't get the chance. Jackie knew that and I knew that and I think it's part of the reason we got to be such good friends to the end, in spite of her early relationship with Mike."

Mike: "What relationship? We were never like that. My mother liked her, though."

Louise: "Jackie did love her yellow roses. Whenever I gave her a plant or just some flowers, which I often did, I'd make sure they were yellow. It was a good luck charm for her. She had a thing about good luck charms. Superstitions. She was always painting 13s on the sides of her airplanes, wasn't she, Mike?"

Mike: "Yes, 13s. You know, it's sad that Floyd's family

never got along with Jackie. Even when Jackie made a place for them right out there at the ranch."

Glennis Yeager

Jackie never walked through a room if Floyd was there without going over to him to give him a little pat. I thought the world of Floyd. He was really a fabulous person. Jackie was always doing things he wished he could be doing. He was there from the very beginning of her flying and he was the one who had pushed her. He loved doing things like that—pushing people to do things. It made life interesting for him.

Jackie and Floyd had a kind of sixth sense about each other. They could always tell when one or the other was in trouble. They just knew, without communicating directly, that the other needed help. Floyd would know it. Jackie would know it.

When I was sick, so sick in a hospital in San Francisco, Floyd knew about cortisone because it was used in the treatment of arthritis but it was expensive then. They had to extract it from the adrenal glands of female hogs or someplace like that, and each shot was three or four thousand dollars, I think. Maybe I'm exaggerating, but I don't think so. Floyd wanted to pay for it for me. He let me know he'd be there for me if I needed him.

Floyd was a young man when he became so sick. It was a shame.

———————————

When I first met Floyd, he used to tell me that he was going to retire as soon as this happened, or that happened, or he passed fifty, then sixty. But my husband couldn't and wouldn't ever retire. He loved doing deals too much.

We lived in a twelve-room apartment in River House, 435 East 52nd Street in Manhattan, which had the most wonderful view of the East River. I decorated that apartment. In the entrance hall the walls were covered with paintings of airplanes I had flown or owned. Facing the door, eventually, were the awards I'd accumulated: Harmon trophies, Bendix, the Distinguished Service Medal. Inlaid in the floor was the design of a compass. Floyd and I collected miniatures, and my needle-points accumulated over the years. Before the ranch became our home base, we would rent a summer cottage at Sands Point on Long Island. Floyd and I used to throw the most exciting dinner parties up there. They went on forever. Floyd used to say it was my fault—that I would even take a backgammon game to bed to keep the action going.

But Floyd could be pretty funny too. I remember the year he gave each of our friends stock certificates to various companies and wrote silly poems tying the gift to the individual. You know, "This is for Ann—some American Can." He had such fun with people.

Sometimes I think of the sawmills, the hunger, the work, of the earthquakes and hurricanes I've lived through, fires in the sky and mishaps on the ground, visiting with queens, presidents, and two private audiences with Popes. Then I think of Floyd and how privileged I was to be able to spend forty years of my life with that man. He divorced Hortense in 1935. We got married in 1936.

OTHER VOICES:

Vi Strauss Pistell

Jackie and Floyd wanted to avoid publicity about the marriage, so they chose Kingman, Arizona, and took George Marshall and his wife along to stand up as witnesses. George was managing the ranch in those days and he had invested in a sheep ranch in Arizona. That's what they were doing in Kingman. The Marshalls remained close to Floyd and Jackie.

Jackie was so happy about being married. She wouldn't talk about the ceremony itself, but she was sure proud to be a wife. You could see it. And she would say so.

RACING

1936–37

The Bendix Cross-Country Air Race was to aviators what the Kentucky Derby still is to horse breeders. They are both American classics. Or, at least the Bendix was. It was the outstanding regular long distance air race of the world. Occasionally, some country would put on a comparable event such as that London-to-Australia race I entered in '34, but the Bendix went on year after year, rain or shine, to open the National Air Races around Labor Day.

The race was, at best, a hard one, even when the skies were clear and smooth. More often than not, the weather was not so good and then it became an exceedingly grueling contest. Always, there were keen disappointments for pilots like me. Oftentimes they were heartbreaking.

The prize money amounted to about $30,000 and, of course, each pilot was shooting at that purse as an immediate objective. But fundamentally, there was much more at stake. This must be so, for I doubt if there was a single year in which the cost to the contestants as a whole didn't exceed the total prize money. In the year 1936, for instance, more than $125,000 worth of equipment alone which had been entered in the race was destroyed either during the race or in preparation for it.

No! It was the urge to do something for yourself and for aviation and not the money that drove us. There wasn't a professional racing pilot who could build any surplus money from racing activities. We'd travel and live the hard way and if you got a windfall, it went right back into better equipment.

I can consider myself a real veteran of the Bendix. By the end of the decade I had been an entrant five times. In fact, I was the woman who got the race open to women in 1934 even though I never made it to the starting line myself. That was the race the supercharger on my Northrop Gamma engine kept blowing up on the factory test block. But three times in the thirties I started. Twice I finished.

In the '36 race, one plane hit such terrible weather that even fully loaded, going at top speed, the ship simply tore apart. In midair! The pilot was shocked into insensibility and only woke up—thank God—in the air, out of the plane, where he had enough sense to pull his parachute cord. He landed safely and an airliner picked him up to take him to Cleveland for the rest of the air events because he was entered in a pylon race. The next day he cracked up again. Two ships wrecked in two days and hardly a scratch on him. I'd say he was leading a charmed life.

That same year—'36—my friends Benny Howard and his wife "Mike" were well ahead of the field of racers in the Bendix and reaching for a new record in *Mister Mulligan*, their plane, when they lost the propeller over New Mexico and in the resulting crash, Benny lost a leg. It didn't stop him, though—nor Mike either. They were both back in the air, and within a year Benny was testing new transports, doing experimental work for United Airlines.

Energy must have fed on pure energy itself in those days because I sure didn't feed it much else. When I think back to one of my first big wins in that Bendix, I shudder. The day after what was a marathon event for me, I found myself on the floor of a plane—it had only one seat—being shaken nearly senseless in a spin arranged by Major Sasha Seversky, who had won his way to the controls in a wager with me. Testing, he told me then, he was testing his ship. And I was along for the ride—always.

Vincent Bendix didn't use his company's name in that race for the fun of it. And it wasn't just the publicity or even the sport that made it worth his while. Companies like Bendix Aircraft got involved in air racing because of what they could learn about an experimental aircraft when it was pushed to the limit. Individuals and individual companies were often behind the beginnings of aviation as we now know it.

Our fast planes built on blood, sweat, and improvisation were the prototypes for what would come later. We were the forerunners. With redesign and rethinking, those airplanes often became the slower, safer passenger planes and the military fighters. And the new gadgets that we tried out developed into trustworthy instruments because of our trial and error. I was always a guinea pig for one thing or another. Sometimes it was a new carburetor, new spark plugs, a new engine for Pratt & Whitney, or a new fuel for one of the oil companies. I was there at the birth of the first oxygen mask. Dr. Randy Lovelace, a young Mayo Clinic surgeon, had a hobby that would change the way the aviation world operated. Randy, a lifelong friend, would later be known as the astronauts' doctor, and his School of Aviation Medicine at Randolph Air Force Base in San Antonio, Texas, would be world-famous.

I had been invited to be on the Collier Trophy Committee in 1937 and I was the first woman to be asked. Donald Douglas of aircraft fame and fortune was present, and General Hap Arnold, who had already made quite a name for himself in the Army Air Forces, was there, as well as Dr. George William Lewis, Director of Research for the National Advisory Committee for Aeronautics (NACA), NASA's forerunner. Honestly, I think it was because I had flown and survived a Gee Bee that I ended up in such esteemed company. I didn't say much throughout most of the first meeting, but I had done some thinking. I was waiting.

"You certainly are quiet, Jackie," a friend sitting next to me says. "You must have something up your sleeve." He knew me.

"I do," I answer, "just wait until they get through."

In England in 1934 I had met Dr. Frederick Banting, a specialist in aviation medicine, and though I didn't have the proof then, I did have information about thirty-five or forty laboratories in Germany doing important aviation research—the kind of medical research our government had no knowledge of. All I had then were rumors about work going on out at the Mayo Clinic in Minnesota. So when my turn came, I asked permission to have the floor for five minutes. I whispered to my friend, "I'm just the cute bombshell here."

"I'd like to submit a candidate, but I don't know what his name is," I say. They don't like this much. But I push on.

"Mr. Douglas," I explain, "you've been trying to build an

airplane that will go as high as 20,000 feet, but that's a waste. I've been pretty high up and I've done more flying at 20,000 feet than most men out there, so before you make your planes fly any higher, we've got to get some work done on oxygen and pressurization. For heaven's sake, let's investigate this thoroughly through this committee, find a hook to hang our hats on, and give the award to the doctors who are doing the work that needs to be done first." I was speaking as a citizen, but I thought it was urgent that we get more research going immediately because I wasn't alone in predicting a war coming. We knew so little about oxygen at high altitudes then and we were doing so little. Nothing, in fact. It was a crime and I knew it. Grumbles and mumbles. That's all I got from the men sitting on the Collier Trophy Committee—at first.

To win the Collier, the applicant was supposed to have completed some kind of aviation accomplishment, but in order to get proper recognition and funding, aviation medicine needed the boost a Collier trophy would provide. I put up such a strong, stubborn plea to award even incomplete research work that they awarded me the distinction of heading up my own committee, a committee of one.

"Surely, there is something we can find to consider a finished product," I argued that day to some pretty deaf ears.

As the meeting adjourned, Dr. Lewis told the other members that he would be delighted if any of them could join me in my investigation of aviation medicine in the United States. Not a one did.

I started by calling the Mayo Clinic cold and ended up in an airplane with exploding chickens.

"Is Dr. Mayo there?" I ask a snotty receptionist. "I'm not sick, I simply want to speak to Dr. Mayo." No dice. For three days we dance around each other. "Is there a Dr. Mayo?" I ask at one point. Perhaps there is no such person, I'm thinking.

"Yes," she says with a "but" in her tone of voice. Finally, I scream, "Young lady, I'm trying to talk to him about something that is vitally important to him and to our country. Put me through to him or to someone else who's in charge."

She was just terrible.

Finally Dr. Charlton Mayo is on the line explaining to me that he is retired but that the young surgeon doing the aviation research is Dr. Randolph Lovelace. It's his hobby, Mayo says. Aviation medicine is simply Lovelace's avocation, not his vocation. I am flabbergasted.

Lovelace, his associate, Dr. Boothby, and another colleague, Dr. Armstrong, were conducting the first important research in the United States on surviving in space and it was being privately funded. A hobby. That's all it was then. Mayo invited me to visit and promised to roll the red carpet all the way out to the airport if that's what I needed to investigate the matter.

I was simply amazed when I saw how advanced they were. Lovelace and this Boothby had actually developed an oxygen mask, a portable oxygen tank, and a low-pressure tank to test individual responses, that I got to try out. I think I was the first woman to climb inside. I also tried out their centrifuge and had something weird turn up. Whenever I experience a shortage of oxygen, I get a pain between my shoulders, and this seems to be true for only one person in every 100,000, they tell me. No one had been thinking about pressurization in those days and there they were working out these fantastic problems on private funds—no government support whatsoever. Their mask went over your nose and then there was an open area around your mouth and tubes hung down around your face, like a little beard. I still have one.

I got involved immediately for what I could learn for myself as well as what I could offer these doctors. I wanted to encourage them. Later, my work won me a spot in the Society of Experimental Test Pilots.

The work was pretty crazy. I'd take small animals up in my plane as high as they and I could stand it. Then, the chickens would explode. Those poor buggers would just explode. What a mess. I'd take up all kinds of small animals to test and record their behavior and the chickens were usually the first to explode at high altitude—sometimes as high as 25,000 feet. We tested at Flat Pass Air Force Base and I'd fly mice but I refused to take the billygoat or the snake. No box would make me less afraid of snakes. Floyd was all for it. But everybody back east thought I was a nut.

But I'd like to believe that my racing and my curiosity contributed to the progress of aviation.

OTHER VOICES:

Floyd Odlum

Jackie has many sides to her character and personality, some of which seem to contradict others. For instance, I have said many times that my wife is fearless and yet she runs wildly from a snake. I've also seen her become almost hysterical from listening to a good old-fashioned ghost story. However, I never saw her back away from real danger and I constantly observed that she moves automatically toward the center of trouble. Certain it is that she is fearless of death and equally certain it is that she considers a barrier only something to surmount.

Even if Jacqueline Cochran had been born with a silver spoon in her mouth, her outstanding accomplishments in aviation would well merit their telling. Her background and beginning only make these aerial feats more remarkable. For more than twenty years she had been pushing high and fast into the little known and sometimes unknown frontiers of the atmosphere, bringing back bits of information which have speeded along the onrush of the air age.

She has out-Marcoed Marco Polo with her travels to most of the foreign lands on the face of the earth, always in search of seeing the unusual. A glance at a new spot on a map is usually, for her, the start of a new adventure.

My wife is the most interesting person I have ever met.

General Curtis Lemay

(RETIRED AIR FORCE GENERAL, FORMER HEAD OF THE JOINT
CHIEFS OF STAFF, AND DESIGNER OF THE STRATEGIC AIR
COMMAND)

Let me tell you about Jackie. She was quite a gal to accomplish all that she did and I first met her during World War II because she had organized the women in the Women's Airforce Service Pilots (WASP) program. They did a fine job—and a job that needed to be done. When the war began, we had about 1,200 officers and only about 10,000 men. By the end, we had expanded to 2 ½ million. The United States may have started out with the Wright brothers and their airplanes right here, invented and designed right here, but we didn't do much about it for a long time. I saw a constant battle for air power ever since I've been involved, and that's a long time. I was born in 1906, three years after the airplane was born, so I've been around in history for a while. It was a battle for air power and more planes from our inception. We had nothing up to World War II. And we did nothing. We even alienated the Wright brothers so much that they gave their airplane to a London museum and we didn't get it back until just a few years ago. As a country, we did nothing for the airplane for a long time.

Those air races that Jackie Cochran was always involved in educated the public about aviation—especially when the military had none, which was right up to World War II. General Billy Mitchell was court-martialed for stepping out of line, for advocating air power. We had nothing for a while. Imagine— from 10,000 people to 2 ½ million in a few years time. A Liberty engine, a few squadrons that had made it into World War I— nothing. My guess is that only a few planes were built for the military. We sure didn't have much.

Those air races were all right. Jackie Cochran was obsessed with the idea of breaking records. And that's okay. Every year she was after something else. I remember her hot rivalry after the war with a French gal, Jacqueline Auriol. Jackie would be in my office in Washington, D.C., demanding a fighter to get a record for the United States. I didn't always look at her plans very well. To give her a taxpayers' airplane to go out and fulfill these ambitions didn't always feel right to me. But she kept at it. And she was a good pilot so the Air Force never had to worry about her cracking up one of our planes. Jackie and those women she trained could fly as well as anybody else. They were well trained and their accident rate probably compares with anybody else back then. We were cracking up airplanes all over the place in those days.

In December of 1937, when President Franklin Delano Roosevelt was about to present the Collier trophy, he asked the roomful of people and no one in particular this question: "I've been giving this trophy for a great many years, but what kind of doctors are these?" Lovelace, Boothby, and Armstrong were the recipients. I was there.

Nobody speaks up. Finally, someone says, "Medical doctors, Mr. President."

"But what are medical doctors getting this thing for?" he asks. Dr. Lewis looks straight at Roosevelt and says, "Miss Cochran engineered this singlehandedly to bring recognition to a great piece of work that is being done to change the face of aviation by private people with private funds. I think Miss Cochran should tell you about her project," Lewis announces. I cringe.

"I am not going to do a Mutt and Jeff, Mr. President," I say. I'd never been crazy about Roosevelt. I didn't like the things he was doing to our country. And there must have been sixty people with us in one of the Cabinet rooms. "Mr. President, it will take at least thirty minutes to begin this story where it started and to tell you what is going on in Europe as well and I think these three gentlemen ought to explain. You might want to make another appointment for them or they can tell you right now. If it's going to be now, however, you'd better pull up some chairs to let everyone sit down."

I never saw Roosevelt push a button or ring a buzzer, but suddenly a man was in the room and chairs appeared. "Change my appointments, Paul," the President said to Paul Watson. Maybe there was a magic wand I couldn't see because it all happened so fast. The President was absolutely fascinated, and within a day or two there was a large sum of money made available from presidential funds for the research.

I had something else literally and figuratively up my sleeve that day too. I held in my hands documented proof of what Germany was doing in aviation medicine. And they had us by miles. They had already developed their own G-suit to mitigate the effects of centrifugal force on the human body going at super speeds. When we all left that day, I left my report for Roosevelt's eyes only.

It wouldn't be the only occasion I offered my advice to a president of the United States.

AMELIA

I met her in 1935.

"I've got quite a treat for you," Paul Hammond said to me one day on the phone in New York. Paul and his wife were good friends and he called to ask me to dinner.

"Having dinner with you is always a treat, Paul," I answered.

"But this time I have a real treat, Jackie. There is someone I want you to meet who will be here too."

"Who?" I asked.

"Amelia Earhart."

This may sound strange, but I believe it was a measure of our closeness: the only person I ever turned my bedroom over to at the ranch was Amelia.

Guest houses dotted my property in Indio, California—a few at first and more as the years went by—and there was only one bedroom in the main house. Guests stayed in the guest houses. But Amelia never felt like a guest in Indio so when I wasn't there, she slept in my bed. And she came often. My home was her home—a home that offered her horseback riding, swimming, pilot talk, quiet walks in the desert but especially peace and privacy. God, the world hounded that woman after she became famous. During the last year of her life, I was closer to Amelia than anyone else, even her husband, George Putnam.

I walked into the Hammonds' dining room the night we met

135

and knew within five minutes that Amelia and I would be friends. It was one of those sure feelings you get occasionally and instantly when you meet someone new. Naturally, I was impressed by her accomplishments in aviation and I was a newcomer then. She had been in the news ever since she crossed the Atlantic as a passenger in the summer of 1928 and then had gone on to set her own records at the controls of her own plane, a Lockheed Vega monoplane with a 500-horsepower Pratt & Whitney engine. Five years after Charles Lindbergh had made his mark, Amelia crossed that same Atlantic alone on May 20, 1932, in 18 hours, 16 lonely minutes. It was a beautiful plane—red and gold—and she was a beautiful person. That's why I loved her. It wasn't her achievements or the glamour surrounding her that caught me. It was her personality.

We two had lunch soon after that dinner at the Hammonds'.

"I'm going to fly west in a week or so. Would you like to go with me?" she asked.

Out we started for our quick trip west in the plane Purdue University had outfitted for her: a gorgeous $50,000 Lockheed Electra which could have seated ten passengers along with the two of us. I copiloted. The trip was hardly a quick one. We were held by weather in St. Louis for four days and then again in Amarillo, Texas. And during that week our conversation ran the gamut of topics—from politics to science, religion, our personal lives, and how much we were both interested in extrasensory perception. Our mutual fascination held surprises for us both. Those six days spent locked in by weather gave me the opportunity to get to know Amelia and to know her was to love her. I had just finished the initial phase of work on my ranch home in Indio so it was natural for Amelia to end up out there with me.

Many people thought that Amelia and I were competitors, particularly after 1935, when publicity about my races had begun to pick up. It was really not so. In that gray area where we both occasionally participated, it was on a most friendly basis. Amelia's specialty was long distance flights, where the engine and the fuel have to be babied for optimum results. My specialty was speed, where you force the engine and everything to the limit.

Great rapport. We had great rapport which bordered on something quite magical. I never had great rapport with her hus-

band, George. Floyd and George Putnam got along just fine, but
I'd never forget one of the first conversations I had with Putnam.

He was always patronizing with me. "Well, little girl," he
said to me, "what's your ambition in flying?"

That was like waving a red flag in front of a bull. "To put
your wife in the shade, sir," I answered. But I never felt competitive with Amelia. I could be positively fearsome when it came
to putting real competition in the shade, but Amelia was different. She was such a gentle lady. I'd joke with her, pick on her,
say things like: "You pick the wrong races, girl. You never give
me a chance to put you in the shade." I have a very strong sixth
sense—something we all have in varying degrees, of course—
but mine was strangely accurate. Every pilot has hunches and
uses them on occasion. My hunches have always been pronounced and personally, I relied on them to a great extent.

Floyd had made a hobby of studying psychic phenomena
and had even been in touch with Duke University, where Dr.
J.B. Rhine was conducting experiments in the normal and
abnormal extent of our senses: seeing, hearing, smelling, tast-
ing, and feeling. Floyd was on a committee that checked facts
for a *Scientific American* magazine article on the subject. That's
how we ended up at a dinner party one night. This party brought
my particular penchant into funny focus for Floyd and the others present.

One of the guests that evening was from Duke University's
department of parapsychology, and he brought along a pack of
testing cards to try out on the guests. Who was most psychic?
Whose hunches were more than mere guesswork? It would all
be in good fun. Five cards, each with a different figure on its
face, were placed facedown on a table behind a screen. As the
man lifted them one at a time, we were to guess the card's face.

Perfect. My score was perfect every single time I played.
Floyd was impressed, intrigued. Some people were astounded. I
honestly wasn't.

Later at home together, Floyd and I would toy with psychic
phenomena. Once we even hired a seer to show us her tricks.
She lifted tables, got herself into a trance, and what was most
enticing for me, she performed what is called automatic writing.
After she left, I told Floyd I could do better, so he pulled out a

tablet, paper, a pencil, and a blindfold. He covered my eyes and I put the point of the pencil to the paper. Then I concentrated on my act. I did think of it as an act at first.

Suddenly, I started writing uncontrollably. My fingers even broke the pencil in two and flung the two pieces into the air. I pulled off the blindfold, shocked. Then we tried it again and the same thing happened. Eventually, I became so successful at automatic writing that Floyd and I needed large rolls of wrapping paper to capture my words, always written in a huge, scrawling hand. I was never conscious of what I was actually writing, but it was me who was doing that writing for sure. There was no mistaking the poor spelling and bad grammar on those sheets. I think it points to the fact that the words came from no further than my own subconscious and not from beyond the grave as some people would like to believe. I always answered Floyd's questions about the living and not the dead. I wasn't reaching beyond or into anybody but myself. What was it all about? I didn't really know at the time and still don't. I don't believe in trying to communicate with departed souls. If God wanted us to contact the dead, he wouldn't pick me or, for that matter, a medium to do the job for pay. So what I am really saying is that extrasensory perception exists—but as an awareness of things living.

I remember being with Floyd on his cabin cruiser houseboat one Sunday afternoon as we traveled down Long Island Sound and into the East River for a docking. I was tired and had fallen asleep in his lap. It was one of those deep, emotional sleeps for which I eventually became quite notorious. I could sleep like a dead rock. Floyd was worried about waking me up, so he began trying to talk me awake long before we reached our destination.

"Wake up now, Jackie," he says to my sleeping form.

"We aren't through Hell's Gate yet. I have plenty of time," I tell him, my eyes still closed.

He's intrigued. "Can you tell me when we are exactly under the Fifty-ninth Street Bridge?" he asks.

"Certainly," I reply. And a short while later, I did—eyes still closed—conscious mind still asleep.

Floyd told me later what I had done.

Sometimes Floyd would put combinations of fingers up behind his back and have me guess how many I could "see." I was always right. He was always fascinated. Perhaps I was reading his mind. I'm not sure.

It bordered on pure thought transmission when Floyd and I used it with each other. We didn't share our secret sessions with very many people. Then Amelia Earhart became a friend.

Back then in the thirties, when Amelia and I first became friends, these sixth-sense notions had burst into full bloom as an extrasensory ability. On Amelia's first visit to the ranch, we heard a radio report about a transport plane en route from Los Angeles to Salt Lake City which had disappeared. Amelia wondered: could I locate it?

That night Amelia and I tried to locate that downed transport plane in our thoughts at the ranch; we sat together for two hours while I offered bits and pieces of critical information. She asked the questions, kept our concentration to a maximum, and I answered: mountain peaks—nearby roads—transmission lines —even the existence of a pile of telephone poles up in the mountains near Salt Lake City. That's where it was—the landmarks I could "see" nearby. Finally, I pinpointed the location, but because neither Amelia nor I knew the area intimately, we called Paul Mantz, a fellow flyer in Los Angeles, to verify some landmarks. He did.

Amelia can't wait. She dashes out into a car and back to L.A., to her plane, so she can set off looking for the wreckage, searching for survivors. Three days later nothing had turned up, and we both assumed we had been wrong, foolish, to say the least. The real shocker came in the spring, when the snow in those mountains had melted and the wreck of the transport emerged where we said it might be. We had been only two miles away from an exact location.

That wasn't the only occasion Amelia and I pushed our powers of concentration. A few weeks later she called to tell me of another plane with passengers en route to Los Angeles that had disappeared. Within an hour I called her back to tell her where I thought the plane might be.

No, I shouldn't say "might." I knew where it was. I could see the people—some dead, some injured, and some uninjured. I could even see the body of the plane pointing down the mountainside in a certain configuration. And my hunch soon proved to be more than a hunch. Search parties proved I was right.

One of the nicest and most touching evenings we ever spent together was the night she returned from her first attempt to go around the middle of the earth in a 27,000-mile adventure. It had ended unhappily in an accident on takeoff in Hawaii. She telephoned me on her arrival back in California and asked if she could come down to the ranch. Naturally, I always had a bed for her—even if I had to vacate my own. Benny and Mike Howard—they were married friends and were both excellent pilots who flew the Bendix—had already settled in, so when Amelia arrived, we were excited about a weekend of flying talk.

We sat in front of the fireplace. She was on the floor near the fire. And she gave us the minute details of the aborted flight from beginning to end. When she had finished, no one said a word.

"What?" she teased us with a cute expression on her face, "isn't anyone going to ask me the big question. Don't you want to know whether or not I'm going to try it again?"

Silence.

No one—especially not the professional pilots present that night—would break the rule of my ranch house: no personal questions designed to put people on the spot.

In addition, we were all worried about the plan. Especially me.

"Come on, Amelia," I finally said. "You know the rules of the house." But we kept talking about the plan. What about her navigator? I wanted to know why she wanted this man. I had questioned her about the guy she had originally had in mind. He was a fine man, but was he up to high-speed celestial navigation? I didn't think he could hack it and I had told her so at one point.

"Take him out to sea for a distance from Los Angeles and fly in circles for a while," I dared. "Disorient the man and then ask him to plot the course back to L.A."

She did and he couldn't. Later, she told me they landed up on the shoreline halfway between L.A. and San Francisco. She hired another navigator, Fred Noonan. My worries persisted and they poured out that night in Indio.

I wasn't the only one. One day Floyd and Amelia got stuck in the desert sand in an old car.

"Do you think I should do it?" she asks.

"Do what?" he says, thinking she wants to start digging the

wheels out instead of waiting for the help to arrive from the ranch house.

"Fly around the world?" she explains. The desert was so quiet, he told me later. Waiting. She was waiting for an answer from a man she trusted implicitly.

This is what he told me he said to her there: "Amelia, if you are doing this to keep your place at the top among women in aviation, you're wasting your time and taking a big risk for nothing. No one can topple you from your pinnacle. But if you are doing it for the adventure and because you simply want to do it, then no one else ought to advise you. No one else should make that kind of decision for another."

Floyd was like that. He could give advice that made you think. He was always able to put me straight. He could make you see things from a new perspective that helped to shed light on subjects you weren't always able to see clearly and offered support when and where you needed it. For Amelia and for me and others too.

Several weeks later Amelia returned to the ranch and brought her formalized plans to encircle the globe. A last, best adventure, it would be. We studied those maps together and that's when she became confirmed in her reverse route directions. She'd fly the equator east to west instead of the west to easterly heading she had been attempting. But I was still uneasy about it all. I insisted that she take a brightly colored kite I had carried along in my ill-fated Gee Bee on the London-to-Australia trip. And I packed fishhooks, lines, and one of those all-purpose, super-duper knives with a blade for every conceivable purpose. Floyd and I as well as Vincent Bendix financed a portion of the enormous expense of her perilous journey.

We decided our powerful play with thought transference might help us, especially Amelia. Could I locate her if she were forced down on her round-the-world attempt? I'd try. Practice would make perfect.

On one of her trips across the country I kept a diary of where and what she had done each day and then I forwarded my report to her. Putnam scoffed as usual. Skeptical, he pulled apart my facts without thinking. For instance, I relayed that she had landed one night at Blackwell, Oklahoma, which was 50 miles off her course. The next morning she had taken off at nine o'clock, heading for Los Angeles. Putnam shot a letter back at me saying that Amelia hadn't taken off at nine but at seven. It soon dawned on me that nine o'clock my time had been seven o'clock in Blackwell. Putnam had never taken time zones into account before he threw out his objection.

I didn't like that man at all, but I did love Amelia with a deep, true affection. When she was in San Francisco on a preliminary flight, I was driving Floyd to Palm Springs from the ranch one Saturday afternoon. The thought intruded like a flash: there was a fire in one of the engines in Amelia's plane. I told Floyd that it wasn't serious and that a crew was dousing it at that very moment. Later that day we heard the story of Amelia Earhart's fire on the radio and the next morning's newspaper carried a full account.

So why wasn't I able to find her downed Electra in the South Pacific when the moment eventually arrived, when she needed me more than ever before?

I did "see" her. I just couldn't prove it to anyone and it would have been to no purpose.

When the news broke that she hadn't arrived on Howland Island as planned, George Putnam called me in Los Angeles and came over to where I was staying almost immediately. "Could I do something?" he wanted to know. He was extremely excited.

This is what I remember telling him. I wrote it down but could never find those scribbled notes in my files. He must have walked out my door with them in his pocket. That was the last time I ever saw him. This is the gist of what he took away:

"Amelia out of fuel...landed in the ocean northwest of Howland and not too far away. The plane is floating. Amelia is not hurt, but Fred Noonan bumped against the bulkhead during the water landing and is unconscious with an injured head. There is an American boat called the *Itasca* in the vicinity and also a Japanese fishing boat."

At the time I knew the name of the Japanese vessel. Now it's gone, along with my notes. I spent three days in a hell here on earth after Putnam left on July 2, 1937. We talked on the phone. I called him the next day to tell him that the plane was still afloat and to add the name of that Japanese boat which "looked" like Maru or Mari to me. Amelia's Electra was drifting eastward, north of Howland Island.

On the third day I called again to tell him that it was too late to rescue Amelia. She was gone. Then I went to the cathedral in

Los Angeles to say a prayer for my friend and to light candles for her soul which had gone from this earth. I never toyed with extrasensory perception again. It hadn't been precise. It hadn't helped.

After Amelia's death I consciously and purposely submerged my sixth sensitivities. They proved of no use to me or Amelia on July 2, 1937.

"Circling—cannot see island—gas running low..." were the last words anyone heard from Amelia, including me. That still hurts.

TESTING, TESTING

In 1937 Jacqueline Cochran finished third in the Bendix Trophy Race, covering the distance between Los Angeles and Cleveland in 10 hours, 19 minutes, 8.7 seconds at an average speed of 313.327 km/hr (194.74 mph) in a Beechcraft D17W.
—National Air and Space Museum, Smithsonian Institution, 1981

It isn't fear. It's something else that I can't well describe now and it would all disappear the moment I climbed into the ship. I was told by good authorities that the number-one racing pilot then, that's Roscoe Turner, would get the most horrible nightmares before his races. He was known to jump up and break the furniture in his bedroom, and indeed on one occasion he tried to jump out the window as if he were trying to bail out of a falling plane. On another occasion he had to be tied in bed by his roommate.

As for the number-two racing pilot back then, I never went quite that far in my physical manifestations or inward nervous tension. I never broke a bed or started to bail out through a window. But almost. And before going up to establish a world's 3-kilometer speed record for women, I sat in the back of an automobile shaking as if I had the ague, which is something like

144

the shakes you can get with a bad chill or even malaria. A crack old-time army pilot was sitting there with me and he said, "I know exactly how you feel. I've done the same thing myself on more than one occasion."

The public used to thrill during the takeoffs in those Bendix races and thrill again when the planes flashed across the finish line. In the beginning they'd see me smile and wave nonchalantly just before the starter gave me the gun. What they didn't see was the way the plane was weighted down with gas until it was more than twice as heavy as the most heavily loaded transport plane. I'd be wondering whether I could reach the end of the field alive. At the end of the race people would see me again smiling and speaking into microphones, but they weren't usually close enough to see the deep lines of fatigue and worry in my face.

I'd lose about six pounds in weight during the race and I only had about 117 to start with. I wonder if beefy Roscoe Turner ever weighed in and out.

We learned from the experiences of each other, but there was so much that we had to learn for ourselves the hard and dangerous way. One racing pilot a few years back increased his speed in the air simply by clipping the ends of his wings off. The plane that pilot Roscoe used in 1937 to win the Thompson Trophy pylon race at the National Air Events couldn't get off the ground when it was first built. The wing load was altogether too heavy. But with alterations, Roscoe not only got off the ground but he bettered the entire field of contestants and won.

Major Sasha Seversky was in the forefront of experimental airplane design and manufacturing. Sasha had been a Russian war ace and he was one of the greatest pilots of his era. His wife, Evelyn, was also a good pilot and their airplane manufacturing plant became Republic Aviation. They'd race their own planes oftentimes. But not always.

"I just wrote you a letter to ask if you wanted to fly my P-35," the major said to me one day in 1937. I was at Roosevelt Field running some fuel consumption tests on a new engine that Pratt & Whitney had manufactured. It was a 600-horsepower engine, but I had installed it in a stock Beechcraft airplane which normally carried 450.

The plane was very overpowered with it, but I had gone through such efforts to obtain it, I didn't dare abandon my plan.

So that's the engine I was testing the day Seversky first sauntered over. I had decided to fly the overpowered Beechcraft in the Bendix that coming September and knew I could take first place in a new women's competition because I was the only woman entered. With a little luck I might grab a second or third overall in the men's division, too, because certain pilots were too hot and hot-headed to realize how much they didn't know about navigation and instrument flying. I knew that I knew more.

When Seversky offered me a P-35 that day, I suddenly saw my hopes soar higher. In his plane I could take first, not second or third.

"Lead me to it," I say to him, "right now."

"No, not right now," he explains, "it's not even finished yet, but when it is, we are putting it in the Bendix with another pilot."

"Why not let me fly it in the Bendix?" I ask.

Seversky's P-35 had been built for the United States Army Air Forces, and they had eighty on order, but there were problems. The operational test pilots kept cracking the prototypes up. Seventeen had been destroyed that way. Sasha knew I was successful flying hot, tricky planes and I think he got the idea that if a woman could fly his P-35 successfully and very publicly, it might show up the men with complaints and help him settle his problems with the army brass.

Sasha explained that he'd let me take the plane up right after the September race because he had put all his Bendix bets on another pilot. He wanted me to meet him at Wright Field in Ohio, where he would obtain permission for me to take it up in a demonstration.

"That suits me fine," I said then.

Two days after the race (in which I took third) Seversky and I flew to Wright. And at a little party the night before my flight test, I happen to be sitting next to a General Robbins. He says, "You have no business flying this P-35. It's a killer. We have cracked up more than twenty of them."

I answer, "Every airplane can be flown, General. And if you

can fly a Gee Bee, as I have, you can fly anything."

No reply.

The next day there is great excitement. The gal is going to take the plane up. I go through a thorough ground check of the cockpit with Seversky because I need to learn everything I can from him on the ground. He's a great pilot, a superior designer, but there's no radio in that plane and a place for only one pilot. I should have taken a piece of paper and a pencil up. But I didn't.

"Don't do anything," Seversky warns. "Just take it up and fly it around. Don't play with it. Just come down and land."

"Right," I say.

There is an all-grass field and a low cloud ceiling—only about 5,000 feet. I want to put the flight off because I do want to play with it. I want to get up high enough so I can get the feel of this killer plane. You can't do that with a ceiling of 5,000 feet. But Seversky is nervous. The ramp is filled with officers and very interested parties.

No trouble on the takeoff. The plane feels good to me. I'm up for about a half hour when I get all squared around for a landing and ready to drop my wheels. When I do this, the rudder pedals start jumping. They practically jump out of the plane.

One of the "off-the-ground" rules Seversky had handed me was: if the retractable landing gear is not down and properly locked, the rudder pedals will warn you by vibrating violently. Don't land until they stop jumping.

God, I wondered, how do I lock them down? And if they won't lock, how do I get down in front of all these men without making an absolute fool of myself as a pilot?

I fly low over the crowd and look over. I'm as slow as I dare go without stalling. How do I ask without a radio, paper, pencil, or a megaphone? I want someone to tell me: are the wheels up or down? I can't see for sure from where I sit because the gear has been designed to come from back to front instead of from the side, as they do in later versions.

I'm as slow and as low as I can possibly go—over a field of men who think I'm showing off. No one answers my unspoken plea. Why didn't I remember paper and pencil? I could have thrown down a note.

After I was in the air long enough to worry about running out of fuel as well as unlocked landing gear, I come up with a plan. Not a foolproof one but a plan nonetheless.

The thought of cracking up that plane just devastated me. I wasn't as worried about me as I was about the reputation I had begun to build. I liked it. I didn't want to lose it. They'd blame it on my being a woman and I didn't want that.

Slowly, I bring the plane down. Pull back. Push my tail down first. Hope that this tail-first maneuver will put a little pressure on the gear to lock it in. Grass strip. Invited guests. Down I go.

Slowly, and so easily. I was down and the wheels were down and locked as they'd been all along.

If it weren't for the fact that I was pretty shaken up on the ground, I probably would have screamed at the fuse responsible for my fury. The retractable landing gear had been fine all along, but the fuse responsible for the jumping pedals had blown. Engineered to save a pilot's life, the mechanism had nearly destroyed my emotional mettle. And on subsequent flights in Seversky planes, I always deactivated that ridiculous rudder-jumping gadget. I wanted no part of it.

The plane? Well, that was a different story. I wanted it desperately. I knew it was the fastest thing I'd ever been in.

OTHER VOICES:

Maggie Miller

(RETIRED MANAGER OF WESTERN AIRLINES AND PERSONAL FRIEND)

Friends like Jackie are hard to come by. Jackie, just by being Jackie, sometimes abused herself physically. She was always pushing herself terribly. She'd tell me, "Maggie, never say *crash* unless someone is killed. If you walk away from an airplane, if you come out of it alive, it's an *incident*, not a crash."

She walked away from so many *incidents*, even she couldn't count them all. I remember her telling me about a plane she left in pieces on a runway in Indianapolis so she could arrive in time to have dinner with Floyd in New York. Her little finger had been broken and was all crooked, but when I asked her when and where it happened, she couldn't recall which particular *incident* had given her pinkie its crooked quality.

Nothing was beneath her. When she would come to my house in Palm Desert, she'd never hesitate to ask me if she could do my nails or help me with my hair. Jackie never forgot who she was and where she had come from. She was generous and very human. I never walked into her home without her coming over to me to give me a big welcome hug. But so competitive and such a hard bargainer too. Listen to this: Telephone calls from her ranch in Indio to my office at the Palm Springs airport, were toll calls, and she hated to pay. So whenever she was playing golf at the exclusive Eldorado Country Club, which was closer to me, she'd make the turn on the ninth hole and use the public telephone they had there. It was a local call then. And she used to talk about her friend Howard Hughes being eccentric about money.

The air was always electric when Jackie was around.

HOWARD HUGHES

On April 4, 1938, First Lady Eleanor Roosevelt awarded Jacqueline Cochran the first of the 15 Harmon Trophies she would win. She received this trophy as outstanding female pilot of 1937 by setting three major records: women's national speed record, 328.068 km/hr (203.895 mph), in a Beechcraft Staggerwing; women's world speed record, 470.254 km/hr (292.271 mph), Seversky Pursuit; New York-to-Miami new speed record, 4 hours, 12 minutes, 27 seconds, Seversky Executive.
—National Air and Space Museum, Smithsonian Institution, summer 1981

A couple of weeks after my first test flight in that Seversky pursuit plane, Sasha handed me the same P-35 with the jumping pedals to make a speed run.

Three hundred miles per hour. I pushed that ship up to about 300 mph, and Sasha became convinced I could win the big New York-to-Miami air race coming up. What better rebuttal could he have than to have his plane flown 300 miles per hour over a measured, timed course and to have it all done by a woman? The Army Air Forces were canceling further orders because they saw the plane as dangerously faulty and not up to the specifications they had ordered.

Sasha installed an extra gas tank in place of a seat for me. It

150

wasn't very comfortable, but what was worse was that the plane had never been test-flown with a full load of gas. I took off and discovered that the center of gravity was somewhere in the nose. God, I nearly put that plane into the bay just south of what is now Kennedy Airport. It porpoised terribly for over an hour, which is a little like riding a "chute the chutes" in an amusement park.

I did get the nose up in time to avoid a swim, but until I burned out most of the fuel in the seat tank, I really had to hold on for a tough ride—up and down in the sky. From Washington, D.C., on, the situation straightened out and I got the record Sasha wanted so badly. What was funny for me about that particular record was who I took it away from.

In 1935, before Floyd and I were married, I had been working on that Northrop Gamma, trying desperately to get it and myself into the Bendix in spite of all the blowups it had the year before. I was terribly short on funds—all those funds Floyd made available to me later—and Howard Hughes was working on his famous Hughes racer. I had seen it when I was testing the rebuilt Northrop Gamma. Howard's plane was just fabulous. Aerodynamically, it was so far advanced that it was far apart from the accepted airplanes of its day.

Hughes's racer was out at Mines Field, which is now a part of the Los Angeles International Airport, and he had stationed an army of police around it. He'd visit it every now and then to run it up and down the runway. I couldn't keep my eyes off it.

One night about 11:30 I was exhausted in my hotel room and the telephone rang. Nobody ever called me that late because they knew how serious I was about my work in the day, whether it concerned my flying or my fledgling beauty company.

"Jackie," the voice says, "this is Howard."

"Howard who?" I say, still sleepy and getting very frustrated.

"Howard Hughes," the man says.

"Howard who?" I ask again.

"Howard Hughes," he repeats.

I thought someone was kidding me, but I stayed on the phone. I had been looking at his racer with my mouth watering for weeks. Maybe it *was* Howard Hughes. We argued about who he was a bit more. Finally, he says, "I want to buy your airplane."

I'm thinking that this is an incredible conversation. "It's not for sale, Howard," I reply. "I'm going to fly it in the Bendix."

"I don't want to fly it in the Bendix," he answers. "I want to fly it cross-continental."

"So do I," I say.

Howard Hughes and I negotiated over the Northrop Gamma for about four weeks. He let me sit in his racer. I let him think I'd sell him my plane. He never did let me take the racer up. He had invested anywhere from a half million to a million dollars in it and even sitting in it was thrilling for me. Do you realize that his airplane is almost identical in configuration to the P-51, which was one of the most important planes the United States had in World War II?

Howard wanted my Northrop so badly, but it would break my heart to consider handing over my rights to it, then or ever. Yet it was costing me so much in lost time and money that when he offered to rent it, with an option to buy, I caved in. When I look back on the refund I received from Curtiss Wright, the engine manufacturer, as well as checks from Howard, I've got to admit that the plane paid me back in spades.

Howard's final rental offer was actually more than I had paid for the entire plane including the repair work. I couldn't afford not to accept. And it was in my Northrop Gamma, refitted with a new nose and cowling, that Howard Hughes had set several records, including that New York-to-Miami race.

I honestly believe that Howard Hughes did more for the development of commercial aviation with his own money than any other single human being in our country. He was so anxious for all those air records to be held by Americans. Yet in 1939, at the outbreak of World War II in Europe, we were considered number seven militarily in aviation. Poor, eccentric Howard ended up more abused and sinned against than he deserved. Yes, he was peculiar and difficult to work with, but I had a lot of respect for him. Floyd and Howard were always buying and selling companies and properties back and forth—which makes me laugh about where the Northrop Gamma ended up.

When the deadline on our rent-with-the-option-to-buy agreement finally arrived, Howard was preoccupied. He was halfway across the United States, the plane was somewhere else, and I was in California. To return it would have been a hassle, so I received a check in the mail for his purchase of my

plane. I was badly upset, of course—I'd kept believing he'd
decide against it—but that was his decision. A few days later we
talked on the phone and I offered to buy it back. He agreed.
Then, when we haggled about the price, we agreed on a sum that
was less than the face value of the check I still held.

You can imagine why I was so pleased to be in Miami and
holder of the new world's record for my flight down the coast. In
Miami there were three or four records Major Seversky wanted
me to try for in his plane. One was a 15-kilometer straightaway,
and another was a closed-course 100-kilometer flight. When I
finished the 100 kilometers and had set the record of the day, I
made a perfect landing. All of a sudden, about halfway down the
runway, that P-35 began jerking violently and literally pulling
itself apart. I couldn't imagine what was wrong. One wing was
pulled off altogether and the landing gear was torn off too. The
airplane fell apart around me. I was shaken but unhurt. But what
had happened?

A movie crew filmed the entire debacle and for a short time I
believed that this film footage was only going to add insult to
injuries. I was going to have to call Sasha Seversky where he
was staying in Havana, Cuba, to tell him what had happened to
his experimental airplane. It was a time when I was honestly
filled with—for me, a strange feeling—dismay.

The truck with the camera on it had followed me down the
runway, through my perfect landing and into the wreckage. It
caught the entire act from beginning to end, and what an eye-
opening act it was. Sasha Seversky was ecstatic when he saw it.
What my movie debut showed was that a tail wheel jumped out
of its locked position and then swiveled wildly. That's what
caused the plane to jerk from side to side with force enough to
tear itself apart. Sasha was so pleased. The insurance money on
the experimental prototype helped him finance the new model
with modifications. When I told him I'd buy some stock in his
company, Republic Aircraft, he promised to let me fly the new
plane in the 1938 Bendix. And I did. This P-35 was the forerunner to the World War II Thunderbolt.

When the Republic Aircraft Company made the ten thousandth
Thunderbolt in 1944, they invited me to the factory to christen it
because I had flown one of the first. There was a huge crowd and

a cardboard facsimile of a French champagne bottle with which I was supposed to hit the nose of the plane. Bubbles would spurt out, I was told. It would look like the real thing, they insisted. It didn't really, and when I looked inside this bottomless cardboard bottle, there imprinted were the words: MADE IN JAPAN. The Thunderbolt, which had given such an exceedingly good account of itself in the war with Japan, wouldn't stop even there. And I was proud to have played a part in its development.

OTHER VOICES:

Vi Strauss Pistell
(RANCH HOUSEKEEPER)

Howard Hughes used to come to the ranch and he was just another character. I remember how he would come for dinner and not eat anything. He'd sit at the dinner table with his long legs spread out and talk. He was always talking with Mr. Odlum underneath a tree outside the house. He wouldn't discuss business where anyone could hear him. Once he arrived with two people from RKO and it was getting late and cold outside. They were waiting outside and Howard and Mr. Odlum had gone into a bedroom. So I walked out and invited the men to come in. "No," they answered, "we can't come in because Howard's inside. We have to stay outside."

Howard really was something else. He'd listen to Jackie and Floyd, turn to them for advice. I remember when he wanted to get married and brought his fiancée to meet Jackie and Mr. Odlum. He called ahead of time and told Mr. Odlum to say nice things about him to this beautiful young woman. Terry Moore—her name was Terry Moore. She was only fifteen and he was in his forties at the time. I don't think she wanted to marry Howard, so Howard was relying on Mr. Odlum to help his cause.

Mr. Odlum never got to tell Terry what a great guy Howard

was because he never let Mr. Odlum alone with her. The men
went to one of our guest houses and talked and talked—alone.
Meanwhile, we sat out on the lawn and then went inside. Terry
had a handful of peanuts we were all eating and suddenly we
saw the two men coming back. "Quick," she says to me, "I can't
let Howard see me eating these. He's so concerned about me
gaining weight and what I'm eating." At that point, in a panic,
she takes the peanuts and shoves them down the cushions of the
couch.

We picked peanuts out of that couch for weeks and the marriage never did take place. But Howard used to go out with all
those Hollywood stars and he'd bring them over. Rita Hay-
worth once visited us. Howard was brilliant as a young man but
became so crazy. It's just too bad it had to happen and he
couldn't have gotten some professional help. He wouldn't even
talk in front of Mr. Odlum's secretary and he used to open and
close all the doors, even closet doors, to make sure no one was
hiding. Jackie knew him well. We were having dinner together
once in a hotel where Howard was staying and when he realized
Jackie was there, he came to visit and the two of them talked
about flying for hours. Jackie knew such great men and I tell
you, her friendships were important to her.

Aldine Tarter
(RANCH BUSINESS MANAGER)

Mr. Odlum sued Howard Hughes. Howard reneged on a promise to Mr. Odlum, and even though they settled out of court, it
was quite a thing. You see, Mr. Odlum retired early from Atlas
Corporation in order to run Howard Hughes's organization, but
when the time came, Howard changed his mind, I guess.

Three months after Howard died, this ranch was crawling
with people searching for the missing Howard Hughes will. But
Mr. Odlum always maintained that Howard wouldn't have written a will. It just wasn't like him. Floyd was dead, so I sent the
investigators to talk with Jackie but Jackie echoed my opinion.
There was no will. They xeroxed everything I had here about
Mr. Odlum's dealings with Howard. Piles of paperwork.

Funny, but in all Mr. Odlum's dealings with Howard, in all
the correspondence from here, there is not one written word in

response. Mr. Odlum would confirm everything in writing. Howard would respond only by telephone. Sometimes they were middle-of-the-night calls.

One of the last calls Howard made to Mr. Odlum was in the middle of a night I had decided to stay over. Most of the time I went home to my own house and husband. But this night I was there and I heard the phone ring. I went in to Mr. Odlum to make sure everything was okay and heard a one-sided conversation that raised big funny questions. Mr. Odlum kept saying, "Howard, I don't have a mattress with a hole in the middle. I never have had a mattress with a hole in it." He just kept repeating this, and I couldn't wait until he got off the phone so I could find out what it was all about. Mr. Odlum said, "Howard, I am not angry with you, but I still don't have a mattress with a hole in it."

"What's that all about?" I ask.

"Howard has really gone into space," Mr. Odlum says. "He insists that the last time he was here, I had a mattress with a hole in the middle of it and he wants to borrow it from me because he has hemorrhoids."

"Did he tell you how he plans to sleep on a mattress with a hole in it?" I ask. "Besides," I say, "he has enough money to have a mattress with a hole in it made especially for him if he wants one. Why is he calling you?"

Mr. Odlum could be straitlaced at times. He'd never malign a soul, not even Howard Hughes or his quest for a mattress with a hole in it. But I sure laughed.

"It's so unfortunate," Mr. Odlum says, "Howard's mind is really somewhere else these days."

WINNING

1938

In 1938, Jackie realized her dream of winning the Bendix race. In a Seversky Pursuit, she covered the 3286 kilometers (2042 miles) between Burbank and Cleveland in 8 hours, 10 minutes, 31 seconds at an average speed of 401.895 km/hr (249.774 mph). After being congratulated by Vincent Bendix and receiving her trophy, she climbed back into her Seversky and flew to Bendix Airport in New Jersey to set a new women's west-to-east transcontinental record of 10 hours, 7 minutes, 10 seconds.
—National Air and Space Museum, Smithsonian Institution, 1981

Superstition seems to be a constitutional part of every southerner, especially someone like me who grew up so close to those southern grass roots and hung around in treetops outside black boogie-woogie sessions as well as revival meetin's. I am chuck-full of superstitions. Some of them are in reverse.

I consider the number 13 lucky and it has been my official racing number for years. The number 13 has constantly popped up in my life in favorable ways. In 1953, after flying a Canadian Sabrejet, the F-86, successfully, I discovered that I had made thirteen flights in it. I bought a Bequine racing plane in 1949 on the insistence of Bill Odom, a young pilot, who wanted to use it in the Thompson Trophy pylon race in Cleveland. He agreed to take the old number off the door and paint the lucky 13 in its place. Two days before the race he called me long distance to say that the plane's paint job was so beautiful that it'd be a shame to ruin it repainting a number 13.

In the Thompson race Odom killed himself and two bystanders—a mother and baby.

Such a ticklish and misunderstood subject this superstition is. I never said a word. But whenever I could, I put 13s on my planes.

The Bendix race was on September first in 1938. As early as July I had my special maps prepared for four different routes with every beacon and radio station and every radio beam carefully marked. Until the time of takeoff, after last-minute checks on weather and wind aloft, I wouldn't know which course to choose. One course was to the south paralleling the TWA flight course to Kansas City. It was longer but had the benefit of many airports, beacons, and radio facilities. The second course was about 100 miles north of this TWA line but did cross over Santa Fe, New Mexico, and one or two dry lake beds that could be used for emergency landings if necessary. The third was the direct great circle route that led right across the highest and most rugged part of the Rockies and for over 400 miles offered no hope to a pilot in distress. It was shorter than the first course by about 15 minutes' flying time and shorter than the second by about 8 minutes. The fourth course led roughly through Salt Lake City, Utah, and Cheyenne, Wyoming. I'd take that one only if storms in the south or helping winds in the north more than made up for the additional distance I'd have to fly on it.

I actually flew route number 2. It would have been better if I had flown route number 1. I didn't know that at the time, and I had loaned my route number 1 maps to Max Constant, another racer. He was flying my own Beechcraft plane in the race and forgot to give them back to me. He chose route number 3 and was well on his way when he discovered the other maps. He claims that his face got awfully red, but neither he nor I saw anything of the earth after the first hour in the air. All the maps were useless.

The only other thing I should have marked, but didn't, on the maps were the points along the way when I would be running out of gas in different reserve tanks. If the engine was drinking the gas correctly, and I was flying according to schedule, the markings would have helped. Marks on maps would have been a nice way to check ahead so I wouldn't have to slow up.

To qualify under the race rules, a pilot had to put in five hours flying time in the ship to be raced. This was a problem for me. It was a Seversky Pursuit, one of Sasha's P-35s, owned by the factory and still under construction. I had flown the earlier model at Wright Field the year before, but this new one was supposed to have wings that were gas tanks and retractable landing gear of a new design. I knew I still wouldn't trust it, however.

About the fifteenth of August I went to the factory on Long Island, and on three successive days I put in two hours of flying time in a similar model. It had the same fuselage that I was going to fly but didn't have the new landing gear. The committee accepted this experience as the required flying time. We were going to be cutting it very close. In its final form, the P-35 wouldn't be ready before about the twenty-third of August or even later. I was worried, but that was the best they could do. In fact, there was no time at the end to install the new type of landing gear. The old version would have to do.

I went to Los Angeles to wait for the P-35. But in the meantime, there were two things I wanted to do: practice night takeoffs and landings and try to get some sleep during daylight hours.

I was hoping to get a race starting time shortly after midnight. I had learned my lesson in that first Bendix about what happens when morning fog rolls in, and a midnight takeoff was my best insurance against it. Then, too, an engine performs slightly better in the night air. So I planned to put in several hours practicing night takeoffs and landings—not that I expected to be landing at night in the race, but you could never tell what might happen.

I started going to bed at noon and getting up and out to the airport around midnight. I wanted to ease my biological clock into offering me a sound night's sleep in the middle of an afternoon. And it worked. But the Seversky was nowhere in sight, so I used my own Beechcraft.

In fact, that P-35 wouldn't arrive until about two days before the start of the race and it came to me after a record-breaking

dash across the country with Major Sasha Seversky, the
designer and builder, at the controls. I fixed him for that by
flying it back to New York in faster time than he flew it out.
When I joked with him about this, he'd tell me he had headwind
and I had some tailwind. Then I'd say that I burned less gasoline
to make it nonstop to Cleveland and therefore took less power
out of the engine. Besides, I'd add, I flew that ship at high altitudes and blind.

But it was all in fun. I recognized that there were few pilots
in the world then who could better Sasha Seversky. He was
Russia's ace when I was still at kindergarten age.

Between midnight and daybreak at the airport that August of
1938, I would fly in and out of the Burbank field in my Beechcraft. It was excellent training. I had done a lot of night flying in
'35 and '36, but I felt a little out of practice. And I flew without
the help of the floodlights or my landing lights. They have a tendency to blur your vision momentarily. Even worse are photographers' flash bulbs. Once, I couldn't take off for several
minutes after someone put one of those things in my face before
a race.

Finally, the P-35 arrived. I decided that I didn't want to take
it into the air for a test even if I could. The racing officials
impounded it because it was a prototype and there was some
kind of rule about untested planes. I would test it en route.

It didn't matter too much to me because I figured that God
forbid, if something happened to it when I was on a test run, that
would be worse. I didn't have the slightest doubt that I could
take it off the ground fully loaded the night of the race, and I
wasn't going to do so beforehand just to prove something to
myself. I saw what had happened to another pilot, Bernarr
MacFadden, when he tried a bit of cavorting two days before
the race. He bought my old Northrop Gamma with its kinks
ironed out, but in one lousy, off-keel landing, he put himself out
of the running.

I just couldn't chance letting something like that happen to
me in that P-35. I wanted to win badly.

Finally, I got to sit in the cockpit. I began to study all the
instruments by the hour. I can almost see them still.

There are about a hundred or more buttons, levers, and

other gadgets to push, pull, or twirl. And there won't be time to get a rule book out if I should need it. It's now or never.

I close my eyes and reach for everything in the dark. And I keep at this until I can get to them blindfolded and with no false moves.

August thirty-first...I put in an extra two hours of sleep. I don't go shopping. So what if I do a bit of hollering in my sleep as they say I do? I'm awake around 11:00 and feeling quite rested. Major Seversky is entertaining friends in the Cocoanut Grove and has asked me to meet him there before we go to the airport together.

I'm sitting at a table in my flying clothes for a few minutes and I spy some photographers who want to take my picture. I refuse. Why? Because I felt that if I were killed during the race, that photograph might be shown and someone might mistake the glass of water before me for something straight. That would be a bad thing for racing as well as for me. (It wasn't that I didn't drink. At another time, in another place, that glass could easily have been a glass of gin. But when I was racing, I never drank. The anticipation of a race alone was enough to make me high on the risks. And physically, I never wanted anything to weaken my reflexes.)

I don't worry about being killed, but I don't want to be wrongfully remembered. Once I was within two seconds of heaven with my friend Amelia Earhart and my only thought was that I was going to glory in good company.

We arrive at the airport just in time for my takeoff, which has been set for 3 A.M. I'm cutting the time close, but I don't want the same experience I had three years before when 40,000 people lined the field, pushing and pulling at me, fog settled in, and I went out behind the hangar and did to my supper what the whale did to Jonah. I choose to cut it close tonight.

The plane is already down at the far end of the runway and fully loaded. Someone has checked it for stowaways because the word is out that a young boy has been boasting that he will make it to Cleveland in a race plane as an unannounced passenger. A stowaway on this Seversky would be too bad. We would never make it to Cleveland and probably never make it off the ground. So I take a flashlight and recheck the little compartment through which the control wires run and which is carrying an emergency gas tank. No one there.

The major is suddenly afraid that I will get too cold. He loans me his leather jacket. The field lights are turned off. I decide not to put on the ship's landing lights either. The light switch has to be turned off before I can get the landing gear up and I don't want to lose even that little bit of time flipping a switch before getting that gear up. The ship is very heavily loaded. Gear down will slow me down. I want it up immediately after we are airborne.

It's very dark. I train my eye on an electric light way down at the far end of the field. Open the throttle. The power is there. So's the response.

I clear the ground before I've gone much beyond the half-way mark. It's a good takeoff. I'm pleased with myself and the ship.

The last time I took off in that previous model, I had been carrying a large load of gas, the plane was way off its center of gravity, and it porpoised on me terribly for well over an hour. "Chute the chutes" was more than I had reckoned for by day, and it had been my big worry. For, at night, and over the mountains, it would have been less pleasant.

Safely in the air, I switch off the belly gas tank and switch on the special wing tanks. I want to rid myself of the off-center load as quickly as possible and the wings are designed to drain in tandem. There's a special flow mechanism from both.

I turn to my flight plan. Checking earlier with the factory experts, I had learned that I couldn't fly at the best altitude for speed and with full throttle and have enough gas to get through to Cleveland. Gas consumption, altitude, and throttle must all be considered for the distance I've got to go. Everyone's decision was for me to fly at 16,000 feet with something less than wide open throttle. If I do this, I'll arrive with 20 gallons of gas left over, they tell me.

The weather shows storms ahead blowing northward from the Gulf of Mexico. This should mean that the farther north I fly, the higher the storm area will ascend. I might miss it completely by choosing route number 2, I decide. I can stay under at 16,000 feet and clear most of it.

I'm wrong. After the first hour the weather gets worse by the minute. Even all regular airline flights are canceled soon after my takeoff because of this storm system. I don't know this at the time. All I know is that ignorance is never bliss in the Bendix. I should have known better.

I need oxygen. A tube from the oxygen tank leads into a pipe stem which I hold between my teeth.

I check my compass and I'm glad I do. It's ten degrees off true. And soon I'll be in the storm and need to depend on it even more. Over Arizona I finally hit the soup. One clear hole in the clouds a little later shows me the top of a mountain I know. I'm still on my course. Good. The whole state is so bad I can't get any radio reception. I'm able to send messages and then, near Albuquerque, I try again to reach an operator to find out if I am being heard. I keep adjusting that radio, but it won't work. So, for me, it becomes a question of instrument flying by compass. Nothing. Not a sound from a soul for 2,042 miles, for 8 hours and 10 minutes. My average speed: 249.774 miles per hour.

I keep climbing slowly, trying to get over the weather. Up around 25,000 I'm still in it and then ice starts coating my cockpit windshield. I can't see anything. I come down a bit to get rid of the ice.

Instrument flying is very tiring after the first couple of hours. For best performance you've got to keep the plane level without gaining or losing altitude or letting one wing get higher than the other. Eyes must keep dancing from instrument to instrument to govern the performance of the engine as well as the flight itself. But it's not monotonous. Flying under a hood was monotonous. No, when you are in the soup like I was, and on instruments, you stay very wide awake.

To add to my woes, the plane became very right-wing heavy. We had installed those special fuel lines through which the gas from the two wings would feed out at the same time. But it wasn't working. One wasn't feeding at all. Was it sabotaged?

The engine stops. I am at 23,000 feet. My windshield is still loaded with ice, and I'm holding the stick with all the muscular control I can muster. Just to keep it in flying position.

I try to switch on that belly tank. It might start the engine. I lean over to do this and when I straighten up, my ship has veered way over on one wing—almost flying on its side.

I go into a spiral.

Pilots learn rules to recover from situations like sudden spirals. But they don't always work. And this was one of those times when the accepted procedures didn't work. What to do? Finally, I put the ship into a shallow dive and straighten it out coming out of this dive. It's the only thing I can think of. And I lose several thousand feet of altitude.

Then I push it over so the empty wing is lower than the full one. Something has gone haywire in this feeding mechanism. By keeping the empty wing lower, I can get gas from the full wing to drain toward the empty one. Then, slowly, I try the switch for the wing tanks. The engine keeps running. By repeating these strange acrobatic maneuvers—dipping my left wing down, draining fuel from the right wing—I can empty both wings dry. But it's not easy flying.

The Wichita radio beam's out of order. I can't get any reception, but I know I've passed Wichita.

It's cold up there. I've come down in altitude to try to free the ship of ice, but I'm still perishing with the cold. My feet feel like chunks of ice. I reach for the hot coffee I've brought along in a thermos bottle, but it has lost its top back there in that high altitude. It's blown off and it's cold coffee now. I suck a few lozenges to keep my throat moist as well as for fun. And I keep sucking oxygen.

The first shot of land I see is the Mississippi River near St. Louis. I recognize some jetties and know I'm within five miles of the dead center of my course. Good.

I start slowly descending, and the next real piece of earth I catch is St. Mary's Lakes in Ohio. That tells me I am about five miles north of my course. I thought I had corrected for this, but when I finally see Cleveland I am still five miles north of my direct course to the airport. And I'm going so fast that I pass the airport, turn around, and come in from the wrong side.

Have I won? The crowds are cheering. It's a standing ovation but it's not over. I'm the first to reach Cleveland but the third to leave Los Angeles and some of my keenest competitors still have forty-five minutes to get in and beat me.

I want to see Floyd. I know he will be worried. The judges come out to the end of the runway in a car to meet my plane and take me back to the grandstand. I make them wait until I comb my hair and put on a little makeup. I've got to tidy up even though the looks I get from them are disgruntled ones. I don't care what they think. No matter how hard the trip, I've got to look my best. And there's nothing wrong with that. Now they insist that I meet the people even though I'm determined to refuel and immediately take off for New York and an intercontinental speed record. An additional $7,000 is at stake. The second leg is voluntary but I'm volunteering.

First things first, I need to touch and talk to Floyd.

Floyd knew that I didn't have an extra half hour's worth of fuel according to my flight plan. My time in the air had run out in his calculations. He honestly thought I was down or dead. The fact was, I went much higher than we had calculated because of those storms, and burned less gasoline per minute at that high altitude going somewhat slower. I landed with less than 3 minutes supply of usable fuel left in my tanks. But in a race of that kind, any margin is a safe margin.

I wasted 40 minutes that day talking and shaking hands. But I did take off again. And when I reached New York, I set a women's record for west to east flight in a propeller-driven plane that still stands today: 10 hours, 27 minutes, 55 seconds. Then I turned around and caught the first regular airline flight back to Cleveland so that I could join the festivities.

I had to be there.

I had won the Bendix.

I was crazy then. I always had itchy feet and I can hear myself the very next morning—after partying all night. Adventure was always just around the corner and I could turn that corner mighty fast.

Had my P-35 been sabotaged in that first big Bendix win? Maybe. Maybe not. When the plane went back to the factory, a large wad of wrapping paper was discovered near the outlet of the right-wing tank. No wonder the drainage was bad. The paper could have been put there by someone who wanted me to lose, or worse. But, more likely, it was paper simply pasted on the inside of the wing during manufacturing. Someone forgot to remove it and it worked itself loose with the gasoline and the vibration in the air.

That reminds me of the time I worked with a new fuel. Pratt & Whitney had a couple of tanks of this stuff, Octane 145, sitting around and I got in touch. I wanted to break a speed record held by a German pilot. It worked and I took that record away from the Germans, who were at war then in 1940. It was a great thrill and pretty fast flying on my part—20 miles faster than that German—and I earned myself a call from the White House later on. Congratulations were in order, for sure, but what the president really wanted to know was: what kind of fuel was it and where could American fighter pilots get some?

It's hard to remember how much pilots like me did back then—testing instruments, ideas, theories, setting up air routes and air lines that exist even now. When I learned to fly, there wasn't an American airline that dared take passengers at night, and look at us now.

I used to tell people that I'd stop racing once I had won the Bendix. But I couldn't. I guess racing was in my blood from the beginning. And I was always looking for something or someone else to better.

On August 8, 1939, Jacqueline Cochran made the first blind landing (solely by reference to instruments) by a woman pilot, at the Pittsburgh Airport. She was congratulated by airport official Lloyd Santmyer. Also, in 1939, Jackie set a women's national altitude record of 9166 meters (30,052.43 feet) over Palm Springs, Calif., and an international speed record for a 1000 kilometer (621 mile) straight course of 489.482 km/hr (305.926 mph).

Again flying her Seversky Pursuit, Jackie set a new world speed record on April 6, 1940, of 530.745 km/hr (331.716 mph) from Mount Wilson, Calif., to Albuquerque and back, a 2000 kilometer (1245 mile) course. Her time was 32 km/hr (20 mph) faster than the previous record held by the German pilot Ernst Seibert.

—National Air and Space Museum, Smithsonian Institution, summer 1981

NOT EVERYONE FLIES BOMBERS TO BRITAIN

JUNE 1941

A fuse blew. There was some smoke and confusion in the cockpit of the Hudson V bomber and in the overcast, over the North Atlantic, we flew blind for a time, on instruments only, for more than four hours, in fact. We didn't know what had caused it, so we couldn't replace it. Breathers on the port engine wouldn't close. It ran dangerously cold. Ice built. Then I remember the fire shooting up past the ship several times. First in front of the nose, then in the rear. I pushed my face up against the glass to see what I could see.

Nothing. I could see nothing clearly. Finally a small break in the clouds gave me a flash of thick black smoke. Could it have been a smoke screen for a battleship below? More likely, a tanker burning? We didn't wait around to see for sure.

This story actually begins back at a luncheon following President Roosevelt's presentation of that Collier Trophy to the aviation medicine men. I was with several people who had been at the ceremony, including General H. H. "Hap" Arnold and a Mr. Clayton Knight. Conversation came around to the English need for planes as well as pilots, because Clayton was head of an American recruiting committee for the British Ferry Command.

"Are you interested, Jackie?" he asks. "Why don't you do some of this flying to England yourself to help dramatize the need. The publicity might help."

167

That was all I needed to be off and running. Of course I'd do it. I jumped at such a chance: to be the first woman to fly a bomber to Great Britain! I was also convinced that our own women pilots might be needed should the time come when our own country needed to defend itself. Women would want to do their part. I'd heard that female pilots were ferrying planes in the English countryside and this was my chance to see firsthand.

Floyd wasn't so sure it was all such a good idea. He neither objected outright nor gave it his full-steam enthusiasm. In the end, however, it was Floyd who helped me get the flying experience I needed in twin-motored heavy equipment. It was Floyd's diplomacy that got me closer to the pilot's seat. And it was Floyd who negotiated my way over troubled waters long before I was over the North Atlantic.

My familiarity with heavy airplanes was nil. I needed experience before I could even consider Clayton's dare. So Floyd called Lockheed Aircraft for me. Perhaps the factory had a plane we might rent? he asked. No luck. The president of United Fruit, a friend, volunteered a company plane, but to fly it, he suggested that I hitch my way to Honduras. That's where it was parked. Out of the question. Next, we tried Cities Service, a big company with big planes, but they couldn't oblige us either. So I waited—not patiently.

Floyd's personal relationship with Lord Beaverbrook, head of procurement for Great Britain, also paved a path through Ferry Command brass for me. And when a Lockheed Lodestar for rent finally showed up at Floyd Bennett Field on Long Island, I rushed out there. A 4M rating from the Department of Commerce would put me closer to qualification for what was called the Atfero Command, the group based in Montreal, Canada, which was in charge of bomber ferrying across the Atlantic. Several hours of instruction and practice over Long Island were followed by a trip to Boston, where old friends at Northeast Airlines answered my anxieties by offering me more help with an official flight check. Flying blind, flying at night, flying on one engine, and landing those big planes put me at ease. After more than twenty-five hours of airtime in those big birds, I thought I was ready for the big time. I knew as much as a Northeast Airlines pilot, and one of my instructors said as much.

I was wrong. I had only just begun, as I soon discovered.

Red tape and sexist insinuations stood mountainously in my way. I went from a Mr. Maurice Wilson, the top boss in the United States for the British Bomber Service, to Sir Gerald Campbell in the British Ministry in Washington, D.C. (well-known for his contributions to the British Spitfire airplane fund at the time), to Clem Keyes, the man who organized our first airline for Curtiss Wright, to Harry Bruno, an influential aviation person and friend, and always I went back to my husband, Floyd. I wanted this feather in my cap badly and I kept encountering obstacles and objections.

Wilson felt that being a woman was a problem. No crew would sign on, he predicted. Others questioned my abilities: could I fly blindly? Could I handle a heavy plane? Was I doing it only for personal publicity's sake? Was my log book up to par? Didn't I know that these flights had to be surrounded by secrecy? Others remained committed to me and my hopes. I was always blessed with good friends.

I arrived in Montreal at St. Hubert Airport, about forty-five minutes from the city, and reported to the command. A Captain Cipher showed up for my flight test. This would end it, I'm sure they all suspected. She'll be out now, the male pilots predicted. They were a diverse group ranging from well-trained flyers serving for patriotic reasons, to ham and homespun pilots who were in the game for the money being offered. I wasn't there for the money and took not a penny from the project. But no matter where these guys had come from or why they were there, to a man, the consensus was obvious: they didn't want a woman in their midst. Even the men who would change their tunes sang discordantly about me in the beginning.

"Have you ever flown a bomber?" Cipher asks me on the first morning.

"I've never even been a passenger in one," I answer.

I'd been told by Northeast Airlines friends that three-point landings at 70 knots were the rule for these big bombers. Cipher disagreed. Keep your speed to 85 knots and touch down on two wheels, I remember him insisting. The bomber had complete dual controls, including hand brakes.

"You think you're pretty hot, don't you?" he says.

"I'm good," I remember saying. "I know how to fly and I know how to fly very well indeed."

He wanted to know what I'd flown and then seemed uninterested when I told him. "I'm going to have fun checking you out," he laughed. I knew I was in for it. It was going to be a horrible time. Those men wanted me there like they wanted the archangel Gabriel sitting on their shoulders. In the face of such open hostilities, my competitive edge became even sharper than it ordinarily was.

I passed the first round of check rides. Back on the ground, the baiting never stopped.

"How do you rate going up so soon, Jackie?" an American pilot asks me when I'm in the administration building, the only warm place to sit. I don't recognize him, but he knows me. "I've been waiting two weeks for my flight test." What makes you better than me?... he is really saying with the cock of his head as well as the tone of his voice.

Another pilot asks me what I'm doing in Montreal.

"Just fooling around," I say, and retort, "what are you doing?"

"Just fooling around," he answers.

On my next test the seat belt has been torn out of the plane. It was a bumpy day and I had rented a car to park at the airport so I wouldn't have to sit in the administration building. I was worried because there was a quartering wind on the runway and at top gust it must have been at least 40 miles per hour. Without a belt I might be thrown from my seat in a maneuver and lose control of the ship. I climbed in anyway and held on to my seat. No problem. Yet.

These flight tests continued for several days, taking up about eight hours a day when waiting time was added. I sat in the rental car alone in between tests. Everything went perfectly from my vantage except for a hand brake that was used for take-offs and landings and taxiing that big ship once you were on the ground. And I did it all from a backseat. At least a half-dozen takeoffs and landings using that damned difficult hand brake sored up my right arm, so I asked Cipher to get us from the runway to the hangar when we came in for the last time. My hand was red and my arm was aching, but I mentioned it only casually. He never said a word then, but the hand brake turned out to be a major millstone.

Two days later I was called to the office and shown Cipher's check pilot report which indicated that I had passed all my tests but was not physically strong enough to handle the hand braking under all conditions. What a dirty deal. The administrative officers sided with Cipher and suggested that I take the title of "captain," but not take off or land. A stronger man than I would do it for me.

I was furious. I wanted to make them sorry they ever heard my name.

Beverly Hanson Sfingi
(GOLF PROFESSIONAL, FRIEND, AND CO-EXECUTOR OF JACKIE'S ESTATE)

I was a brash twenty-one when Helen Detweiller, a mutual friend and another golfer, introduced me to Jackie Cochran and we didn't like each other at all. No one would ever believe that we would start a dear friendship. It wasn't until after a couple rounds of golf and a couple of rounds of drinks that the two of us let our hair down one night.

"I think you are the most stuck-up bitch I've ever met," I told her, and she all but returned the "compliment." We got along fine after that and got to the point where we could say anything we wanted to each other. That was the only way to exist if you didn't want to get crushed around Jackie. She could walk all over you. If you were Caspar Milquetoast, you were going to be crushed. If you stood up for your rights, she respected you. It bothered her when women were blahs. That really bothered her.

Her philosophy was: if I can learn something from you, there's a basis for a friendship. We were friends for nearly forty years.

I remember one day when she was out playing golf in a tournament and shot a terrible score on one hole—a 10 or even 12. The caddy said, "Don't worry, Miss Cochran, Ben Hogan took a 14 on a hole the other day, so you shouldn't feel so bad."

She says, "Who's Ben Hogan?" She didn't know he was

such a famous golfer then. The caddy was dumbfounded and told her all about Hogan's winnings on golf courses. I'll guarantee you that once Jackie started studying something or someone, she never forgot a fact. You never caught her making the same mistake twice.

A couple of years later Ben Hogan came to Palm Springs and I introduced them to each other on the course. There was an amusing twist because there she was in awe of him and he says, "Miss Cochran, you don't remember me, but I was an enlisted man during the war and when you flew into Sweetwater, Texas, one of my duties was to wash down your plane."

Floyd and Jackie threw fantastic parties, and if you were invited, you didn't want to miss out. I remember sitting down to dinner one night next to a woman and in trying to be polite, asking her, "And what does your husband do?" When she answers, "He's a Supreme Court Justice," I nearly fell off my chair. Jackie always tried to mix us up so livewires would be sitting with deadbeats. She was very considerate.

When my sons were baptized in the local Episcopal church, we had to convince Jackie it was okay for her to participate. She was pretty firm about her Catholicism. One of those Sundays, Jackie was there and the rector got wound up in his sermon, droning on and on. In the meantime, the babies had filled their breeches, the church was not air-conditioned, and it was just ghastly in the back. Jackie was with us, dressed in one of her Parisian suits. After the service, the rector, puffed up with pride, knowing who she is—and she was pretty famous in our neck of the woods—asks her, "Did you enjoy the service, Miss Cochran?"

This I couldn't believe at the time. She says, "Well, it was fine, Father, but I was afraid my suit was going to go out of style before you finished your sermon."

I died. He just chuckled. She had that kind of whipping wit. She was so quick on her feet.

GUTS

In order to prove to U.S. and British officials that women could handle such heavy aircraft as bombers and thus play a role in wartime flying activities, Jacqueline Cochran gained the support of the British Minister of Supply, Lord Beaverbrook, and General "Hap" Arnold to allow her to ferry a Lockheed Hudson from Montreal to England. Because of opposition by male ferry pilots, a compromise had to be worked out. On June 17, 1941, Jackie piloted the bomber across the Atlantic but had to relinquish the controls to her male copilot on takeoff and landing.

—National Air and Space Museum, Smithsonian Institution, 1981

OTHER VOICES:

Maggie Miller

Do you know what you call that? Guts. Jackie would get in there, in a race, in a contest, in a jet trying to set a new record, and she'd keep pushing because she had the guts. And concentration, of course. She'd get herself all geared up to accomplish something and keep her mind on business, no matter what. Did you know that Jackie never took a written test for her pilot's license? She did it all verbally and everyone tells me that doing it like that is three times more difficult. She had a fantastic memory, a photographic mind, but was never embarrassed to say to anyone, even a president of the United States, "I don't understand what you are talking about. Tell me again."

The people who criticize her don't understand where she came from. There were some who hated her. Well, so what? That's bound to happen with a woman like Jackie Cochran and whatever they say about her may be true. She could manipulate herself through the muddiest waters I've ever heard about. But she was a real woman and real people are capable of being very possessive. When she made up her mind to get something, come hell or high water, she'd get it. But she was awfully good to me. We met when I was manager for Western Airlines at the Palm Springs Airport and became good friends. I miss her a lot. Jackie was sensitive but wouldn't let very many people know that. To let them in was to risk being hurt, being too vulnerable. And that was something she wouldn't do because of what she had learned growing up the hard way. Sometimes I think that if she had had a formal education, she might have been smarter than Floyd.

Captain Grafton Carlisle let me in on the scuttlebutt. The pilots were organizing to stop me and were especially angry with him because he had called them fools and signed on as my navigator. I wasn't looking for any glory I couldn't earn, so over lunch at Carlisle's home with his wife, I told him that if he were the one who took the Hudson off the ground and brought us back down, he ought to be captain, not me. I'd take the first officer's position. He liked me and that's when I learned that the hold-up on my special visa was not because of a paper log jam. It was purposely being delayed because one of the pilots had a friend in Washington, D.C. In a contest of power and friends, I knew I could win, so I contacted the American consul in Montreal, who called the Passport Department in D.C. and, *voilà,* the visa arrived sooner than someone else ever predicted.

There must have been forty or fifty pilots at a Monday morning meeting. Hot—they were really hot-headed. I stayed away. Floyd stayed on in Montreal after the weekend and he went to plead my position.

"She's on a publicity stunt," was one objection.

"She'll belittle the rest of us who have been involved in this dangerous work," one argued. "This isn't women's work. It's for men." I don't think this guy wanted anything, let alone the knowledge that a woman might be able to do it as well as a man, to take away from his image as a "hero."

"The Germans will shoot her down because the news is out already." Someone had tipped off a Hearst reporter in Boston and a small story had appeared. But it didn't come from Floyd or me and when Floyd called the head of the Hearst organization to explain our secrecy agreement, they promised to keep the story under wraps, in Boston only, until the flight was successfully completed. Later I learned that one of the Atfero pilots protesting that I would break the code of silence had himself called the Boston reporter with the news.

"Putting a woman into the cockpit of a bomber for ferrying purposes is taking bread out of our own mouths," was another argument Floyd heard.

In his defense of me, Floyd told the men that it wasn't a stunt. I had been asked to do the ferrying for a good cause, and I'd fly under the same secrecy limits to which they had all agreed, but the British Information Service had the right to use my flight as they pleased. Floyd also reassured them that I was not an advocate of women stealing the aviation jobs from men. Mine was a special flight approved by the authorities for special reasons. I had the experience, had passed the tests, and did all their objections boil down to one point, he asked: Did they object simply because I was a woman?

Mumbles, grumbles but that, in effect, was the only reason.

A Captain Bennett spoke, taking my defense from the offense: "Taking a woman into our organization will be disruptive," he said. "We've disapproved of your wife being here from the very moment the question was raised. We've simply been overruled by higher-ups. But now, now," he continued, turning toward his fellow flyers, "we're not running this organization and we've no right to issue an ultimatum to anyone, not even Miss Cochran."

Floyd left the meeting. Carlisle stayed, and when next we

met, his steam was showing. He was so furious with those men. They were threatening to blackball him from any further flying jobs if he went along with me. Some of the noise they produced was hollow, empty. But Carlisle considered some of it serious. He made his living in the air and expected to keep at it. But his fury brought my project closer to fruition.

"Let's just do it. Right now. Tomorrow morning."

A radio officer agreed to join and we sat down in the administration office to hash out commissions. Carlisle took captain. I was first officer, but I'd be able to fly, not on takeoffs or landings, but up there, in the air, over the Atlantic, I'd fly the bomber.

Tuesday morning. June sixteenth. The airfield is quiet and I check the equipment as part of my job. The oxygen has been hooked up wrong. The emergency tank of antifreeze fluid for the propellers is empty, and tools are missing. One is crucial. Mrs. Carlisle and the radioman's wife drive up and wait in a car with sandwiches. They haven't come because we might be hungry, however. Threats have brought them. Three women present might wet-blanket the angry male pilots, make them think twice about the physical threats being rumored about. But all's quiet. After sandwiches and an end to my search for a new tool—I bought one from a mechanic—the takeoff is nothing.

As soon as we're up, on our way to Gander, in Newfoundland, the first leg of our trip, Carlisle hands me the controls and goes below to work on navigation. That first night, I stayed with the airport manager's wife in Newfoundland, which was no big deal, but the next morning we were stymied for hours. A broken window in the cockpit. The same tool stolen again. Six hours of generator work. I wanted to scream, as only I knew how. I patched the window with adhesive tape instead and went looking for another all-purpose wrench. We didn't need the kind of ruckus I knew how to create. I paid a dollar for the damn tool, an outrageous sum considering it was probably the same tool I purchased the day before. A wrench may not sound like much, but without it, we wouldn't have been able to operate the oxygen system. Someone was angry enough to be acting irresponsibly.

Ready for takeoff into the dusk, Carlisle rattles us down the runway and it feels like we are rolling over logs, lots of logs. No speed, no lift. We fail to get off and he throttles back. Maybe it's the shock-absorbing oleos on the landing gear. In cold weather they can be a problem. Anyway, we check it out, pump the tires back up, take 50 gallons of gas out of the tanks, and try again.

An hour later we stagger down the runway at only 70 knots, heading across the Atlantic with a destination of Prestwick, Scotland. How we managed to get into the air and stay there at this speed is a mystery to me. Before we even made our turn into the right direction, Carlisle turned the ship over to me.

My job was to hold course and altitude, watch all the flying and engine instruments, and keep the log. Ferry pilots were told to keep their speed to 135 miles per hour, but in anxiety, above dark ocean water and trigger-happy Germans, some pilots would try to make better time at higher speeds, only to run out of gas. No heroes or heroines were we. We simply plodded along because I kept to every regulation in the book. I had studied my manual religiously. And Carlisle kept at his own station. He was able to get several checks on our drift because we all caught glimpses of the ocean below. Our Hudson never veered more than 40 miles off true course. The radio operator, who wasn't allowed to send signals on such a flight because silence was the rule, was in his compartment behind the pilot's seat receiving any offered.

I'll never forget that night. Soon after dark that fuse I mentioned before blew. The lights went out, and while we were able to get them back on, something went haywire with the port engine. It didn't quit. We just couldn't close the gills on it. In the dark, however, I saw the aurora borealis, the northern lights, for the first time, and let me tell you, from an airplane they are weird but entrancing. Distant lights shoot up out of nowhere in the north, fooling the world into thinking the dawn's early signs have arrived. Makes you think of Santa Claus—but it's not so friendly a sight as that. That flight took us through a long night, but it was dark little of the time. Our latitude, the summer season, and those eerie northern lights made the cockpit pretty bright.

Then we hit the soup. Overcast is never fun when you find yourself in it for four hours. I glued myself to the instruments. Just before daylight we must have been spotted, because suddenly, tracer bullets came up in front and around us. The three of us jumped. I sat back still, but Carlisle rushed up to me and the radio operator came running too. Grabbing what was called a Very pistol, he opened a hatch to fire a signal bullet of a certain color. If it had been fire from friendly sources, the signal would stop the bullets from flying. But our shots did no good because the light would never have been seen on the surface of the water. The firing continued and I thought of the angry words from the pilots' meeting: would the Germans try to make an example of me—and my death?

But the bullets stopped flying as mysteriously as they started. We could find no noticeable damage on the bomber.

Sunup, and a hole in the clouds allows us a glimpse of the sea. My face to the window, I catch sight of thick black smoke and tell Carlisle it might be a ship burning. German or English? We don't know and don't dare waste fuel flying low enough to say for sure.

The coast of Ireland in the distance was the friendliest sight I had seen in weeks. Seriously, I could feel my body untense after weeks of pent-up emotion and what would finally tally up to be nineteen hours airtime. But it wasn't over yet.

The route from Ireland to Prestwick was a tortuous air tangle guaranteed to protect us from enemy intelligence. It had no pattern and jumped one way, then another. Twelve hours from Gander, I handed the controls to Captain Carlisle for the last time and he brought us in easily.

OTHER VOICES:

Major General Fred Ascani

I would never have questioned Jackie's ability to fly anything you put her in. She wasn't fearless. That's the worst, most dangerous kind of pilot. I saw her when she was apprehensive, but that's good. That's a sign of a good pilot. She always had the natural apprehension that a good pilot should have. It helps to keep you aware because when you get anxious, all your senses are on. Jackie's inquisitiveness about anything that flew was probably successful in suppressing any fear she felt. She always wanted to know exactly what the airplane was going to do in a steep bank, and so forth. A good pilot is aware of his limitations, and she was. You want to plot it all out and you need to crank in all the what-ifs.

I accepted her as an equal because she had the capability in my field: aviation, piloting experimental airplanes. It was like a bond, a cult. We all respected Jackie for the pilot she was: a good one.

It was a testament to her: the way she didn't abuse being a woman among all those men. She was smart, knew her business as well as her limitations, and made a point of learning her airplanes very carefully. I'd put her way above average in pilot ability. I can't recall a single incident where there was discrimination because of her sex. But she could curse like a man, you know. It was very deliberate on her part. She just wasn't above letting loose with a few choice remarks. See, I admired that in her. She always seemed to land on her feet. She was one of those people who decided what she wanted to do and then went out and did it. Just like Chuck Yeager.

In Prestwick, I opened up a bag of goodies and watched lemons, oranges, orange juice, and sandwiches disappear like wildfire at the airport. Our allies hadn't been eating so well. They needed everything. In fact, I stashed a few oranges and lemons into my purse to save for London, and they turned out to be good as gold in a city under severe food rationing. Beaverbrook himself bargained like a trooper for two oranges when I offered one in exchange for a cartoon of himself I spotted in his office. The Battle of Britain was definitely on, and I was in London the night the East End burned, watching from the roof of the Savoy Hotel.

Goddamn it, but being the only woman in the history of World War II to fly a bomber to our beleaguered British allies was exciting and worth every ounce of energy I had spent manipulating my way into that airplane. The trip served me well in terms of future references too.

AMERICAN ATA-GIRLS

AUGUST 1941

No one gets more nervous than a pilot when things are going wrong and he isn't at the controls.

Fourteen of us and a radioman sit in the bomb-bay of a B-24 being flown by a British crew. There was no number 13 on the side of this plane. Loose boards serve as a floor, and each of us has a pallet for sitting or sleeping. There are no windows except two small ones off a tiny platform near the rear of the plane. Four people crowd around those two openings, four heads turning toward the light in the same way a plant turns toward the sun. The rest of us in the semi-darkness fight about space and cigarettes. Heavy winds on this trip back across the North Atlantic force us to skip just above the waves. Someone is sick and the hours add up. Twelve, it should only take twelve. But it's been fourteen now and word comes back that we are heading for Montreal, not Newfoundland after all.

I was nervous and the truth was that our pilot was off course and didn't know just where or when we would get in, if at all. We had very little food along, a few cheese sandwiches stowed in the toilet and, as time wore away, only the ten cigarettes I had up my sleeve in my favorite cigarette case. I passed a few around and made a deal. If I got a chance on the platform by the windows, where I could straighten my back and see the light, I'd divvy up the rest of the smokes. Okay? Okay. I stretch and look out.

I was on my way home with a plan in mind to put American women pilots to work just as the British were doing. In London I had met with Pauline Gower, who headed the group of English women ferrying airplanes for the government and freeing men for more serious tasks, combat, for instance. The English were so in need of warm bodies for war when I was over there that I'm surprised that they didn't put women into combat. I tried to get into it. I had set up a plan to get taken on a mission, but the only guy who was brave enough to bring me along got taken prisoner before my turn came up. I missed my chance.

I was exhausted when I finally arrived in New York, went to bed, and left word that I wasn't to be wakened by anyone other than the President of the United States. I was determined to sleep till noon the next day.

Nine A.M. the phone rings and President Franklin D. Roosevelt proves my exaggerated plea to be more than a joke. A mad dash through my closet and a police escort help me keep the lunch date at Hyde Park that noon, where I met with Roosevelt to tell him what I had seen in Great Britain and what I had planned for American women pilots. Later that week I met with Eleanor Roosevelt, Assistant Secretary of War for Air Mr. Robert A. Lovett, and General H. H. "Hap" Arnold. Eventually, I found my way to General Robert Olds's office, where he was just forming the Ferry Command, later renamed the Air Transport Command.

General Olds wanted to put women pilots to work on an individual basis, hiring them whenever and wherever needed. I wanted a more organized program because I felt that a few good women pilots amidst all the men would simply go down as a flash in the historical pan. I wanted to make a point with my planned program. So I put together my thoughts for training, organization, controls, and regulation of women pilots and submitted it to Olds, who wanted to kill it right there. I made sure Arnold saw my ideas, however. That was the end of July 1941. I waited for his answer. Olds still wanted to hire women immediately and, it seemed, Arnold soon objected to hiring them at all.

In the meantime, an English contingency had asked me to help with the recruiting of qualified pilots—male or female—on a more direct basis than what I had been up to. Here was my opportunity to prove a point: an important point about women flyers. I began combing the records of all American women with pilots' licenses, and I spent days at my desk at 630 Fifth Avenue at my cosmetics firm thinking of nothing but flying, war, and interviewing women. Cosmetics could take care of itself, or so I hoped.

September 19, 1941. Finally, a letter from General Arnold in answer to my plea to put women to good use comes to the conclusion: not yet. Hap didn't feel there were enough qualified women pilots ready and willing to fly for the Army Air Forces and of the ones who would and could, he foresaw big problems in housing, messing, and training them along with men at Army air stations. His argument encompassed more, of course, but in a nutshell, it was no.

I wrote back on October 4, 1941. Some of the facts at Arnold's disposal had been twisted to meet Olds's needs, and I wanted to set my side of the debate straight. There were more women pilots available than Arnold had quoted, and I wanted to rest his mind that I never envisioned women taking jobs away from men, something he had hinted in his two-page letter. Women, as in England, could form an auxiliary air corps with military or semi-military status and be given sufficient responsibility and discipline so that in case of need, they would form the nucleus of a women's active auxiliary. They would replace no one and merely be readied as leaders for a larger corps. I called it preparedness in my response to Arnold. In England, at that point, women had moved more than 4,000 airplanes with the loss of only one pilot and two minor accidents.

I ended my letter with questions: May I hope to hear from you? Wouldn't it be advisable to experiment in a small way to determine what women can do? When you reopen the subject, will you permit me to submit my plan in detailed form? Arnold answered that he had read my letter with interest. He'd be in touch.

General Arnold and I had lunch in his office together. That's when he urged me to complete my English experiment and to get the experience I would need when the time came for American women to rally to our defense. Go on to England, he said to me, I'll get in touch. I'll keep Olds away from the women pilots. So that's what I did. And that's what he did—for a while at least. I went to England to prove to General Hap Arnold and others in Washington, D.C., that American women pilots were just as capable as English women pilots. Twenty-five young American

December 1948: "The House That Jackie Built" was a favorite expression
Floyd used to describe the desert ranch.

All eyes for Cary Grant in London, 1942.

Winning a race would only fuel Jackie's desire to win another and then another.

After WW II, Jackie lobbied hard
—in and out of airplanes—for an
Air Force separate from the Army.
It paid off.

General Henry (Hap) Arnold gave Jackie her
Distinguished Service Medal of Honor in 1945 but
Eleanor Roosevelt had begun the parade of 15
Harmon Trophies back in '37.

Selling products like her beauty "Perk-Up" cylinder, she flew 90,000 miles a year after WW II.

Receiving the French Legion of Honor in 1949.

With Floyd at a New Year's Eve Party.

Only a flyer in love with flying would decorate the foyer floor of her New York apartment with compass markings.

Testing color combinations for Jacqueline Cochran
Cosmetics and touting "Women With Wings" on
radio with Jinx Falkenburg.

women and I did it to prove a large point to the folks back home. I wasn't there on English soil to prove myself as a pilot. I wanted to show my administrative skills and I spent long days hashing out organizational issues with British Air Transport Auxiliary (ATA) officials, among whom I held the rank of flight captain, and working with the U.S. Eighth Air Force which was just getting set up in London then.

More than a month before Pearl Harbor brought World War II to America, I was off on my own wartime project—a project that would take me away from Floyd and home for nearly three years.

OTHER VOICES:

Aldine Tarter

She cared and she worried about Floyd, but it was a long distance marriage for many of their forty years together. The telephone bills were horrendous. The cables came regularly. She wasn't a good letter writer when left to her own devices. With a secretary alongside she was prolific, but she didn't always have a good secretary. Some were great; others weren't so hot.

Jackie always had a large sense of her own worth, of what she could do for her country herself, or of what women were capable of accomplishing. Those ideas and goals came first and she was self-centered in that way, but she and Floyd would talk almost every night, or send their wires, or arrange elaborate ship-to-shore communiqués. Once she called from an airplane in the middle of the night and this was long before they had these portable phones that exist now.

It was three o'clock in the morning and my phone at home rang. This was when General Hunter Harris was head of the Air Force in the Pacific theater and Jackie had gone with him and Mrs. Harris. A young man's voice on the phone says this is Sergeant So-and-So, calling from Topeka, Kansas, and you are speaking on an air-to-ground phone call. Ma'am, when you speak, I will flip the switch on and when you are finished speaking, say "over," and I'll flip it over. Then your party will be able to answer. Don't start talking until I signal you.

So before he signals me, I say out loud, thinking no one can hear me, "Never mind me, honey, it's three o'clock in the morning and I know who the phone call is from and I won't get a chance to say anything anyway." At that point, Jackie chimes in, "That wasn't very nice of you, Mrs. Tarter."

I turn to my husband to tell him that I've finally blown it. Of course, I hadn't. Jackie and I were friends. I remember her typically southern expressions. She'd laugh at me when I would remind her of one or another. For instance, once I was talking about someone being very tall and I said, "That guy can shake hands with Jesus." Another time, when a friend of hers, a Roman Catholic monsignor, fell into the ranch pool, I said he was "as high as a Georgia pine." She didn't laugh then because we were all trying to fish him out without any fanfare.

She was calling me that night so she wouldn't wake Floyd at that hour, but she wanted him to know where she'd be, and that air-to-ground call would be her last chance to make contact for a while. I called Mr. Odlum first thing in the morning with the news. Jackie did a lot of things that Mr. Odlum couldn't do. He lived vicariously through her. There he'd be, in his wheelchair, watching her trying to win a race or set a record. And there she'd be, never letting the fact that she had a rich husband stand in the way of anything she wanted to try.

Ann Wood
(ATA-GIRL)

The bombing of Pearl Harbor wreaked havoc with my classes up in Maine. I was teaching flying at Bowdoin College up there and my students all started to sign up, go off to war. I wanted to do the same. But women weren't really wanted in the American war effort. So, the bandwagon was about to leave without me. Then I received the wire from Jacqueline Cochran about accompanying a small group of American women going to join the Air Transport Auxiliary in England.

I was terribly excited about the telegram and had some recollection that she was a famous woman pilot. This was the early forties and she had made her mark in the Bendix races. I was young and responded immediately.

My expenses would be paid to travel to New York City, where I'd be interviewed by her personally. Who wouldn't want a free trip to New York?

She was using her cosmetics business office on Fifth Avenue in New York to meet qualified women pilots for the program that would take us to England. So patriotic. That's what I remember.

I've always been struck by her looks. She had such glorious big brown eyes. They could be absolutely piercing. But she used to have a problem with her figure. It would get soft on her even though she was physically active and always a big sportswoman. She loved golf, played a lot of it, and abused herself in the sun. In those days we all did.

I became a friend as well as one of her youngest recruits in England. I had only the minimum number of hours required—350—and I think I jacked those up a bit on my own. It seems rather ludicrous looking back now, but I felt less qualified than the others. There were some women who had been out there flying for ten years longer than me. Helen Richie, for instance, was in her 30's and had better than 1,000 flying hours to her credit. I was twenty-one.

In the early selection process, Jackie met us singly, on a one-to-one basis. I recall her River House apartment and the glass case along one entire wall which contained all her memorabilia. And her cigarette case: the rubies on it were for her *stops* and the emeralds for *go* and they were strewn—along with diamonds—across a glorious gold box she carried. The design followed the routing of a Bendix air race and Floyd had given it to her. He used to give her such lovely things for one race or another.

She was a woman who wanted to make something happen all the time and she knew the very people to make it all possible. She had automatically risen to a higher power base by flying that bomber across the North Atlantic to Great Britain. She always did have that uncanny ability to envision where she wanted to be and then get there. There was something absolutely magical about her.

This is a different side. When I was having marital problems in England, years after this ATA experience, Jackie and I were corresponding back and forth and she told me she was coming to Paris. She was a director of one of the major airlines then, and she flew back and forth across the Atlantic a lot. Her schedule was tight. I called her.

"Ann, don't do anything yet. I'll fly over from Paris. I need to talk to you about all this. Meet me at the airport in London and we can discuss your problems," she says. Immediately, I'm feeling relieved that someone else can want to help, to take over my problems, to relieve me a little.

She flew over. We met in the waiting room and then she said to me, "Don't make any move now. I'll be home in ten hours and I'll discuss all this with Floyd. We'll get back to you."

Floyd and Jackie had this unique kind of relationship. It was wonderful really. He was a bulwark for her and made so much happen. I don't think she made very many big decisions in her lifetime without first talking to him about it. You weren't conscious of the physical attraction. He had begun to be sick by the time I knew her. But you could always see the equal admiration society they belonged to. She used to say to me, "Ann, I don't know what I'm going to do if he gets really sick." But she knew what she would do.

Jackie Cochran didn't like to be in private meetings with important men when no one else was around. Even when they were good men friends, if there was a way to avoid it, she would. Sometimes I was the other woman who had to come to her rescue. "Ann," she'd say to me, "can you be here at the Statler by five-thirty. So-and-so is coming by and I need you here." So, I'd go. And oftentimes, I'd be the third wheel in what was a business conversation.

We were all living in such anxious times then. I believed I was going to an exciting war theater to make a real contribution. And I was going to love it. I might not come back, but that didn't matter.

PROOF POSITIVE

OTHER VOICES:

Margaret Boylan

(EX-WASP)

If Jackie Cochran were threatened, she'd respond like a tigress. And she had an awful lot of power. Some people hated her guts for this reason. I saw lots of evidence of that. She could be ruthless when she wanted to pursue something, and she'd go at her goal with an intensity that wouldn't stop. People got stepped on en route.

She especially didn't like to feel competition getting too close. I mean she could eat you alive when you were working for her if something went wrong. She'd turn around and look at you and you'd think, "Oh, boy, here we go again."

I liked her. I remember one time when we landed out near the Grand Canyon, and once down on the ground, Jackie walked back from the cockpit into the cabin of the plane and said to me, "Margaret, wasn't that the smoothest landing you've ever experienced? Wasn't it great?"

I said, "Jackie, you're supposed to wait until other people compliment you. You're not supposed to brag about your own landings when you're the pilot."

"Well, I don't know why not," she said to me. Then she got mad.

"Oh, come on," I answered. "I was just teasing you. Look at it this way. You only tease people you really like."

Then she smiled.

1942

You got accustomed to the bombing in England and you'd simply carry on. In fact, there was a lot of carrying on, partying, worrying, and theorizing that you were spending your last night alive, so why not make the best of it? You'd be sitting at a dinner party, eating, drinking, playing backgammon, and you'd hear the bombers overhead. They'd swish right over my little house at 41 Ovington Square—behind Harrods department store, a block or so away from the antiaircraft guns in Hyde Park. Those planes would make a terrible noise. Then there was silence and you knew they had to be somewhere near.

You'd travel by subway, and many Brits lived down there with their own little stations picked out, neat and tidy. They'd sleep down there every night. Along with others, I didn't like it and preferred the air outside—even if it wasn't always so free of danger. I could not be part of the underground life. And I sat on the roof of the Savoy Hotel the same night the entire East End of London burned. Once, I chose the top of my front steps on a beautiful moonlit night of dogfights over London. Wrapped in a blanket, I saw windowpanes shatter all around me, watched the searchlights, the antiaircraft fire, and the flash of planes. A house up the street went to pieces, and another one, just a block below me, was hit. I often thought that there was some mysterious force at work there protecting British monuments like St. Paul's Cathedral, the Parliament buildings, the palace, and the bridges. But London was pretty much a shambles. I'm not a fatalist, but I used to think that my time would come when my number was up, so I went about my business openly. I didn't see myself dead just yet.

The "going off to war" giddiness probably originated in Montreal, where the American women were checked out in powerful, complicated aircraft. There was a feeling of exhilaration among the forty girls. Fifteen failed to pass. That's how we ended up with twenty-five. And for some, the answer to the wartime anxiety was to have a glass in hand from eleven A.M. on. Everyone up there was shipping out, waiting for transportation to some war zone. It was party, party, party.

Small groups of three or four together left for England by boat from the mouth of the St. Lawrence River. I had hoped to have the chance to fly another bomber to Britain, but it wasn't to be. A typhoid shot to protect me from getting sick gave me one of the worst reactions possible. An oozing sore on my leg, where the shot had been administered, required sulfa dressings for weeks. I didn't dare trust myself for the flight over. I had wanted to meet each group of girls as they arrived first in Liverpool, or at least in London or near Maidenhead, where some of the difficult British training began. So I took a British plane to Bermuda and made my way through the war zone using that connection.

Organizing the American group of ATA-girls was a tough assignment on all fronts. The British Ferry Command was unprepared for us when the first group arrived. Then I had a nasty run-in with a British physician who insisted on giving the American women complete physical examinations before they began any flying training. That sounded fine to me, but his idea of a physical and mine were miles apart. He wanted the women to strip naked for him. No way.

There he is—adamant about his damn procedures.

There I am—not about to take off all my clothes or to let the other American girls be subjected to such ridiculous procedures. Where was it stated that England needed its pilots to be examined in the buff in order to qualify for a training program? I marched off to Pauline Gower for answers and from there to the commanding officer of the Air Transport Auxiliary. He let me cool my heels in his outer office for a day. Was I angry!

I won that round but then went to battle about written examinations. Some of the women in the American group had master's degrees, and I didn't see the need for general retesting. When it came to understanding the English battle scene, that was a different story, of course. There was a lot to be taken in.

Flying air corridors set off and hemmed in by captive balloons was tricky, particularly in sticky weather. Navigating through the English countryside was also difficult, and flying both new and disabled aircraft wasn't going to be easy. I finally convinced the English to adjust the period of indoctrination and testing to accommodate the special needs of my American women.

OTHER VOICES:

Ann Wood

(WINNER OF THE PRESTIGIOUS GEORGE MEDAL
IN ENGLAND FOR WARTIME SERVICE)

We had some crazies in our group and I think that's where the strip search started. Somebody complained to Jackie, and her prudishness about things of that nature got the better of her. My feeling always was: if he wants you to strip, so strip. I can handle it from there. I don't even remember what happened. But Jackie made a great big scene about it and wanted to know what he thought he was doing with her girls. She always saw herself as our protector. She'd moan and groan and spend hours fighting our battles, battles that weren't really so important in the long run. But that was Jackie. She felt inferior to the British and she'd pick fights that were silly sometimes.

There's an important thread that runs through her life and shows itself in episodes like the British insistence on strip-search examinations: Jackie was a prude. I can't tell you how many times she'd invite me along just so I'd be there. If you run this theme of prudishness through her life, it comes out in her choice of women to take to Europe with her. She was so strict with us, wanted us to represent the United States and be above reproach. She could party hard and be a good time all by herself, but we had to be good girls. We were in an exciting war theater and believing all the time that we were making a great contribution. We had everything going for us. And Jackie didn't want anything to spoil it. But I went to London every chance I got to party.

My training was reasonably long, two or three months easily, and I made at least forty trips through various areas to familiarize myself with the airports, factories, and cities. I learned how to navigate using their navigational aids. For instance, if you were taking off from the London area, and heading for the midlands, you might be going to Birmingham, Nottingham, and there are other big towns there. As an American, you might be scratching your head, thinking, "My God, they all look alike from the air, which is the one I want?" Whereas in the United States, you might take off from Boston, head north, and there is only one Portland up there in Maine. You can't confuse it with four other Portlands. We flew during the daytime because there was always a blackout at night.

I had a couple of accidents, really of a minor nature. I once had to land a plane early in my training because the engine just stopped. I picked a good field and the farmer came out with a pitchfork in his hand, thinking I'm a German, of course. But I progressed up to Spitfires, those wonderful airplanes. You could turn over so fast in those planes. The story I like best about me and the Spitfire is the one about the Bristol Bridge.

One day I was flying along with two ex-RAF pilots somewhere in Scotland, and the name of their game was to fly under the Bristol Bridge. That was fine. They, each in his own plane, told me exactly how to do it and then put me in the middle. Johnny Jordan went first, then me, and then my other friend. It was such fun that one day when I was alone, traveling near Bristol, I decided to try it again.

I'm thinking, well, I'll get down here and I'm heading for the bridge when it suddenly strikes me that the opening beneath the bridge and above the water is so much smaller than it had been the day the three of us accomplished our stunt.

"Oh no!"

I hadn't calculated on the tide being in, and it was too late to turn back. I could do nothing else but head for my slip of a chance to make it through.

God. It was frightening. I did get through but I can tell you: *tide is a serious factor*.

There's always been confusion about Jackie Cochran and

the ATA-girls. She became great friends with the generals in England and worked with a military man named Peter Beasley. She would be investigating one problem after another with Beasley's help and wasn't there in England for those eleven months simply to ferry airplanes from point A to B. She went to England to get us there, to prove her point, and to return to the United States. The women who are critical of her role over there, who contend that she did little actual ferrying work, never understood her mission.

Only one of those twenty-five women never made it home again. Mary Nicholson, my own secretary, had a plane's propeller exceed its thrust capability and fly off. It was a runaway engine and she flew straight into the hills. The other twenty-four fulfilled their eighteen-month contracts and some, like Ann Wood, stayed until the war was over ferrying Hurricanes, Spitfires, and as many as five different aircraft in a single day's span, landing and taking off from nearly impossible fields. They would move planes from factory to field or vice versa, or pick up aircraft that had put down in emergency situations. The idea behind it all was to free the men for combat work or more crucial positions. And it worked.

At one point when the war had pushed England pretty desperately, they had a maximum of only forty serviceable fighter aircraft. They made the best of what they had and it was the most heroic job I ever witnessed. I recall about 300 ATA pilots who came from all over the globe: at least thirty different nationalities. To my knowledge, there were never any security leaks about those planes.

I was based at White Waltham and had my enemies there. Authorities in the lower administrative echelons and out in the field never knew that I believed my battles were better fought on the ground in the political arena than up in the air. Because of my knowledge of military channels, I was even asked by the Eighth Air Force to spend several weeks in organization. The whole air effort and the American role in this English battle were being argued. General Arnold, Admiral John Towers, and Air Marshall Arthur Harris used my little apartment at the

Savoy Hotel one night to debate the question of nighttime versus daylight bombing. The Americans wanted a round-the-clock effort, but the British, who were badly in need of more planes, didn't even want to envision how costly the light of day might prove to their men and machines. The upshot was a compromise where the Americans took the daytime bombing raids and the English stuck with the night.

Besides the bombs, I remember the food. God, it was awful. Tripe, they ate tripe, and the memory of that pig-sticking and stinky smell in my childhood returned like a flash. I couldn't stomach it. The British didn't know what to do with hominy grits, however, and as a result, it was one of the few unrationed items. I jumped on this knowledge, laid in a goodly supply, and got some canned hams shipped over from America. Do you know what I did with all this? I put it in a bank vault. I knew that even in the event of a bomb raid on the bank, the vault would probably be okay. So like any good capitalist, I'd go to my bank to make periodic withdrawals—but for dinner!

The hams and hominy grits didn't help me the night Captain Paul Hammond and a few other friends started speculating— and wouldn't stop—on the marvelous taste of an old-fashioned southern fried chicken dinner. Mouths were watering all around. Impossible, someone said. And I agreed. Single white eggs were worth their weight, literally, in gold at that point. Where would the ingredients come from?

"Not impossible," someone insists.

"Well, I'll do my part," I say. "I'll cook it. In fact, if someone can get white flour and chicken, I'll cook you all a dinner worthy of General Robert E. Lee," I promise, never thinking they'll be able to obtain the impossible: food such as that.

White flour showed up from an American cruiser. Chicken came from Northern Ireland. And in the apartment of the American air attaché, I found the odds and ends I needed to complete my feast. A dozen military men, including several British admirals, sat down to home-cooked southern fried chicken one night. Considering the situation outside and above us, it was a night never to be forgotten by any present.

OTHER VOICES:

Aldine Tarter

Fried chicken. Sometimes when I think of Jackie, fried chicken pops into my mind at the very same moment.

"The funniest thing happened to me last night," Jackie said to me one morning. "Last night Floyd and I were having a drink and all of a sudden, I was aware of being on the floor, not how I got there, just that I was there. Floyd says I drank too much and fell off my chair. He claims I got drunk. But I wasn't drunk, Aldine. I wasn't drunk."

I was scared. Jackie must have been sixtyish at the time, but she was a woman who denied that she could get sick enough to die. She had this big bruise on her forehead, and I said, "Oh, God, Jackie, look at your forehead." She says, "Aldine, that came later. After I got up from the floor, I went to get ready for bed, sat at my dressing table, and just fell forward again. It's a very strange feeling," she was saying to me. And at that very moment I saw her eyes glaze over and she slumped down in her chair and I thought she was dying. I screamed, "Jackie!" Then she came out of it and said, "Do you see what I mean?" She was calm. I wasn't. "You've got to get to the hospital. My God, this is serious."

"I think I'll go to Albuquerque," she says then.

She had put all her faith in Dr. Randy Lovelace and the Lovelace Clinic in Albuquerque. But Albuquerque was at least an airplane trip away or two days of driving. I was worried. While we were all arguing about what to do, calling the Lovelace Clinic and calming everyone down, she had another attack. The doctors out in Albuquerque didn't want her to fly. My first thought was to charter an airplane and zap, get her right over there. They nixed that, however. So we began loading up the ranch station wagon and getting two of the housemen set to take turns at the wheel. There was enough room in the back for Jackie to lie down.

All this is going on and suddenly, I see the wagon being loaded with giant boxes of grapefruits and lemons. The damn thing was packed with gifts for the doctors and nurses at

Lovelace and it was Jackie who had ordered it done. There was hardly room for her to sit in the backseat. I was furious about this and I couldn't find her. Maybe she was dead already somewhere. Then I caught a scent of something and I knew what she was up to.

Chicken. She was frying chicken in the kitchen all by herself and I was so mad.

"We've got to have fried chicken to eat on the way, Aldine."

WASPS

The success of the British ATA convinced the U.S. Army Air Force to organize its own women's pilot program and recall Jacqueline Cochran from England to become director of women's flight training.
—National Air and Space Museum, Smithsonian Institution, 1981

General Hap Arnold was really something. That man was a powerful, strong, intelligent, forceful, unbelievable human being and he would get so mad that he would beat on the desk and yell, "Goddamn it," and I would say to him, "Shut up, you are going to go to hell if you keep talking like that."

He came to London in June 1942 and that's when the fight about the American women pilots heated up. I like a good healthy fight every once in a while. This one went on for too many years.

Lord Beaverbrook was going to have a dinner party to honor General Arnold and wanted me present, so his "man Friday" arrived at my doorstep in the Midlands, where I was working. The invitation came with a message: "His Lordship said he knew that you wouldn't mind being there with only gentlemen." Of course, I loved it.

I had to take a train in, slept all the way, and then missed cocktails, where I was hoping to be able to snack. I was so hungry, but when they brought out dinner, that piece of meat was crawling on the plate and bellowing. I just couldn't eat it.

The next day, at a meeting with Arnold, he said, "I want you to come home with me."

"I can't just yet," I explained. "I do have a contract to work for the British a full eighteen months. There's a clause in it which would release me if and when the United States was at war, but I'll need a formal letter from you asking me to come home. It'll take thirty days, I'm sure."

"I want you to come home to form a group of women pilots," Arnold said.

In the meantime, trouble was brewing. General George had circumvented Arnold to give permission to Nancy Harkness Love, an accomplished American pilot who was married to Colonel Robert Love, deputy chief of the Air Transport Command, to set up an ATC auxiliary of women who already had their pilots' licenses. These women had at least 500 hours' flying experience and were to be designated the Women's Auxiliary Flying Service, or the WAFS. Floyd had been forwarding newspaper clippings describing the situation and it was evident Arnold hadn't been kept well-informed.

"I understand you already have women pilots," I say. He was furious.

"I don't have any," he insists. When I show him the news articles, his anger flares. "If they think they are going to get away with this, they're wrong. I don't care who has authorized this, even the Secretary of War."

Lovett Stimson, the Secretary of War, was the coldest potato I ever met in my life with the most beautiful command of the English language I've ever heard.

"I don't want to come back and start some fight," I say to the general, though he knows me well enough to know how much I enjoy a good battle. "I'm perfectly happy where I am, and I might as well stay here in England." He stops me and insists, "You come home. We are going to have a women's organization in the Army Air Forces and I am going to set it up and I am going to close that Air Transport Command women's outfit down as soon as I get home."

"Why don't we both think about this?" I suggest.

"I've done my thinking," he answers.

"Okay."

And that's where one hinge of this ongoing battle began. A complete autopsy of the situation would be nearly impossible and certainly a bore, but it began with Arnold pitted against the officers of his own Ferry Command. WASP skirmishes seemed to spare no one: the United States Congress got in on it, the press, the Army Air Forces administrative officers, including Colonel Oveta Culp Hobby, the woman I loved to hate, the civil services administration, and the unemployed pilots left standing in unemployment lines by the shutdown of all the pilot training programs. In one final battle scene, Arnold's character would be questioned and I'd be called "the shapely pilot, with a cause célèbre, a composition of windblown bob, smiling eyes, outdoor skin...It's whispered he's (Arnold) battling like a knight of olde, or olde knight for the faire Cochran." It was all so silly and unfair. And the other victims, the wonderful women who flew for the United States Army Air Forces during World War II, wouldn't get the credit they deserved until it was almost too late. The program would also become a casualty—by dying too soon. But I couldn't predict all this at the time. And even if I had been able to, I would have insisted on jumping in where few other angels had trod before: head-on into the American military machine.

It took me about a month to put my English life in order, get on an airplane, and end up in Arnold's office in Washington, D.C. I remember asking him point-blank: "What do I do now?"

"You work directly out of my office, write down your directives, and let's train 5,000 women."

"That seems like a ridiculously high number, but I want to think this all through carefully, go back over my reports from last summer, and analyze the problems. Can I see you tomorrow morning?"

"That door is open to you anytime you want to come in," he says.

And it was.

Between September tenth and the fourteenth, a two-pronged women's program became evident. The experimental squadron of experienced women pilots would remain part of the Air

Transport Command under Nancy Love. Secondly, I would take charge of the women pilot training program and come under the direction of the Flying Training Command. I was to train 500 women pilots, though that number was later increased to more than 1,000. I was pleased.

By October 1942 I was really busy trying to set up my side of it all. I didn't worry about what the women under Nancy Love were doing for the Ferry Command. I just didn't have time. I was assigned to Colonel Luke Smith, a general staff officer in Washington, D.C., and we never got along for a second. Later, when he considered me banished to Texas, the program finally got underway. Commander of the Fort Worth training command, General Barton Yount, one of the loveliest men I've ever met, was crucial as my first training class came together. We needed everything: aircraft, instructors, a field, sleeping and eating facilities for the young women. I couldn't even get a bunch of cats and dogs and I had at least 25,000 applications once the word was leaked through the media that the United States Army Air Forces would be starting a training program. All applicants claimed that they had the equivalent of two years of college, were at least 5 feet 4 inches tall, and were between eighteen and thirty-five years old. I kept saying to myself as well as anyone who would listen: "We are going to train only 1,000." There was so much mail, more than anyone, even a trained staff—which I didn't have—could honestly sort through. How to interview the women and then find a place for the training program were big problems. I looked for clean-cut, stable young women who could show flying hours properly noted and certified in a log book. We asked for 200 hours flying time at first and later reduced that number to 35. I was to serve with the general staff of the Flying Training Command based out of Fort Worth, Texas.

On the morning this decision was made, I was standing in Arnold's office.

"Barton, Jackie Cochran will be down there in a few days and I want her to have anything she wants. Will you see to it? She'll fill you in on it. Good-bye." Yount told me later that Smith had also called to warn him of the "bundle of trouble" headed in his direction. According to Smith, "I was a very determined, obstinate woman." He was right about that, but Barton and I usually agreed with each other. Once in Texas, I chose Houston as a command center. Later, we would take over a British training base in Sweetwater, Texas.

It was all happening too fast, even for me. My worries were nearly overwhelming. Without chief administrative officer Leni Leoti Deaton, I would have drowned. To compound the issues, word of the bomb to end all wars was leaking. I worried that the war would catch up to us, and the need for women would be over before I had a chance to see that they were properly trained. This was partly behind the decision to hire the trainees as civil service employees. We were too few in number compared to the armed forces totals and too inexperienced in those early stages to know how it would all turn out. I could wait. A bill to militarize my women pilots was in order, but in the meantime, Arnold and I had to find a way to pay those girls, to organize them without going through all the Army's bureaucratic channels, to work fast, to set aside worries about uniforms and chain of command. It backfired later, but at the time, it got us up and flying, off the ground.

I had three objectives: (1) to see if women could serve as military pilots and if so, to form the nucleus of an organization that could be rapidly expanded; (2) to release male pilots for combat; (3) to decrease the Air Forces' total demands on the cream of the manpower pool. American industry was producing tens of thousands of airplanes and in the fall of 1942, no one could tell whether we had enough young, qualified men to fly them. All the other services were drawing heavily on available manpower. If a woman could handle a trainer plane, then a man could be released for active duty. That's what I thought, that's what I had seen at work in England, and that's exactly what I would prove in the long run. But it was a very long run.

At the start, the total training occupied 23 weeks. Later, it was lengthened considerably. Our flying equipment was claptrap stuff in the beginning. It got better, and looking back on it, we had something over 200 airplanes of standard types: PT-17s, PT-19s, BT-13s, BT-15s, AT-6s, AT-17s, UC-78s, UC-43s, and UC-81s. What a maintenance nightmare it was.

Margaret Boylan

The challenge appealed to Jackie. She had been told "No." Women couldn't do it, we weren't needed and that first "No" made her all the more determined to get the program off the ground. The other spur in her saddle was that Nancy Love had her program started. When she made up her mind, Jackie Cochran was like a steel railroad going right down the track. She had a great sense of her own worth and she knew she was good. She bathed in the recognition. It's hard to sit back today and know the real motivation for someone like Jackie Cochran. But I really believe that her competitive spirit was what got the WASP program up and going. She had a great sense of history.

The Women's Airforce Service Pilots program really proved something. It was a marvelous period of history, made possible by Jackie Cochran. When you consider how competitive this woman was with other women equal to her, it's amazing that she worked so hard for our benefit. We flew a lot. I can tell you that whenever she was threatened, she'd get under way full speed. People didn't know what to do with Jackie Cochran. So the success of the WASPs was a tremendous, stupendous effort on her part. I don't know anyone else who could have done it and been as successful as she was.

I first met Jackie when she arrived in Houston at our training center in her souped-up Beechcraft. She came roaring in and we all went out to meet her and gather around her airplane. The propeller of that plane cleared the ground by only six inches. There, on the side of the plane, were the words: WINGS TO BEAUTY. They made me smile and I said to someone, "That's a weird name for an airplane." I may not have used the word weird, but it was some such phrase. Jackie heard me. She had ears like you wouldn't believe.

"What's wrong with that name?" she asks.

Uh-oh, I think. And I say, "I don't know. It just seems kind of strange to me."

"Well, it's the slogan for my cosmetics company," she explains. "I like it a lot. Why don't you meet me later today in my office."

All I needed was to get into trouble with the commanding director of the women's pilot program. The entire operation was new then and I was brand new. Sometimes I think it's amazing that Jackie got the program going before very many people realized what she was up to. Anyway, I went in to talk to her.

"We've got a lot of bugs we need to get out of this program," I tell her. "For one thing, we are being taught by civilian instructors and then tested by Army Air Force pilots and the training and testing are not consistent with each other. We're losing a lot of women because of this. They are washing out because practices are not standardized."

She looked at me strangely. Her big brown eyes could bore holes in you if she'd let them. "You come back here tomorrow," she says abruptly.

"Are we finished talking?" I ask because I had been in the middle of a thought.

"For today," she answers.

The next day I was called back into her office and she explains, "I wanted to take a look at your record to see if you were about to wash out yourself before I took your comments seriously. You might have been talking through your own hat, but I found out you aren't, so I'll listen. What else did you want to say?"

I was surprised and explained that I had said most of my piece the day before.

There were always conflicting aspects to Jackie's personality, and you never knew what was going to set her off. She competed with an intensity that stepped on other people in her route. A lot of the WASPs took offense at the trouble between Jackie and Nancy Love. And while I know some of the stories about their differences, I do have a story that will point out their similarities:

The two of them—Jackie and Nancy—were supposed to be participating in an Army Air Force program at some base, and Nancy, who was a very beautiful woman, was just recuperating from the chicken pox. She was over the contagious part of the disease, but she still had all the pock marks and scabs on her face. There these two enemies were, getting ready for a dinner at this base, and Nancy complaining to everyone within earshot about the marks on her face.

"That's no problem," Jackie says matter-of-factly. She pulls out her whole bag of cosmetics, sits Nancy down in front of her, and just does a magical job of covering every one of those blemishes, beautifully. Nancy looked wonderful and it was because Jackie Cochran made her so. She could be ruthless, she could be arrogant, and you didn't want to get on her bad side. I really liked her a lot.

And it was Nancy Love who told me the chicken pox story.

WASP STINGS

1943

My gosh, we had knock-down, drag-out fights. The Army had its WACs. The Navy had its WAVEs. The Marines had their women's group. I believed that there was a reason for the Army Air Forces to have a separate women's group. *Separate* is the key word as far as I could see.

So help me God, this is a true story. I am not telling fairy tales or being bitchy. Though I certainly know how to be bitchy.

I was in Fort Worth only about six months when General Arnold called me back to Washington. You know I wore at least three hats for him. I was always a sounding board for that man.

"You are wanted in Washington by General Arnold," General Yount informs me.

"What for?" I ask

"We didn't ask," Yount says.

"Well, I'm still a civilian. I don't have anything to fly there," I say kind of sassylike. I had sold my plane to the government for $1.00 and then they would sign it back to me.

"You've been dying to take a B-25 for a ride, so do it," Yount says. I had gotten myself qualified on everything they had: the B-29, B-70, the works, so I took off with a green copilot and not much experience in this B-25. I flew to Washington, D.C., that night in the worst weather you've ever seen. It was ghastly. Then I went to the Mayflower Hotel, where Floyd's company had a suite and ended up occupying couch space until they could throw someone out of a corner room somewhere for me.

Seven A.M. I'm in Arnold's office.

"How'd you get here so fast?" he asks.

"This better be important," I say.

"Have some coffee, Jackie," he says. Trouble. But I just adored the man, so I poured myself some coffee and sat down.

"How would you like to have your girls become part of the WACs?" he asked.

"How would you like to be back in basic training?" I answer.

"Don't get fresh with me," he says.

"Those girls will become part of the Women's Army Corps over my dead body. No way. And I *am* fresh with you. I thought I was here today to discuss legislation to make these girls part of the Army Air Corps, not this. Hobby has bitched up her program and she's not going to bitch up mine."

"Well, it's under consideration," Arnold says.

"She's not going to get them."

"Well, you'd better go talk to her," he says.

"I'm not going to talk to anyone until I go to bed and get myself a long sleep. Then I'll be able to tangle with her. I can tell you this: I wouldn't have flown all night in bad weather to battle with Mrs. Hobby."

"Colonel Hobby," Arnold corrects me.

"All *right*—it's Colonel Hobby."

Arnold gets on his squawk box and Colonel Hobby answers. "Miss Cochran will be available to see you at your convenience from eleven o'clock on tomorrow."

"Let me get my calendar, General," she says. Then, after a long wait, she says, "I think I can see her at two o'clock."

I decided right there in Arnold's office that I'd give her fifteen minutes leeway. That was all. If she wasn't there by 2:15, I'd be on my way back to Texas. Arnold laughed at me and arranged for one of his colonels to be present. Someone needed to keep me civil. He knew it. I knew it.

While still in his office, we got to talking about Baltimore prostitutes. Not the kind that comes immediately to mind.

The B-26 bomber was being built in Baltimore and had a bad reputation. Because its wing area seemed too small to support its body, it was said to have no visible means of support. That's how it earned its name. Its reputation wasn't enhanced by its performance on the job either.

"What do you hear about it?" he asks. The accident statistics looked bad. Pilots were afraid of it. General Barney Giles, my chief at the time, had even test-flown it to look for some basis for all the bald-faced rumoring. Later, I would ask General Arnold to put girls on the B-26 program so we could prove the plane's reliability and shame the men into their senses.

For the time being, I was handed some literature on this prostitute: a letter from Arnold's friend and some technical data on the plane. So, the next day, out of my pocketbook came the B-26 reading material while I waited impatiently for *Mrs.* Hobby's return from lunch. I had gone up to the front desk on my arrival and informed the secretary of my appointment. A Colonel Carmichael from Arnold's office was along with me. Poor guy.

I had on a beautiful French suit, a lovely mink coat, and was dressed to kill. Thirty minutes—fifteen more than I had offered to give—went by before I walked over to the desk to give the girl my card and explain that I had to take off for Texas that afternoon. I was still wearing my coat. No one—not one of those women working for Hobby—had been polite enough to ask me if I'd like to remove it. It was hot in that outer office. But I was hotter and not because of my coat. My chip showed badly on my shoulder. I didn't care.

Carmichael asked me to give her a few more minutes. Finally, though, I went up to a secretary, asked for a piece of paper, and began writing: "Dear *Mrs.* Hobby, if you want to see me, you can find me in Fort Worth, Texas. Jacqueline Cochran."

"Oh, you're Jacqueline Cochran," the girl says. Who she thought I was, sitting there all that time, I can't even guess. I get so nasty every time I think of this episode and that woman. "I have no more time to wait," I say, turning to leave and obviously making poor Colonel Carmichael, Arnold's man, very uncomfortable. He knows he's in the middle of a hen fight and he can't win.

At that point, *Mrs.* Hobby walks in, right past me, and on into her office. I turn and head for the door. It was obvious that Arnold wanted Hobby and me to discuss the matter: should the women pilots become part of the WACs or ought Congress to pass a separate bill incorporating them into the Army Air

Corps? I wanted to be part of the Air Corps, of course, because I saw plans down the road for a separate Air Force. Besides, I wanted no part of *Mrs*. Hobby herself.

We did sit down to talk that afternoon. She opened the discussion with casual remarks, off the record, that made my blood boil. She really doesn't know one end of an airplane from another, she says. I am still wearing my coat and trying very hard not to move a muscle. You know, there is nothing more disarming to a person than to have someone use silence as a weapon. I decided to open my mouth as little as possible.

The chitchat deepened the hole she was digging for herself. "My seven-year-old son is just crazy about airplanes," she says. God, I was angry. I flew all that way to have it suggested that my program be taken away from me and by a woman who talked about airplanes on wallpaper—children's bedroom wallpaper.

One of the points to my argument that day was that pilots, even young women pilots, are temperamentally different from women signing up for straight army corps work. "They're a different breed of cat," I insisted. If she didn't understand airplanes or the kind of women who flew them, then she had no business being their commanding officer. It was my job and I wanted to keep it. I just couldn't see throwing my girls in with that bunch. I was so proud of my pilots. Practically all of them were well placed later in life, one received her doctorate in aeronautical engineering and went to work for a helicopter company, some married ambassadors, but they all went on to lead lives of great accomplishment and excitement. They were just a fabulous group and we reunioned at my ranch. I resisted Hobby openly and at every turn, and Arnold laughed for weeks about my fury. Later, it wouldn't be so funny.

"Her office is twice as large as yours," I told Arnold later that day.

"She's a powerful woman," he explained.

On August 5, 1943, the training program and the women ferry pilots were merged to become the Women's Airforce Service Pilots (WASPs). Jacqueline Cochran was named Director of Women Pilots.

—National Air and Space Museum, Smithsonian Institution, 1981

1944

A motor scooter would definitely have helped me get around that maze of Pentagon offices when I was trying to sell my plans for a separate WASP. Some were arguing that we should simply remain on civilian status, but to gain the recognition as well as the rights, both political and economic, we needed to be militarized. Why I couldn't convince enough people of this frustrated me to the end. I did make a lot of friends in my rounds. As well as enemies.

Several questions did get settled once we merged with the women in the Ferry Command: I became official director of women pilots, Nancy Love took WASP staff director in the Air Transport Command, and something almost just as important finally got settled: WASP uniforms.

Trainees had been provided with coveralls and some functional clothing, such as leather jackets, but for a uniform look they all dipped into their own pockets to purchase khaki slacks, a cap, and a white shirt.

At the very first graduating class out in Texas, the girls were all dressed up in those khakis and blouses and they arrived in beautiful formation...just beautiful. We never really taught things like that per se or gunnery and we didn't have enough planes for all, but we picked the best in that class and put on a show for General Arnold, who was there to pin wings on each. Newsreels were rolling, everybody was there.

The first girl steps up and she's awfully pretty—beautiful in fact. Arnold takes the wings, and to pin it on the blouse, he almost has to put his hand down it. He didn't think a thing about it, but it didn't look right at all. He wasn't a man who ever got fresh with any woman.

I walk over to him and make my suggestion. "Perhaps you should simply hand them to each girl?"

He looks a little surprised, but then it dawns on him. He just smiles.

Later that day he said to me, "Don't you think those girls deserve a uniform?"

"Yes, sir, I do."

I started working on the project with the most arrogant, impossible human being alive, a lieutenant colonel who produced 30,000 hideous old WAC suits. I told him right away, "I don't want these cast-off clothes."

"Well, I don't think you've got much of a choice," he said to me. He knew I was losing my battle with Hobby and things didn't look good in Congress. I went to Bergdorf Goodman's department store in New York City, and with my own money I paid to have WASP uniforms designed. They were really handsome suits, with a cute beret and I knew they would make the girls look young and fresh. But I was crying for money. I went to a General Meyer and said, "Now, look here. This is the design that I want and I am not going to take those old WAC suits."

"There is a lot of material in storage somewhere. You can have it made up any way you want."

When I saw the fabric, I was aghast. First of all, there was enough of it to make a tent to cover the entire United States of America. Why in God's name the Army would have purchased so much from someone made me wonder. Secondly, it was terrible stuff. I told Meyer, "You can give this to the starving Armenians. I'm not going to take it."

"You don't have any choice," were the words I got again.

"Yes I do," I replied. "If my girls have to pay for their uniforms out of their own pockets—and they will, I believe—or if I have to put up   the money myself, we'll just do it that way."

I went to General Marshall to uncover the truth about all that fabric. Jeepers. When I started digging, getting my fractions together, I told him that there was someone sitting in a woodpile somewhere. "General, this is the story I've been getting—do you know anything about this program? Has anyone ever bothered to figure out how many pairs of socks the Army needs, or how much fabric it takes to clothe these men and women? I think there is something funny going on." They started an investigation into who had been ordering so much and discarding so easily.

To prove how terrible the fabric was, I paid to have it made up into a uniform, had one of the most beautiful women there in the Pentagon wear my beautiful Bergdorf Goodman suit made of Santiago blue fabric, and I had someone else wear the old WAC outfit. We marched into Arnold's office one day and asked him to choose. He couldn't. So we marched over to General Marshall's office and he says, "Well, I like the one you're wearing, Miss Cochran."

"You can't have this one," I answer. It was a simple but expensive gray suit I had purchased in Paris before the war.

Then he admitted, "The blue one is the best. And you'll get your uniforms. We'll pay for them."

It wasn't easy being director of women pilots. Not because of the basic premise of the program so much as the hassle of breaking such new ground for women in what had been a highly prized corner of a man's world: flying. My training program, my operations, the WASPs—everything worked, and in fact, it worked extremely well. We were proving a point about women flyers, providing competent pilots to the ferry operation, towing targets—a nasty job—working on tracking and searchlight operations, simulated strafing, smoke laying, and performing other chemical missions, radio control flying, taking care of basic and instrument instructing, engineering test flying, as well as handling the administrative and utility flying. We had to prove points as basic as the fact that women could fly during any time of the month. Menstrual cycles didn't upset anyone else's cycle. WASPs flew nearly every type of airplane used by the Army Air Forces, from small primary trainers to the Superfortress (B-29), including the Mustang, Thunderbolt, B-17, B-26, and C-54.

More than 25,000 women applied for training. Eighteen hundred and thirty were accepted and 1,074 made it through a very tough program to graduation. These women flew approximately 60 million miles for the Army Air Forces with fatalities of only 38, or one to about 16,000 hours of flying. Those statistics compare favorably for male pilots in similar work. Women had as much endurance, were no more subject to fatigue, flew as regularly and for as many hours as the men.

OTHER VOICES:

Margaret Boylan

As I look back on the WASP story, I think it's one of the most incredible stories I can think of. Given the times—the 1940s—and the way women were looked upon, it wasn't the easiest program in the world for anyone to sell, not even a Jackie Cochran. Even after Hap Arnold said to her, "Go ahead," no one knew where to go ahead to.

Maybe it was the abrasive way she operated at times, maybe it was a sign of the times, but the failure to become a permanent part of the military had some basis in what was going on in Congress then. I believe Jackie could have kept us going. She really could have. She just wasn't willing to pay the price it was costing her. And she was the type of person to make a cut-and-dried decision. If she couldn't do it her way, she'd just as soon not do it anymore.

It came as a great surprise to us when we were disbanded, folded. It was really a shame because there was a definite role we were playing and could have played out to the end of World War II.

There are almost as many stories about why the WASPs were disbanded as there are pages in this book, and I don't know the real reason. We were not allowed to come into Washington, D.C., for several months while the battle for WASP militarization was being fought in Congress. Many people believe that Jackie lost the battle for the WASPs because of her animosity toward Hobby. She didn't want to have to submit to Hobby's power. Others say that she and Arnold lost the political battle because unemployed male pilots across the country had launched such a powerful media campaign against women taking men's jobs, and others say that Jackie just lost her appetite for the whole thing. The stories vary tremendously. The ending is always the same.

PROSTITUTES AND OTHER PROBLEMS

SUMMER 1944

"**Y**ou know that men are walking off the B-26 program there in Oklahoma at Ardmore Air Force Base," Arnold says to me.

"Yessir, I've heard that and I've read the material on the plane," I answer.

"I want you to get out there and fly that airplane and come back here and tell me what you think of it," he says.

"General, I'd like to be checked out in it by somebody," I explain. "I haven't been flying anything but a desk lately except for my time between Sweetwater and back here. Can you get me the best pilot in the whole damned Air Force—someone who has a lot of time in it?"

"Have it your own way, Jackie. You'll do it anyway," Arnold says. He could get very cross with me.

"Yessir, I guess that's all."

A major by the name of Sweet Burnett turned out to be a real pro on this Baltimore prostitute. He was a charming, delightful guy and I asked him to tell me everything he could about the plane, to boil ten hours into one or two, because I needed to make some recommendations on it.

"Major, why don't you start by flying it out there so I can watch you, okay?" He put the plane through some pretty good paces, and when he came in to talk, I ask, "How much load do you have on board?"

"Oh, you caught on?" he asks, smiling. It turned out that the

212

crazy plane would not fly with a full military load. "It won't fly on one engine with that much load," the major explains. "And when you come in on an approach, you always feel the need to gun it because it wants to roll on you."

"You've got to have plenty of airspeed to keep it high enough," I surmise, and then ask, "Do you think a couple of feet on the wings might cure it and not take too much speed off?"

"Maybe."

And that's exactly what we did with the B-26 to polish away its prostitution rap. I took the plane up after our little analysis, flew it for a while, and then reported back to Arnold: "I'm not an engineer, but I am pretty certain that if they put one more foot on those wings, you won't get this rolling sensation. And you'll increase the aileron control." It was the same old problem. It always bugged us in the early days of flying—lack of aileron control. It killed more pilots than anything I can think of. They don't have this problem anymore because they've learned. Those little dinky ailerons were something you had to handle and the rudder wouldn't take care of it.

The second recommendation I made to Arnold on the B-26 was that women ought to be flying it.

"There will be an awful lot of cry and hue," he predicted.

"Do you want me to do it or not? You are running the Air Force, but if we put some girls in the B-26 program, have them tow some targets for B-24s, it'll take care of the trouble."

I went to General Yount to discuss the possibility and also to General McNaughton. Then I went on over to a Colonel Northrop, who was head of the B-26 training in Oklahoma. He liked women, liked the idea of women pilots in the B-26 outfit but didn't like being in Oklahoma.

"When my grandchildren ask me what I did in the war, I'll say Oklahoma," he told me when we met. "Why do they want to keep my nose here on this training for the whole war?" he wanted to know.

I told him I had a cure for what ailed him: girl pilots. He was all for it, and ten women who had never heard the scuttlebutt about the Baltimore prostitute were moved into his training program. They soloed in six to eight hours and did such a beautiful job that Colonel Northrop couldn't keep them around his men. One of the reasons they did better than the men was because their classes were separate from the men. They didn't pick up the fear. One hundred and fifty women ended up flying the B-26 with only one minor accident, not a single fatality, and over 75,000 operational hours to their credit. They were a marvelous bunch of women and always ladies. I used to say to them, "When a man wants to put your parachute in the airplane and take it out, let him. That's what men are for—to be nice to us. If you are going to run around trying to act like men, they are going to treat us like men. If we act like ladies, we'll be treated that way."

I lost the battle for militarization of the WASPs in Congress in the summer of 1944 and I believe I lost because of *Mrs.* Hobby and her powers. But, looking back at the outcry of telegrams from congressmen who voted against us, I don't think they all knew what they were voting away. Arnold's office was deluged and so was mine. That was in the summer of 1944. There are still WASPs who opposed the plan then not knowing that they could and should have shared in the benefits of the GI bill, received compensation for injuries or proper recognition overall.

The arguments in Congress against the continuation of my training and flying program were strange. People vented their spleens about something they knew nothing about—and didn't care to learn. We were putting male pilots on bread lines, we were teenaged schoolgirls, stenographers, clerks, beauticians, housewives, and factory workers piloting military planes in a startlingly invalid program, we were wasting millions of taxpayers' dollars to train women in a frivolous program, the women were my pets and poor General Arnold had been persuaded by me to make secret trips to lobby for us in Congress. All of it was untrue. All of it was demoralizing and so very destructive of the truly heroic dimensions to which the WASPs had risen. I was disgusted. There was even a move on to have Arnold court-martialed. That got stopped. But the program was lost.

The Women's Airforce Service Pilots program was deactivated on December 20, 1944, but not without a storm of protest. And it was with deep regret that I took on a task officially ordered by General Arnold in a directive to me, as Director of Women Pilots, on October 1, 1944: "—submit promptly to me your plan for deactivation to take place not later than 20 December 1944."

The end coming five days before Christmas took some of the sting out. Every girl got a ride home for the holiday.

JANUARY 1945

I walk into General Arnold's office and say, "Well, it's done and I've gotten myself a job."

"What kind of a job?" he asks, sort of surprised by me.

"I got a job as a correspondent for *Liberty* magazine. I don't know how to write, but I'll get to Asia this way."

He looks up at me—absolutely furious.

"But you don't need my services anymore," I insist. "I want to see the end of the war."

"You stay on as my consultant," he says. "I'll write your orders."

In a matter of weeks I was on my way. And it was Arnold's orders that got me where I was going.

OTHER VOICES:

Doris Brinker Tanner

(FORMER WASP AND ASSOCIATE PROFESSOR OF HISTORY
AT THE UNIVERSITY OF TENNESSEE, WRITING IN
AMERICAN HISTORY ILLUSTRATED, 1977)

On September 20, 1977, a select congressional subcommittee on veteran affairs in the House of Representatives heard testimony on Bill 3277, designed to provide long overdue recognition to the Women's Airforce Service Pilots and deem their World War II service to have been active duty in the armed forces for the purposes of laws administered by the Veterans Administration.

During the hearings, committee member Margaret Heckler questioned witness Bruce Arnold as to why he had devoted so many hours to the cause of the WASP. Colonel Arnold replied:

"This was one of my father's desires...he would have been right here doing this too if he were alive, and...I am carrying on some of his unfinished work. My father worked on the principle of 'get it done now and work out the details later.'"

It was indeed later. But despite forceful opposition, Congress finally recognized the WASPs.

1979

On May 21, 1979, the Assistant Secretary of the Air Force, Antonio Chayes, presented the first authentic WASP discharge, stating that "the efforts and sacrifices of a talented and courageous group of women have been accorded (retroactive) status as military veterans...and inspire the forty-seven thousand Air Force women who now follow in their footsteps." The unknown, gutsy women of the World War II Army Air Forces at last occupied their rightful place as the first female military pilots in American history.

WANDERLUSTING

SUMMER 1945

The second atomic bomb was dropped just about the time I reached San Francisco on my way west. The Army Air Forces were alerted to send all available crews forward as fast as possible and this took precedence over all, especially me. It didn't look good, but I had friends who felt I deserved to be in at the kill. They'd put me on board a plane as overload. So I limited myself and my baggage to 200 pounds, got hoisted aboard a DC-4 just ready for takeoff, and was off in the middle of a warm summer's night.

First stop: Hickam Field in Hawaii. The commander of the base had been one of my strongest opponents as director of the WASPs because he didn't like women in general and me in particular. He told me I hadn't the slimmest chance of making my way any farther west. I'd be in Hawaii for the duration of the war if it were up to him. But of course, it wasn't. It was up to me.

OTHER VOICES:

Shelley Mydans
(WORLD WAR II CORRESPONDENT
FOR *LIFE* MAGAZINE)

Yes, I remember Jackie Cochran very well although we knew each other only briefly. Her personality was so engaging and her strength so apparent, one couldn't forget her. We were together in Manila as World War II ended and again in Tokyo and Shanghai after the Japanese surrender. From Manila we flew up to Baguio together to cover the surrender of General Yamashita, who had commanded the Japanese troops in the northern Philippines. This was in August 1945.

I especially remember an incident when Jackie's aviation background saved us from an accident. The pilot was one of those happy-go-lucky youngsters who flew around the Pacific in those days, and as the plane began to taxi, Jackie looked out the window and saw that he had forgotten to check the ailerons. The blocks were still on. The rest of the passengers, most of us correspondents, were oblivious, but Jackie turned pale and called out to the pilot just as he prepared to take off. I was impressed by her reaction: as a seasoned pilot she was experienced enough to be alarmed, and as a passenger, she was sure enough of herself to take charge.

I was in the Philippines as a correspondent for *Life* magazine with my husband, Carl, who had flown ahead to Japan with the first troops to land there. And it sometimes seemed to me that Jackie and I were watching each other with an eye to the way we were carrying ourselves in our particular role as women in a war zone. Her career as a businesswoman and a pioneering aviator was far more impressive than mine, but perhaps she saw in me, a foreign correspondent, someone who led a very glamorous life—though it wasn't always all that glamorous. However, I might have had some of the same experiences she had being a woman in a man's world. You had to keep your sense of proportion. You had to be a little tough-skinned, perhaps, to survive the extraordinary attention. You could have looked like Godzilla and it wouldn't have made much difference to those men in the Pacific, who were starved for women.

Jackie was tough but she wasn't hard. She was always thoughtful and generous the times I observed her. Tough, not hard. And this toughness was part of her character. She was someone who knew her own worth and took no nonsense, and I liked her for it. She had been swimming against the current all her life. At a time when women were expected to marry and set- tle down, she fought her way to the top in a field that was sup- posed to be exclusively for men. Certainly she was a woman who would never have been stopped by the notion, "This is not something a woman ought to do."

General Barney Giles was in Guam and that's where I went in the first B-24 converted for passenger use. I never even slept a night in Hawaii because I ran into a friend who offered me din- ner, a free ride out, and a package that came flying through the open door of that plane just as the engines roared. Inside the cramped B-24, with its bucket seats that were more like real buckets than their modern day namesakes, those boys were pic- tures of misery and exhaustion.

I open my package and inside is a limp-looking rubber.

"What is it?" I ask everyone and no one in particular.

"Fabulous," one boy says. "It's a rubber mattress."

By rolling it in the opposite direction from which it had been rolled, it automatically inflated itself. I put it in the aisle, some supply bags became pillows, and the boys took turns taking naps. I couldn't sleep. I was too excited.

After refueling in Kwajalein, an island bathed in moonlight, we flew into Guam about 2 A.M., where Barney met me with a bear hug amid a chorus of catcalls and whistles from my fellow passengers. General "Tooey" Spaatz had plans to take me fishing first thing in the morning, but the gin rummy and the poker stand out in my mind. We never did catch any fish.

First it was a game of gin rummy with General Jimmy Doo- little. I won. He wanted me to pack his bag for home and I refused because packing was never my strong suit. I compro- mised and cooked him a meal while he packed, and we talked. Two things you'll need for Japan, Jackie, he told me, tossing woolen underwear and a roll of toilet tissue in my direction. We laughed. But he was absolutely right.

The next night in Guam it was "spit in the eye"—"spit in the ocean"—"one-eyed jacks"—and a poker game even Floyd couldn't have prepared me for. Floyd had given me lessons, but I was out of my league with the team around that table: "Tooey" Spaatz, Barney Giles, Doolittle (who had hung on another day), General Curtis Lemay (we met there for the first time), General Kenneth McNaughton, General Tommy Power, and others. Before the night was over, I started holding my own at this poker party of powerful men. In fact, it took a few of them another night of chance to get square with me. While I missed the naval surrender of the Japanese on the *Missouri* by staying and playing in Guam too long, the chance to meet Archbishop Spellman almost rewarded me in kind.

The church is a Quonset hut. Puddles of water from the constant rains sit on the floor, and Spaatz has overslept to miss the Mass entirely. I'm worried. I'm uncomfortable. I'm in charge, or so it seems. I'm the only Catholic they can find.

"Don't worry about kneeling," the archbishop suggests to the motley crew wondering whether to put knees straight to puddles. It's uphill from here for the archbishop and me, I can see.

Later, after Spellman ate with great gusto the breakfast I had cooked with great trouble, our friendship was secured. That man came back for second helpings and then thirds of those scrambled eggs, bacon, biscuits, and freshly squeezed orange juice.

"Where has all this wonderful Air Force food come from?" he asks.

"The Navy," I say.

Helen Lemay

We were in Rome together and Jackie and I had a lot of fun one night at a dinner with Cardinal Spellman. There was a count with him who always took care of his needs when he was in Italy for papal conferences, so he was there in a lovely suite with a big living room. Of course, Cardinal Spellman was quite a gourmet. He loved his food, just adored it, and anything he served was always top-drawer. It was served beautifully that night too.

After dinner he says, "I want to show you gals something. I don't think any woman has ever seen a cardinal's underwear, and you two are going to be the first."

We shake our heads "No" and can't believe what he's suggesting.

"I'm going to show you my underwear," he says again with a smile.

Then we all march into his bedroom, where he opens drawers in a little dresser. I have never seen such lace in my entire life.

Women in little Italian villages made the garments, and there was a little tunic, very long pantaloons of lovely handkerchief linen with lace along the bottoms. It was gorgeous lace and done in the pattern of the village where they came from. Little houses were designed into it. Then above the houses was a tiny red satin ribbon that ran through the eyelet lace with a small bow on the side. I'm telling you, it was gorgeous. It could have been in a museum, not in an underwear drawer.

Jackie and I both loved fine clothes, Spellman knew it, and we just loved looking at the cardinal's underwear. He was so dear.

Word came down from the hills in the Philippines that Japanese General Yamashita would surrender up at the summer palace in Baguio. The naval surrender had already taken place by this time. Major General E. H. Leavey invited me to attend the surrender up in Baguio as a personal friend, and the only other woman present was correspondent Shelley Mydans. Shelley was on the broken-down DC-3 with the lousy bucket seats, with a pilot who hadn't been shaving very long, when we were nearly killed on our way to an airstrip on Luna Beach. This pilot had forgotten to remove what were called gustlocks from the controls, and I noticed them as we taxied to the end of the runway before takeoff. I rushed up to the cockpit. He looked startled, then explained he was about to remove them. Not to worry. Hell, not to worry! We could have been killed.

It's crowded. There are reporters at one end of the room, a fireplace at the other, and there's a long table with gaudy chairs along one side for the American contingent. Simple camp chairs on the other for the surrendering Japanese. It had been a banquet hall in its heyday, but we were there for no banquet that day. I stand by the fireplace because there's a raised area in front and I'll get a little bit better view of the proceedings.

Our generals are there. I recall Leavey, Styer, Wood, Wainwright, Percival. I can see fat, gross, vulgar-looking Yamashita. When he spies Jonathan Wainwright and C. E. Percival, muscles sag all over his body. He must have been shocked because both generals had been imprisoned by his order not so long before.

Very, very thin, Wainwright has a bounce in his step that is unmistakable. He holds his head high. He had been the one to surrender Bataan to the Japanese, while Percival had given up Singapore. I swear Yamashita turned into a pile of flabby flesh at the sight of these men. I wish I could have been there later when the rope was tightened around his neck, right in the same prison where so many Americans and Filipinos had been tortured and starved, some to their deaths.

Following the ceremony, Wainwright and Percival both took a few minutes to speak to the crowd. Percival stammered, cried, and I'll remember Wainwright's remarks always. He had lost his self-respect in having to surrender, and now he fully appreciated what freedom and democracy meant. I don't believe there was a dry eye in the room, and as he turned to leave, he saw me, a woman, not someone he knew, just a woman, an American woman. General Wainwright kissed me soundly on both of my wet cheeks.

TO AND FROM KYOTO

OTHER VOICES:

Major General F. L. Ankenbrandt
(UNITED STATES AIR FORCE, DIRECTOR OF COMMUNICATIONS)

31 May 1949
Mrs. Floyd Odlum
River House
435 East 52nd Street
New York, N.Y.

My dear Jackie:

Recently when I saw you in the Pentagon dining room with Ken McNaughton and continued our discussion of the pleasant visit you had to Japan and the Orient at the close of the war, it occurred to me that you might appreciate some little testimonial from me which you could, on proper occasion, show to your friends (or at least to Floyd, to prove to him that you were really there!).

Enclosed herewith is a certificate which it gives me great pleasure to forward to you as an accurate statement of the circumstances of our trip to Kyoto on September 25, 1945, when, so far as I am able to ascertain, you were the first American

woman to enter the city after V-J Day. We can find no evidence
that there were any other American women in any other recon-
naissance groups or in the advance party which helped in the
arrangements for General Krueger's occupational headquarters...

   ... I recall pleasant memories and the start of a lasting friendship...

                              Cordially,
                              Anky

Anky actually did provide me with that certificate to show Floyd
and friends that I did what I said I had done. Japan was a mess.

   Nothing I can say will adequately describe the destruction
and desolation I saw there after the war. What struck me at first
were the safes littering the roadway as I traveled to Tokyo.
Some salesmen must have had a heyday selling these safes to
families worried about earthquakes or fires. Had they considered war? Now the families had built lean-tos of cardboard and
tin alongside their safes—the only thing left standing where their
homes and businesses had been. It was awful.

   Hiroshima wasn't to be for me. I wanted to see the bomb site
badly, and tried on several occasions, but the weather was horribly uncompromising in its insistence that I not see what I
wanted to see. Fog, clouds, rain—perhaps someone was trying
to tell me something. I do remember the first time we flew over
the area, however. I was sitting in a jeep! That's right, it was in
an airplane—a jeep parked inside the plane, and I had a front
row seat.

   Kyoto is the Japanese city of shrines, so when General Ankenbrandt, a small party of Army Air Force officers, and I set out
to survey this ancient capital, I had no idea we were in for a surprise. The men were on a fairly routine inspection mission. I
was along for the adventure.

   Trouble started when we circled and could see only a medio-
cre grass strip where the Tachikawa Air Field should have been.
We were in a "bucket" C-47 and wondered what would happen
when we put down on the water-soaked grass. There was a
small hangar in view, a few dilapidated airplanes, that short

grass strip we kept debating, and nothing else. No signs of Americans.

On landing safely we discover that the grass conceals a hard-surface runway. An old Japanese man comes out of the hangar alone and greets us in sign language. Signing back and forth like that, he finally figures out that we want to get into town and that he should guard our plane. Funny, but he brings out an old rocking chair that undoubtedly had hailed from America and sits down beneath one wing of our plane. He starts rocking. The chair, so far, is the only indication that America exists for Kyoto. Had we won the war? Where were the others? We decide to leave three enlisted men in the plane.

Out of the C-47 comes a jeep, and Anky and I as well as a few other guys climb aboard. We head toward Kyoto. There's no smoke. No people. But the occupation of the city was to have taken place two days before. Where are the Americans? We move on.

Kyoto was so quiet it felt dead. We reached the heart of the city without hearing so much as a heart murmur. Should we go to one of the temples? Ankenbrandt isn't so sure we should leave our jeep. Then I notice a curtain flutter once—then twice. Someone is behind. I tap on the window. Anky is quite concerned. "Let's stay longer," I say to him. He's anxious to get out of there.

I tap the window a second time and a face appears. I smile. It smiles back and in perfect English someone asks: "Is there anything I can do for you?" This man with the perfect English is wearing a top hat, striped trousers, and a cutaway coat in anticipation of the American occupation of his city—dressed to kill? No, he was simply ready for anything. Tea—in fact, he and his wife served us some tea.

The American occupation hadn't happened yet. Anky and I and those few Air Corpsmen were seven hours too soon. General Walter Krueger, Commanding General of the United States 6th Army, wouldn't enter Kyoto until after we had departed. That didn't stop me from wanting to explore.

"Where are all the people?" I ask our greeter in the get-up. He smiles.

"We're the advance guard," I tell this poor guy, who explains that the entire population is behind closed doors waiting to learn what the occupying forces will want them to do.

General Ankenbrandt wants to leave because he is worried
about the military protocol. I want to look around. He capitu-
lates and we head for a department store. It makes me think of a
phrase: "When the going gets tough, the tough go shopping."
Inside the store the scene is simply amazing. Scores of workers
are hauling in cheap goods, and the ink isn't yet dry on price
tags. American soldiers will buy anything they've been told…so
are they getting ready to please American soldiers? Or profit
from their own failure? We took our shoes off, went inside, and I
negotiated a very fair price for some fine silk.

*At the end of World War II, Jacqueline Cochran was the first
American woman allowed to visit Japan. She returned to Tokyo in
1953 on an inspection tour as a lieutenant colonel in the USAF
reserve. Also in 1953, Jackie toured the Tactical Air Command
bases in Korea with U.S. Air Force officials. Seoul was one of their
stops.*
   *—National Air and Space Museum, Smithsonian Institution,
1981*

From Japan I moved on in 1945 into China, where a group of us
wanted to be part of what the Chinese call the Double Ten
celebrations—a feast on the tenth day of the tenth month. It is
one of the biggest days of the year for the Chinese. That was fun
but fighting battles for the American press corps, lunching with
Madame Chiang Kai-shek, and then meeting Mao Tse-tung
were even better. It was living life on the same kind of edge I
had known as a teenager making my plans around what each day
offered. And boy, did those days offer me memories—as well as
the contacts I'd need one day when I went about lobbying for a
separate and strong American Air Force.
   I was in Shanghai when the war correspondents in China
were ordered out of the country within thirty days by our own
military men. A month wasn't enough time for those men and
women to tie up loose ends and secure passage home, so a group
came to me to ask me to pull any strings I had with the military. I
was glad to help because the entire press corps had been so

accepting of me in spite of my "fake" papers. I knew I wasn't a writer for *Liberty* and so did everyone else. They were asking for a sixty-day extension with a promise of military passage as far as Hawaii, where most could obtain accommodations on commercial transportation.

It took me nine hours to get to Chungking to find General C. B. Stone, but before I could plead my case, Stone insisted that I head on over to a reception for Madame Chiang Kai-shek. Right then. Right there. I was aghast, had been up since four o'clock that morning, and was in crumpled slacks. Impossible, I told Stone. Not impossible, he replied. Go change in the plane, and so I did.

Madame Chiang Kai-shek was enamored of things American, including the chance to converse with an American woman. We met that day briefly and later had lunch in her Connecticut-style cottage. Clapboard siding, New England-style furniture, and its beautiful gardens made me think of home and Floyd. In fact, I ran into Floyd's Canadian cousin, General Victor Odlum, who was in China serving as ambassador for his country.

What a fight. Stone sent me to General Stratemeyer to straighten out the war correspondents mess, but Stratemeyer would not listen at first. Seems a story had been leaked without first being censored by him and he was furious with the press. He'd have none of me or my side of the issue. He wasn't going to rescind his order, he said. He wanted me out of his office and them out of the country.

He didn't know me. I had already drafted a cable to my friend, Secretary of War Robert Patterson, explaining the problem and asking for advice. When I showed a copy to Stratemeyer, he was furious.

"Who the hell do you think you are, Jackie Cochran?" he screamed. "And what makes you think that cable hasn't already been stopped by my censors?"

"It won't be stopped, General," I answered, "because I'm going to ask the Canadian embassy to send it out in their diplomatic pouch. You can't touch it."

He claimed he could still interfere, and I was worried. I had one more card up my sleeve, however: my orders from General Arnold as a special consultant to a commanding general. A catch-all phrase asking me to report back to Arnold on matters of benefit or interest to the United States Air Force caught Stratemeyer's eye when he read through my papers.

"I intend to report to General Arnold on what you are doing to these war correspondents," I said.

"Get out of here," he insisted.

"But I want an immediate cancellation of this thirty-day order," I said.

"I won't commit myself right now, but I will go to Shanghai to talk to the group," he finally agreed.

"I've got a plane here in Chungking that can get you there," I said. He was really shocked at that point. He couldn't believe that General Kenney, air chief in the Far East, had put a plane at my disposal. Sometimes I can't believe it either.

General Stratemeyer and I flew back to Shanghai together two days later and he extended the effective date for expulsion of those newspapermen. Sixty days. I got them sixty days and I think my membership in the American War Correspondents' Association came as a result of that battle. I sure didn't earn it as a writer in World War II. I met Dwight D. Eisenhower for the first time as a result of that association. The future president of the United States sat next to me during one of their dinner meetings in New York City. He was the guest of honor but would soon be my friend for life. The correspondents believed they owed me one back then, but when I look back on my life, I owed them more.

How I got myself around the war-ravaged world in not much more than eighty days is difficult to describe—but that's what I did. Before I'd reach home and Floyd, I talked to Chairman Mao Tse-tung for two hours, flew over India to Egypt, and got lost in a Beechcraft trying to cross the Suez Canal to see Palestine. (I had always believed that the Suez would look a little like the Hudson River but it was more like an oversized irrigation ditch.)

Landing in Rome in a B-25 at dusk and making my way through dark streets to my hotel whetted my appetite for more moonlight adventuring. There were no streetlights on in Italy yet. Windowpanes were still blacked out. The war had just ended. One night, after a day of sleep and in anticipation of a visit with the Pope the next day, I put on those long woolen undies Doolittle had given me, pulled on an extra sweater and a trenchcoat, and asked the concierge for detailed directions in Italian to and from the hotel. Sure he thought I was crazy. I knew I was being prepared. I took my pistol.

Unforgettable and enchanting. Everyone should chance a tour of that immortal city by nothing but moonlight. I tramped until two o'clock in the morning to the Coliseum, the Forum, St. Peter's Cathedral, and down some pretty dark streets. I tramped until I was quite lost in my own maze of wandering. Then I saw a coffee shop with a light.

I show my paper to the waiter. He speaks no English, obviously. Out of the shadows an American appears and interrupts me as I try to reach for my Italian directions.

"It's none of my business, of course, but what do you think you're doing out and about Rome alone at this hour?" he asks officiously. "Let me get you back to your hotel."

"That's right," I reply. "It's none of your business."

And it wasn't. I made it back to my hotel in one piece, alone, and the pistol was exactly where I had put it in my pocket so many hours before. Eleven o'clock the next morning, I met His Holiness the Pope.

The next day I was on my way to the Nuremberg trials.

OTHER VOICES:

Yvonne Smith

(CALIFORNIA FRIEND AND A POLITICAL CAMPAIGN
COORDINATOR)

My friend Jackie Cochran had tremendous courage and would do things with a drive and competitiveness that not many women of her generation had. It gives her more of a glow because she did her thing when other women weren't. There wasn't anything in the world she liked better than traveling, and we had a great time when we traveled together to the Orient, to Spain, to Rome, all over Europe. That woman could paddle three boats at one time.

We met after she got involved in politics and I remember the day we got caught in a dust storm. She was flying her own plane, a Lockheed Lodestar, though we had a copilot and engineer on board. Anyway, she took us off the ground and the wind or dust or something apparently clogged up an engine. She called back to me and said, "Yvonne, I think we have a little engine trouble. I want you to move clear back to the back of the plane as far as you can get and the minute we land, you get out and get out fast."

She's just as calm as she could be. Nothing to it. Meanwhile, I'm scared to death.

We landed with no problem, though I got out of that plane as fast as I could. Nothing happened. We were at the airport in El Centro, California, and it was just some dust.

She just loved pilot talk, to be in the center of a group of pilots, being a pilot. I can still see her metal seat. It was there in her house for years, moved from closet to closet. And it came from the 1946 Bendix race. In order to get more range out of the plane she flew that year, she had her seat designed around an aluminum gasoline tank. Would you want to sit on a tank of gas in a high-speed plane? Well, she would—and did.

GERMANY AFTER THE WAR

It was November 1945 and the Nuremberg trials in the Palace of Justice had been running for four days when I arrived and wheedled my way in to catch glimpses of Goering, Hess, and others. Good luck and good friends got me in.

U.S. Supreme Court Justice Robert H. Jackson was in charge of the trials and only he could permit entry. When I heard his name standing at the Visitors' Bureau in Frankfurt, I knew the impossible was possible. Precisely at noon, when the trials recessed for lunch, I arranged for a private wire to reach Justice Jackson. Almost immediately, he was on the end of a telephone line and enthusiastic about seeing me. Floyd and I had known the Jacksons for years.

One piece of testimony caught my ear the next day: Field Marshall Erhard Milch was defending Goering and made it clear that Hitler had not been informed of how fierce our bombers had become. Milch had been forbidden to report the news that American and British planes could reach into Germany with little problem. Only good news had been passed along to the Führer, and shortly after his arrest, Goering even admitted to General Hoyt Vandenberg that when he personally saw those Thunderbolts and Mustangs over Berlin, he knew it was over. He just couldn't tell Adolf Hitler. Sasha Seversky's efforts to put longer and longer range into our pursuit planes had been right on target. And I felt good about my own involvement in pushing those planes to their limits.

Buchenwald, Dachau, Berlin. Misery crowded around me as well as around the German people on all sides. I saw feet wrapped in rags, people living in topless basements, where once there had been homes, and hungry women and children roaming everywhere. In a car with an American medical officer on a snowy night, I drove around a Berlin square—occupied militarily by both American and Russian soldiers. A woman with at least five little children came up to the car as we stopped. The officer I was with spoke German and he tried to get her story. Her husband had disappeared in the fighting. She had nothing to eat and nowhere to go. I reached into my purse on the car seat and could feel only a chocolate bar. It had started to snow. I was numb. I wanted to do something for her, something more.

We drove off and traveled at least a block, when I remembered the trunk and what goodies it held. "Stop the car," I order the driver. He thinks I'm crazy. "We've got to go back and find that mother," I say.

"Why?" he wants to know.

"Because there is some food tucked away in the trunk of this car," I explain.

OTHER VOICES:

Maggie Miller

Where Jackie went, there went food. The first time I played golf with Jackie at the Eldorado Country Club in Indian Wells, she brought a surgical knife with her. Now, in order to appreciate this story, you have to picture this very posh country club. This is the club where the Eisenhowers lived after Dwight was elected President of the United States. He had his home there.

Why the surgical knife? Well, the golf course is lined with grapefruit trees, and Jackie's got her surgical knife so she can reach up, grab a grapefruit, and peel it to eat. She also brought along her own sandwiches and drinks in one of those Styrofoam coolers. I wasn't embarrassed. I loved being with her even if she was more competitive than anyone I ever knew. Before teeing off on the first tee, Jackie wanted to bet a quarter a hole. If I happened to get a good shot off the first tee, she would say "All bets are off." Everybody knew her tee-off time and her tricks. In fact, that very first time when she had her cooler and her surgical knife along, we got out there on the first tee and the phone rang.

"It's for you, Jackie," someone says. I'm standing there thinking that I can't believe this woman in the big floppy hat.

When she got off the phone, she says to me, "It was Dolores calling. Hell, she always calls me when she wants money."

There was some sugar, cocoa, a couple of hard-boiled eggs, cans of fruit juices, and some big lumps of German bread in the trunk. I never go anywhere without some food. I guess it's a hangover from my childhood.

"It's like looking for a needle in a haystack," this guy insists. "Why even try?"

"Because—"

Luck was with us. And with her. We found her, and the image of her face is etched in my mind's eye. There she was, standing there on that crowded street, arms full of food, tears streaming down her cheeks, snow falling. I had a good cry too.

The Reichschancellery was where Hitler supposedly ended his career. It was guarded by the Russians and they didn't want Americans wandering around inside. They did want cigarettes, however.

Inside, the Russian captain with the hefty smoking habit showed me around what had been a fabulous underground home. It was worth the entire pack of smokes as well as the $10 bill I had slipped him. The place had been flooded in some spots and as much as a foot of water stood in some rooms. Boards served as bridges over these low areas, and I made it into a library, into the bedroom where Goebbels's six children slept before their deaths, and to the spot where Hitler's body was supposedly incinerated. I saw no evidence of fire, however, and

I often wonder, as others did, if Hitler died there or elsewhere. The Reichschancellery reminded me of the Pentagon, with its large, architecturally beautiful structure. Gutted, looted, and flooded when I was there, I could envision what it once was. For two more cigarettes I walked away with a doorknob to show Floyd where I once had been—to remind myself of how lucky I was.

It was rare for Floyd and me to be alone together. Two days together with no houseguests, no hassles—that's one of the things I wished for back in Rome when I threw my coins in the fountain. I'll bet in all our married life together, that only happened once or twice. There was always somebody or something happening. But I had things to talk to him about after that trip and that's all I wanted as I headed home: talk and time with Floyd.

Something terrible was happening to him. He was sick, so sick and I had to get home.

OTHER VOICES:

Vi Strauss Pistell
(COCHRAN-ODLUM RANCH HOUSEKEEPER)

We spent years of our lives together, Jackie and me. She was good to Mr. Odlum, and it wasn't always so easy. Arthritis began crippling him, causing him terrible problems when he was really just a young man in his forties. Then, too, he didn't always want to share his business dealings with her, and he could be so quiet, so introverted, concerned only with what was going on in his head. She wasn't a quiet person, but she was good to Mr. Odlum all right. She loved to entertain and have people around her. He tried and was a gracious host, even when he was so sick.

In the very beginning I mistook his quiet side for a coldness. I took it too personally. I didn't think he liked me and I said to Jackie once, "Gee, you're so friendly and you talk to me all the time, but Mr. Odlum doesn't say much. He doesn't pay any attention. Is there a problem?"

"Don't pay any attention to him, Vi. He's off thinking about something. It doesn't mean a thing. He just gets lost in his thoughts," she explained. Later, Mr. Odlum and I talked more. Even still he rarely talked about his business with her. For instance, he never told her about the money in the end. She didn't know how much money he was losing. Maybe she didn't want to know. Maybe they should have talked more. But the pattern had been set. I remember when she wanted to start an orphanage out in the desert and couldn't get it going because of complications with the state. Then she wanted to adopt three little Spanish boys and she came to me to talk about it.

"Jackie, you've got to talk to Floyd about this," I said to her.

"Why should I talk to him about it? I'm going to do it." Funny, but in spite of all that, Mr. Odlum used to know what she was thinking. Jackie didn't always like that.

Aldine Tarter
(MR. ODLUM'S RANCH BUSINESS MANAGER)

Mr. Odlum first came down with arthritis in 1941, but it wasn't so bad then. He claimed that it was the frustration of working in Washington, D.C., during the war that brought it all on. He was being paid $1.00 a year to help Donald Nelson on the War Production Board, and Mr. Odlum was used to running his own show, I think. Overwork and frustration got him down. Then, too, Jackie was gone so much of that time.

He tried everything from what I understand. Every single treatment known up to that time—he did it all. He went from the Mayo Clinic to Johns Hopkins University Hospital and up to New York City to Columbia-Presbyterian for a spell. He was told to stay in bed and not move a muscle. And I know he tried that approach for months. Some doctors believed he would be hopelessly crippled for life. But Jackie wasn't about to let that happen. And he himself was never a man to give up. He used a cane when I knew him and then progressed into a wheelchair. But you didn't think of him as an invalid out there in the desert. He was a very active, spry guy.

The desert air gave him back his life. Jackie Cochran did that.

Floyd and I kept the River House apartment for years and years, making the trek back and forth from California a lot. Floyd preferred the train, but I couldn't stand that kind of confinement, even when I thought such a leisurely ride might do me some good. Once I got off halfway across and caught a regular airliner. We didn't get rid of the River House residence until the '60s, and even then we took some regular rooms at the Waldorf Towers to be sure we had a place to call home in New York.

But in 1945, after I came home, Floyd and I found ourselves out west more than back east. And I was always dropping in and out of Washington, D.C. That place started giving me the willies, though. Almost every time I had a heart attack, it was in or near D.C. in later years. But sometimes good things happened to me there.

For her work as founder and director of the WASP program, Jacqueline Cochran was awarded the Distinguished Service Medal in 1945. It was presented to her by General "Hap" Arnold.
—National Air and Space Museum, Smithsonian Institution, 1981

I received the DSM in 1945 and I learned of it, being in the military channels, via a phone call from the surgeon general of the Navy, Ross MacIntyre. Ross was a good friend of mine and he was the doctor who put President Roosevelt to bed almost every night. No kidding, Ross MacIntyre was devoted to Roosevelt and called me one day. "The President signed the citation," he said. "You're going to have the DSM."

"What the devil is that?" I asked him. I had never heard of it, never checked up on it, didn't know the importance of that medal. There isn't anything higher than the DSM except the Medal of Honor.

"That's nice," I told Ross then.

"President Roosevelt would like to present it to you," he said.

"I wouldn't like that, Ross," I explained. "If I deserve anything like this, it's because of General Hap Arnold and Hap Arnold alone, and if he can't present me with the medal, then I don't want it."

Ross was surprised.

"Mail it to me," I said. "I can't actually turn down the President of the United States, so you've got to stop it here. Don't invite me to the White House for this. Tell him I'm so loyal to Arnold, that it must come from him. Hap gave me the chance to do this work."

I've always believed that without loyalty and devotion, you can't work for anyone effectively, especially someone at a top echelon. I had complete faith and respect for General Arnold.

"You know Arnold is very ill, Jackie," it was explained to me, "so he can't do it. He's just had a heart attack."

"He'll be back," I said, and I could feel it in my bones.

One morning, not long after he did return to work at the Pentagon, I walked into his office wearing my WASP uniform.

"I thought you got the DSM," he said, looking at me closely.

"No, I didn't get it yet," I said. "I'm waiting for you to give it to me. Any morning that is convenient for you is fine for me. Now or three months from now. Otherwise, they can mail it to me."

I thought he was going to cry. "You don't turn down the President of the United States, Jackie," he said to me.

"Well I did," I answered.

"That's a little bit of loyalty," he said. And three days later he called me. "Whom do you want me to invite to the ceremony?"

In a big conference room at the Pentagon, dressed to the hilt with generals, admirals, and colonels, Hap presented me with the Distinguished Service Medal and I couldn't keep my tears back. It was a lovely ceremony, and from there I went on inactive Air Force duty. Though "inactive" was hardly the word for what was to occur between me and the Army Air Corps. It was still a stepchild of the Army. But it wouldn't be for long if I had anything to do about it.

RACING AGAIN

1946

I swore I'd be the one person in the world who'd never write a book. I had an idea there were too many of them and I didn't have much to add to the list. After the war, back in the harness of my own life, I changed my mind.

I'd get up about eight, read all the mail and newspapers—especially the advertisements. It's always seemed to me that the ads are the best part of the paper. I'd go through them to get ideas and then be out of the apartment at River House and over at my cosmetics office a little after 9:30. It was a small office, just a desk and three chairs, but when I was there I would talk to anyone about anything. A couple of days a week, when I was in New York like this, I'd spend time at our plant in New Jersey.

I was flying about 90,000 miles a year seeing various account executives and buyers in department stores that carried my products. In New York there was always dictation to do by the end of a day. At home, at night, with Floyd—that's when I began writing this book. Floyd always said to me, "Do it, Jackie."

The Air Force had field after field of surplus airplanes for sale after World War II ended. There were masses of them and I could not resist. Another Bendix race wasn't in my plans for 1946. But I got itchy feet when I saw all those P-51 Mustangs as well as the price tag: only about $3,000. Then Floyd (again!) said, "You can do it, Jackie!"

Two weeks—I had only two weeks to get ready for that race

238

by the time I made up my mind. Using old P-58 "Lightning" wing drop tanks—those buggers were longer than the Mustang wings were wide—I'd get greater range from the small fighter. A better idea was to take the machine guns out of the wing emplacements and convert the entire wing area into fuel tanks by giving them a plastic coating on the inner sides. But I had no time for that. I did need the extra space for more gas, so that's how I settled on the idea of exterior drop tanks. And a seat tank. I had my seat built around another gas tank. I'd be slower because of all this outside baggage by about 40 miles per hour, but with no head wind and a little tail wind on my side, I might make up the difference after I had used the gas and dropped the extra tanks free of the plane.

There were twenty-three men in the race—in those Mustangs, Lightnings, Thunderbolts—about 9 P-38s, 15 P-51s, a P-39, which really should have won the race for its pilot, a Major Tucker, with bells and decorations all over his chest. I think he had shot seven Germans down. There were two or three old-timers like myself, but the rest were new to the Bendix.

I had problems. Big ones at first. The Mustang wing tanks were held in place by specially made racks. Between those racks, those huge tanks, and the landing gear, there was such an air suction that it was nearly impossible to retract the gear once you were off the ground. I couldn't fly and expect to win with the wheels down, but I couldn't get them up. God, it drove me crazy for a while. Finally, I discovered that if I pulled them up while the wheels were still spinning from that trip down the runway, I could just make it.

What happened on takeoff that September was that I created quite a stir among the onlookers. It looked like I was trying to create some dramatic effect.

I reached the California border, racing toward Cleveland, with no problem at all. In Arizona my radio went dead in the middle of a weather check, and though I turned, twirled, and twisted everything connected to that damn radio, I couldn't get it going again. I kicked it, got a sore toe, and then worried about breaking it all over again.

It was overcast all the way to Cleveland. I couldn't see the ground. I couldn't hear weather checks and I had to rely on my compass.

Bad weather near the Grand Canyon and I'm flying at 24,000

feet. I decide I can top the storm by climbing to 30,000 feet. Meanwhile, the operating manual for that model Mustang warns that just before a fuselage tank of gas drains to less than 30 gallons, the plane shouldn't be in turbulent air. There's a problem with control under those factors and incidences of uncontrollable spins. That I don't need.

I climb to 27,000 feet and I'm not in danger of spinning. I am in danger of dying, however, because the engine simply quits. Then it starts. Then quits again. Sudden bursts of power, then no power, make the plane swing back and forth in the sky. I feel like I'm in the seat of a swing attached to miles-long ropes. God, what is it? It's called cavitation, I know that, but what was making it cavitate so?

Turns out that this Mustang shouldn't have gone higher than 25,000 feet, and when it went higher, it couldn't suck in that fuel efficiently. I turn the nose down and head back into the storm to fly by instruments only again. Going on instruments under normal conditions is pretty routine, but the plane was still rocking back and forth, and when I hit the full force of that weather front in that condition, it nearly knocked me senseless. Like diving into a pool of cold water from a platform on a long pole swinging in the wind.

I don't dare throttle back because that might change the attitude of the plane and necessitate a change in trim. I haven't got time to trim. Finally, it settles down, the swinging stops, the storm passes.

I thought it would be clear sailing from there. But I was mistaken.

The exterior wing tanks were such a drag on my speed that I had decided to detach and drop them as soon as they emptied. But I wanted to be over an unpopulated area too. In an overcast, I couldn't pinpoint my position accurately enough to do this, so I waited. So over mountains, with a little more fuel, I decided to waste it and pull the tank release controls while I knew where I was.

There was a violent—and I mean violent—jerk. It felt like a collision up there in the air. But there had been nothing to collide with.

I look over at the left wing and discover that the tank is still there. I can't see enough. Because of where the cockpit sits, I can catch only the upper side of the wing. But I see enough to know that I've still got those tanks and now they are dragging low, pulling my wings apart.

The release mechanism designed for shorter, stubbier tanks won't work right. The connection between the front part of the wing and tank is cut, but the back won't let go. Still fastened like this, the rear ends are caught in the airstream and are swinging violently up and down, swiveling up to snag the trailing edges of my wings.

I couldn't see all of this in the air. I could feel it.

To keep the wind resistance down to a minimum and get the last mile of speed available, I had cellophaned those leading edges on the wings and along all the rivet lines. What I could see from the cockpit was all the cellophane ripped off and pieces of wing sticking up two or three inches in places. They acted as air brakes and I toyed with the notion of taking my leave.

The plane was badly out of trim, and even after I adjusted the trim tabs to the extreme, I had to hold the stick by sheer force to maintain a flying attitude. Finally, the tanks let go, but I was really worried that the plane might disintegrate on me, that I had damaged my internal gas tank and sprung a leak. If I could have seen what I saw once I reached Cleveland, I know I would have bailed out, or at the very least, landed somewhere right then. But I didn't.

When I decided that I had to be over Cleveland, I came down without benefit of radio and hoped to God I had a ceiling beneath me as well as no other airplane below me. I had no way of knowing where anyone else was, so I pulled a little off course and behold, I broke into the clear at 9,000 feet and saw planes all over the place heading for Cleveland. Why there were no collisions that year is a mystery to me. I started passing P-38s as if they were standing still, flew over the finish line, and went around again to land.

As I got out of the plane to look for Floyd and friends, someone said, "Jackie, you are all bloody. What happened?"

And so I was. I put my hand up to the back of my neck and was suddenly aware of being very wet with my own blood streaming from a cut on my head, down my back. I hadn't even felt the blood or the pain before that, and I never did know when it happened. During the cavitation in high altitude? When the wing tanks collided with the wings? It didn't matter. What did matter was that I had to start wearing my helmet more religiously. I had buckled myself in with shoulder straps, but the helmet had been sloughed aside. I must have hit the canopy really hard, because the gash was wide and another lump on my head was the size of an egg.

The big surprise, however, was not the blood, the egg, or the fact that the plane was far worse than even I had imagined in my worst moments up there. The surprise was that I had come in only six minutes behind the winner. I had taken second place in spite of it all.

Hotshot Tucker and some of the other newcomers couldn't believe it. In fact, an aerodynamicist speculated that I lost at least forty miles an hour from what he could see in the damage. I smiled when I received a six-page handwritten letter from an airline captain who wanted to explain all the reasons why he lost to me. He had come in ninth or tenth and screwed up in his navigation.

Navigation did do the trick. My flight map in that race, as in others, was a well-prepared set of accordion-pleated sheets fixed up like a book. Landmarks, radio checkpoints—which proved to be worthless that time—changes in compass courses as they related to minutes of flying time, and my precautions against turbulence came in very, very handy. You are immobilized in the cockpit seat in a race like that, so I made sure the map wouldn't get too far from me by tying it to my leg with a heavy string. It landed way back in the fuselage during some of that rocking and banging, but I just fished it back to me. Without that map, without those compass corrections, without that string, I would never have placed in that race.

The sturdy little Mustang helped, however. In fact, the first three spots in the '46 race were Mustang, Mustang, Mustang.

After the war, Jacqueline Cochran resumed her racing career. In the 1946 Bendix Race, she finished second, flying a North American P-51C. She covered the Los Angeles-to-Cleveland course in 4 hours, 52 minutes at an average speed of 623.48 km/hr (420.925 mph).

—National Air and Space Museum, Smithsonian Institution, 1981

Tony Levier
(LOCKHEED TEST PILOT)

After World War II, a lot of new people got into the aviation act with lots of money. It really blossomed because of the war and thousands, thousands of war planes were sold for pennies on the dollar. You could buy most any airplane. I bought a brand-new P-38, a brand-new one for $1,250. Jackie, I think she bought a P-51. She raced it too—raced it in the Bendix. The engines used to be the biggest cause of trouble in those races. You'd push them so hard they'd simply blow up.

I spent thirty-three years working for Lockheed as a test pilot. I started there in April 1941, but I remember meeting Jackie at that first Bendix race she won back in 1938. I remember it clearly because I won the Greve Circular Trophy Race that year and Roscoe Turner took the Thompson. There were three major races which were part of those National Air Races each year.

Jackie was prominent, qualified to do anything. She knew everybody even back then and she was never afraid to tackle anything. She'd get right in there, speak her piece, and be her own person. Certainly nobody would be able to dominate her unless she had a great deal of respect and faith in them. I think Chuck Yeager is an example of someone she trusted with her life. And I had a few occasions to do the same sort of thing for Jackie.

We became good friends because she liked pilots, and hot pilots in particular. Of course, that's why she idolized Chuck. And I was another she admired.

A SEPARATE AIR FORCE

1947

Maybe it was the chemistry. Maybe not. All I know is that whenever General Hap Arnold and Secretary of War Patterson were in the same room together, the sparks would fly. That added fuel to Hap's hope for more autonomy for his Air Corps. The general didn't like everyone else in on his every decision. And on several occasions we talked about it. It bugged him to have to go to the Secretary of War for so many approvals. He wanted his arm of our country's defense separate.

"The only way you are going to do it, to ever get it accomplished," I said to Arnold after the war, "is to take it to the public and fast. On its own, without a swift kick, the Army is no more going to let go of its Air Force than they are going to cut off their heads. To get it done, take it public." And he agreed.

That's why I went back to work for General Arnold about a year and a half after the war ended. I was his assistant and I told him, "This transition has to be done by a civilian, and neither you nor any man in uniform should touch it or even get near it. Stay out of the campaign. Let me have your cooperation. Let me know you are there if I need you. And let me have a man who is discreet, who knows how to keep his mouth shut, who will feed me the facts, and I'll start right in."

You see, I had to cover the United States traveling to my cosmetics business customers anyway, and in 1947 I was dying to put together an organization which would start screaming for a separate Air Force.

It was a hot topic at the time. Those men carried the bomb. They beat Germany to its knees in the final analysis. The British had weakened the Germans, but American fighter pilots had killed them. I wanted to make sure the Army Air Corps got this credit, so I began by buying advertisements. I was a businesswoman at the time. In fact, I was once declared outstanding businesswoman in America by the Associated Press, so it was nothing unusual for me to take out an ad describing how the Air Force had been and was still being kicked around by the Army. I was a civilian and I had a perfect right to do such a thing.

I would tell Arnold, "When I get through with the Army, they are going to want to get rid of me." Sometimes I sound like I did little else but go around picking fights with people. For the Air Force to have begun their own campaign would have looked bad. They would have been washing their dirty linen in public. I could do it. They couldn't.

I spent a year making speeches all across the country. Arnold assigned a staff person to me. Jake Smart was a colonel, bright, personable, articulate, could set up those speeches for both me or himself, and insinuate like mad without getting his tail caught in the Secretary of War's gate. Mind you, I liked Secretary Patterson personally. He was Arnold's problem, not mine. I simply set out to create a case for a separate Air Force.

Jake Smart came to my New York apartment in 1947, and we planned a year and a half of strategy. You know, it would be, "You take Denver, Colorado Springs—I'll take the governors and people like that." I went around investigating who had swung the sticks for the service people, who had sons in the Air Force, who could help, who wouldn't. I raised $100,000 within six months.

We had some real tearjerker speeches, put together by great writers. I kept feeding stories to the newspapers about what the Air Force had done to win the war, went about seeing bigwigs on my own, and speaking out whenever I got the chance. Jake kept me posted on things around the Pentagon. I had registered as a lobbyist then and didn't set foot near the Pentagon for eight months. I didn't want to get in any more trouble with congressional groups about my efforts.

Colonel Smart was a marvelous liaison between me, Arnold, and Stuart Symington, who had been Assistant Secretary for Air and was later named First Secretary of Air. As soon as I had a bloc of votes on my side, I'd let them know.

Most of the opposition came indirectly from Army supporters. The Navy was a little anxious about a cutback in appropriations, but we kept insisting that we weren't going to be putting anybody out of business, we were simply going into business ourselves. Sometimes I'd take these guys factually back to the beginning of the war in '39, when we had about thirty airplanes, a lot of eager beavers, and no gas. We didn't have the money then and we needed it.

I know this well because Floyd put up the money to finish the P-47, the marvelous Thunderbolt, just in time. I made two world records in it and that long tail is still there. There wasn't time to re-engineer it even though I always considered it home-made engineering designed simply to keep the tail up in the prop wash. That and the P-51 were the two backbones of our defense. The P-39? It was a sorry airplane, the boys didn't like it much and it was a killer.

OTHER VOICES:

Aldine Tarter

Mr. Odlum told me that Wall Streeters used to say that airplane manufacturers were nuts. He never thought so, but maybe that's because he was married for so long to an airplane nut of his own: Miss Cochran. Mr. Odlum was in and out of the airplane business for thirty years.

I understand that he first got involved in Convair in 1947 and people just laughed at how stupid he had suddenly become. We were heading into peacetime, and there wouldn't be much need for airplanes anymore. But you've got to remember that he had

Jackie beating his ear all the time about the future of air power, and as I've said before, that man did his homework. Jackie was working on her Air Force doings, but he was working on the notion that the future of our Air Force would rest in airplanes. You know that he invested in Republic—Major Seversky's company—as well as in Jack Northrop's company, and he was involved in Pan Am doings, too.

He took over Convair and found out they were doing worse than he had surmised. He started selling off pieces of it—some to Piper, for instance. And by '48 he had cut his losses there a little. But he still needed a miracle. Or at least that's what I understand from reading between the lines years afterward.

His miracle was the B-36 intercontinental bomber that had been sitting around on drawing boards for several years. It was pushed at the public by 1949 as the hope for the Western world, a mainstay of our defense in the cold war. And you can guess where it was being made: at Mr. Odlum's Consolidated Vultee plant in Texas. It was part of Convair, a part he hadn't sold off. He got so many orders for that airplane, and the Pentagon was his biggest customer. But some people weren't so happy all the good news was going in his direction. And the B-36 was taking some of the steam away from the Navy's Flying Boat and Sea Dart. Mr. Odlum, Senator Symington, and Secretary of Defense Louis Johnson ended up in front of a congressional committee investigating the deal. A House representative from Pennsylvania, James Van Zandt, had accused Johnson of giving Floyd the B-36 contracts as a payoff for helping him in the Democratic campaign. Mr. Odlum told the committee that the charges were crazy, and he kept his cool throughout. He was always cool-headed. He could get angry with Jackie, but most of the time he was very calm.

Mr. Odlum sold Convair in 1952 and here's what he said about it in an interview with Martin L. Gross for *True* magazine: "Convair had expanded to 53,000 workers and was getting to be too much trouble—even though I enjoyed handling it. After all, I had built it from skim milk to whole milk and there was plenty of cream left for the next guy. It doesn't matter to me whether Convair stock is going up to forty dollars or not next year—we can't let people get the idea Atlas sells only at the top. Once our job is done, I've got to move on.

"We produced a lot of new Air Force equipment while we

were there. I'm especially proud of the Convair F-102. Despite all the recent publicity on the F-100, I'm sure the 102 is going to replace the Sabrejet as our standard fighter. Production of the B-36 had about stopped, but we were already in a program for a new jet bomber to replace Boeing's B-52 in a few years."

Ex-Senator Stuart Symington

Floyd Odlum was very unfairly criticized when the B-36 bomber came up. That airplane was very much wanted by the Air Force, and it was built on the theory that we would be able to bomb Europe from the United States. The Navy objected to that. They had always been our first line of defense, and they didn't like the idea of a long-range airplane taking their position.

I was very fond of Floyd and Jackie. I've never known anyone as competitive as she was. She was right there up front. Tremendously competitive. She had to win, but that's what made her so great. We'd even compete on her golf course and play a little game called straddle. But you never saw anyone so insistent on winning.

Floyd was her mainstay, her backbone, and she was terribly eager to please him. He was a brilliant trainer for her and used to see himself through her eyes. They set each other up. He had been interested in aviation all along, but it was Jackie who stimulated that interest. He lived through her, especially after he became crippled with arthritis.

Not very many people know that the whole American missile program was carried on by Floyd Odlum when our government decided to drop it. My job as Assistant Secretary of Air had been assigned to me by President Truman, and we felt terrible when the Defense Department decided to wash its hands of the MX 774, as it was called then. A guy by the name of Bossart at Convair had been working on it for years, but the Pentagon decided to stay with bombers only, to let missiles go. A group of us went to Floyd to tell him how we believed in the missile, but there was no more money for it. He did a very patriotic thing. He said to me, "I'll carry on the program through my company." He had purchased Convair then and was the boss. So the Atlas missile program, for it was named after Floyd's Atlas Corporation, was made possible by one man, Floyd Odlum. He poured a lot of money into it before being vindicated. The Atlas carried us into space and the country owes Floyd as well as Jackie a debt of gratitude.

I stayed with Jackie and Floyd at their ranch quite a lot. It was luxury on the best possible scale, not ornate but pleasant, homey. I can still see Floyd in that pool, on the telephone. I can see her too. She had to score, and was so passionately fond of anything she was fond of. A word to describe Jackie would be thorough. She was thorough in her likes and dislikes, in all her efforts in life, but you know, you don't achieve goals as she did, especially when those goals are in a man's world, without making enemies along the way.

I remember when we first met. I had heard about her and she was considered to be the number one aviatrix by the air people. She came to see me because she wanted me to support her drive for a separate Air Force. I had anticipated a tomboy, so when she walked in I was surprised. Attractive and very well-dressed, she was obviously proud of her physique. She could be a seducer.

Years later, when we were closer friends, she said to me, "Senator, that first time we met, you were looking at my legs." I guess I was. We laughed about it.

Chuck Yeager and Jackie Cochran met in my office and I didn't realize how close they became until some time later. Chuck and Glennis Yeager were always out at the ranch. Floyd felt that Chuck was the same kind of man as Jackie was a woman. They were alive. She had a deep, deep affection for airplanes and the pilots who flew them.

For us, in the Air Force, she was a great thing—a kind of ambassadress because she had Floyd to support her—and because of her own brass. Her passion was to get attention and she wouldn't hesitate a minute if she were certain she was right about something. That's good. You see, if she wanted to see someone on Wall Street on Air Force business, it was no problem. There's a tremendous amount of politics in government and Jackie could do something about it. You might say that she knew where all the bodies were buried. Around the Air Force, she was sort of a goddess.

In my lobbying campaign for an Air Force separate from the Army, I went for the jugular. "It's your own lifeblood," I'd emphasize in my talks. "Without a strong Air Force, look what might happen, and we haven't a prayer of not having somebody on our backs sooner or later."

Big foot armies will never be needed again. World War II proved that. Looking back over casualty lists, I concluded—and it's only my opinion, of course—that what the ground forces gained could have been had easier with a bomb from the air. If you look today, Army Aviation is still bigger than the United States Air Force in numbers. They've got more helicopters than anybody. They built their own air force. But back then I'd build my case from my position as a private citizen who had been there in the Battle of Britain, who was there when Dunkirk happened, who saw improperly trained pilots losing their lives. I still get chill bumps when I think about the men who died behind the lines. It didn't have to happen that way, and we needed a strong, separate Air Force.

Women would walk away from our speeches with tears in their eyes—women who had lost sons in the war and were left with serious questions about why. I'd say, "We don't want to catch ourselves in that position ever again. But as long as the Air Force remains under the thumb of the Army, that possibility exists."

The upshot of all this effort—and it wasn't all mine—was a separate Department of the Air Force and a separate United States Air Force. The National Security Act of 1947 became law on July 26, 1947, and the lawmakers created what is officially called the National Military Establishment as an executive department headed by a civilian Secretary of Defense—James V. Forrestal became the first man in that job—and defining three coordinate departments: the Army, the Navy, and the Air Force. The law created a civilian position of Secretary of the Air Force as well. Stuart Symington, a good and true friend to both Floyd and me, was appointed by President Truman to that position.

Jake Smart became a four-star general, and I'll bet my report is still there in his 201 file. I've always been a very good salesman. My whole life has been built on promotion and sales and it doesn't matter whether you are selling washtubs or cosmetics or human ideas. If you can present it well, you can make people believe you. If there is a bigger principle in back of it, you get what you want.

Stuart Symington

Chuck once said to me, "I can't teach Jackie Cochran about flying. That woman knows how." And coming from Chuck, that is quite a compliment. He's a fascinating guy. The only reason he's still alive is that he takes incredible care for his own safety, I think.

When Chuck got his Medal of Honor from President Gerald Ford, Jackie couldn't be present for the ceremonies. There had been a special bill passed in Congress allowing him to have the medal because it wasn't earned during wartime—and Jackie had been instrumental in his receiving it. Anyway, after the ceremonies were over, I said to him, "Chuck, if there is ever anything I can do for you, just let me know."

He says to me, "Senator, there's something you can do for me right now."

"What's that?"

"When you get back to your office, call up Jackie Cochran and tell her we missed her."

LYNDON JOHNSON

1948

Stuart Symington

I went to Dallas on May 12 in '48 for an Air Force Association event and Lyndon Baines Johnson was there. He was running for the Senate and was feeling very, very poorly, not because he was the underdog in the campaign then. He was sick and had been in terrible pain for days. I found him in a hospital bed. We talked for a while and he was worried. He thought it might be a kidney stone, but the Dallas doctors couldn't seem to do anything to help. And Lyndon didn't want anyone to know just how sick he was. He was in the middle of a tough political race.

"I know that Jackie Cochran is in town because I invited her myself," I told Lyndon. "She's got her own plane here." Johnson knew Jackie from way back when but not very intimately. They first met when she was on the Collier Committee the year they awarded the trophy to the aviation medical specialists. Jackie had done some of the investigating for the trophy committee up there at the Mayo Clinic.

This is a story that has never been told.

Stuart Symington invited me to a big clambake in Texas. The Democratic party was honoring him and he did me the honor of asking me along. I told him I would think about it and ask Floyd, because I hadn't been involved with either political party up to that time. Floyd said I'd be foolish not to accept. I liked the Johnsons and I liked Stuart Symington.

I checked the weather for flying my lucky Lodestar and called Symington back. "Okay, I'll be there." He told me he'd meet me at the big luncheon, and I decided to take a young flight engineer named Steve with only 10 hours flying time, and Ellen, my maid of thirty-seven years.

I arrived a little late for cocktails on purpose because I didn't want to have to mingle too long with the men. There were only a few women amidst about four or five hundred men. I spied Symington right away because he is so tall and handsome; he towers over everyone and you can't miss him.

"I thought you'd never get here," he says.

"I told you I'd be here in time for lunch," I explain.

"Well now, Jackie, I've turned out to be your mailman."

"Well, you're a pretty handsome one," I say as he hands me an envelope.

I put the envelope into my purse and looked around to see if I could find Lyndon Johnson. He wasn't in sight. That was strange. Then, I began combing the room for Lady Bird, who was supposed to be present. No sign of her either. The newspapers announcing this big wingding had made a big deal about Lyndon, a very successful congressman, now running for the Senate, who would be at the lunch. Where was he?

I went out into a hallway to find a quiet place and opened my envelope. Inside was a message: "Jackie," it said, "Lyndon is in XYZ Hospital. Go to the back of the hospital, where you'll find some steps. Walk up, and on the second floor in room number such and such, you'll find him. Please don't announce yourself. Just go and find him. I don't want you to be recognized." It was signed Stuart Symington.

Because of the political campaign, Johnson was trying to keep his illness a secret. I ate my lunch and then excused myself.

"I've got a terrible headache," I told one of the men. And I wasn't lying. The room was full of smoke. It was stuffy and I was tired. I left before the speeches began. It dawned on me as I walked out of the room that I was anxious. I had a real affection for the Johnsons. Lyndon had helped me with some of the twists and turns my career had taken. He had been there to straighten out visas for the twenty-five ATA-girls. He had been there when I made my case for the aviation medical men. He had been supportive of my schemes and dreams all along.

Down in the lobby I decided not to take a taxi but to rent a car. There was a U-Drive-It desk there, and after I looked up the address of the hospital in the telephone book and got myself a map, I was on my way. The steps in back of the hospital were emergency steps, not a fire escape, but emergency steps just the same. I figured it must be an emergency. The door had been left ajar a little, and I found the room upstairs easily.

I knock lightly, not knowing what to expect.

Warren Woodward, a brand-new legislative aide to Lyndon, opens it. "Stuart Symington sent me," I explain. He pulls me inside. Lady Bird is sitting in a chair and both she and Woodward look like they'd been dragged through the proverbial mudhole. I'd never seen two more exhausted people in my life.

"My goodness, what's the matter?" I ask.

They show me into a connecting room, where I am absolutely shocked. Lyndon Johnson is in a bed and he is sick, sick, sick. His color's bad. There's a bad odor in the room. And a local doctor is there. I pick up Lyndon's wrist to take his pulse, and it's fluttering, not beating, fluttering so fast you can't count the beats. He was in shock. His skin felt terrible and his eyes had that look. Eyes tell so much when someone is ill.

I slip out of the room and back to Lady Bird. "Either you get proper medical aid for this man or he's going to be dead within twenty-four hours. I think he's dying. What have the doctors here done? What is this all about?" I ask.

Lady Bird Johnson explained that Lyndon had been in the most excruciating pain possible for three days and that the hospital staff had used an instrument called a cystoscope to try to remove or break up at least one kidney stone. They hadn't been very successful. I could see that. It was obvious they didn't know what they were doing because Floyd had suffered with the same problem and it never came to this. Later I would learn that Lyndon Johnson was in serious trauma probably because of the botched procedure. In the meantime, the debate about his political career was going hot and heavy.

Lyndon Johnson wanted to hand in the towel right there. He was exhausted, sick, and could see little reason to continue. The odds of his winning weren't even in his favor.

"Listen," I say, "there's a doctor up at the Mayo Clinic who has had fantastic success with a special new procedure to remove these stones without surgery. His name is Dr. Gershim Thompson, and we've got to get Lyndon into his care." Gershim had brought Floyd through it with flying colors. Lady Bird was exhausted. She had been up with Lyndon all night and all day in his marathon. But it was obvious that she didn't want him to give up the campaign. "Lyndon is so stubborn," she said to me. "Make him do something. Let's get the Mayo Clinic on the phone."

Ordinary surgery in those days for stones was difficult to perform and difficult to recover from. I could understand why they were all debating the problem. Did they really want it all to end right there?

I got Dr. Thompson on the telephone and put the local doctor on the extension. Could the man be moved? Could Gershim come to Dallas? Why the shock?

"Get him in your plane and bring him up here," Gershim says.

"What if he dies en route?" I ask.

"Jackie, moving him can't really do that kind of harm. In fact, the movement might make the stones move, and that can only be good," Gershim explains. Thompson started getting the medical details from the Dallas doctor. Lyndon's stones were between kidney and bladder and they hadn't moved since his original attack. That worried Gershim a little, but he still believed that getting Lyndon to Mayo was his best bet. And that I was the person to do it.

"If they want this all kept quiet, Jackie," he said, "we'll keep it quiet."

It must have been four o'clock in the afternoon by then. I was really worried. Steve wasn't the experienced copilot I'd need along given the circumstances. After I had my heart attack years down the road, I used to cringe thinking of all that flying I did, taking other people's lives in my hands alone, without good back-up. But you do what you have to do.

Lyndon still looked sick enough to die on me.

"Who's going with me?" I ask.

Lady Bird, Woodward, Steve, Ellen, and I make plans. The

first thing I did was call for weather reports. From Dallas to Rochester, Minnesota, would be at least six hours and the weather up there didn't sound good. I decided to delay our leave-taking until after midnight. We could cruise in the Lodestar at 235 mph and I could carry enough fuel to go nonstop, but I worried about head winds hampering our progress. I telephoned Ellen. "Go to the store and buy two pillowcases, some big soft bath towels, a plastic pan of any decent dishpan size, two quarts of rubbing alcohol, and make sure we have some blankets aboard. Do we?" Ellen was always wonderful in those situations. She never stopped me to ask screwball questions. I'd tell her later. She took those pillowcases and towels to the Laundromat and washed and dried them too.

What I wanted to be ready for was pneumonia. I think pneumonia is the most dangerous threat to a patient in Lyndon's condition. Then I told Ellen to call Steve, to tell him we ought to be ready to take off sooner than planned.

It was cold for May and while I waited for the weathermen to call me back, the Dallas doctor asks, "Have you ever given anyone an injection?"

"Yes, sir, I was trained as a nurse many years ago," I answer.

"I thought so," he says. "When you talked about his fluttering pulse, I suspected as much." He wanted to give me two or three injections of the pain-killer Lyndon had been taking. I asked for more. "I may need them," I say. "What if something happens? What if we have to put down between here and Minnesota?"

Three o'clock the next morning, Ellen, Steve, and I arrive back at the hospital to pick up our party. The plane is ready. Steve had managed to pull it around behind a hangar, out of sight so no one would see us.

"Lyndon," I say, repeating what Lady Bird and Woodward have said about our plans for him, "you're going to the Mayo Clinic, Lyndon, and I'm going to fly you there. You're very ill, and if we don't do something soon, you'll die. Your doctor here, Lady Bird, Woodward, and I have all decided. We're taking off now in the middle of the night so no one will see us and no one else need ever know."

He squeezed my hand. That's all. He was so sick that he was on the verge of tears. Great pain—that man was in great pain.

The doctor was there with sterile injections of some narcotic, all wrapped up individually in towels, ready to go. Otherwise the hospital area was empty. No one saw us leave.

They put a bathrobe on Lyndon. And between Woodward and Steve, he dragged and shuffled his way out of there and into my rental car. In the backseat, with his head in Lady Bird's lap, he looked pathetic. He had bitten his lip in pain. The trip to the airport was murder. Then I didn't know what the hell to do with that rental car.

I parked it and toyed with the idea of taking the keys with me. Then I saw someone. "Will you hand in these keys for me when it opens in the morning?" Funny how things like that worry a person at times like that. I never heard another word about the car, so I guess it got back safely.

Inside my airplane is a thin long bed along one side of the forward cabin. Opposite the bed is the engineer's seat, with its table, and Ellen took that spot. We strapped Lyndon into that bed which is closest to the cockpit. I put an oxygen mask on him and said, "Now, keep that on. You must. It will help you breathe better and I'll fly better knowing you're safe." In the back Ellen had put extra blankets and pillows where the seats slide way back. Lady Bird and Woodward were buckled in and practically snoring before we taxied out onto the runway. Completely dead. They were both completely dead asleep from all that had happened.

I whisper more to myself than to him, "Lyndon, are you okay?"

We start rolling down the runway fast and the ceiling is just minimum for takeoff. At that time of the morning there is little air traffic, so I ask to be programmed onto my course immediately. I tell the controller I'm in a desperate emergency to get to my destination. Up above the clouds I find the most beautiful weather, daylight coming in, and the sun coming up. Once we're up and away from the storms around Dallas, I want to lower our altitude to 5,000 or 6,000 feet so I can take the mask off Lyndon. Not yet but soon. I know it must be uncomfortable in his condition.

It's quiet. I calculate six hours, fifteen minutes flying ahead, and I put the plane on automatic pilot, wondering if Steve knows enough. Can he handle this plane alone? Stay asleep, Lyndon, stay asleep.

Suddenly there's a scream like I've never heard from a human being before in my life. It's just bloodcurdling, and when I look back, Lyndon has ripped off his oxygen mask. I jump from the cockpit and say to Steve, "Watch it, boy."

Sweat. The sweat was just pouring out of him. He looked like someone had poured a bucket of water on him, and Ellen had jumped up. Not a sound from the back cabin, however. I had closed the door so that Lady Bird and Woodward could catch some sleep. They didn't hear that howl.

I wasn't dainty about it. I pulled Lyndon Johnson's clothes off with Ellen's help, got the dry sheets and blankets, and began swabbing him with the alcohol. I turned him over to give him a shot and then he began to be sick. Thank God for that dishpan, which helped a little, not completely, however. I may be one of the few women in the world to have been vomited on by a future president of the United States.

Stripped of his pajamas, swabbed with the alcohol which would help stop the pneumonia, wrapped in blankets, Ellen and I watching, Lyndon finally fell back to sleep. Twenty minutes had passed.

I'm always nervous out of a cockpit even when a plane is running perfectly fine on automatic pilot. If anything had happened, you wouldn't be there to recognize the signs—what if a fuel line had broken, what if the plane needed trimming, anything. But Steve was fine. The door to the cockpit had been left open and I kept one eye up front.

I wondered: should I land there and then? I kept saying to myself, "My God, what is the moral thing to do here? What is the best?" The retelling of this tale nearly forty years later still makes me sweat with the anxiety and enormity of it all. I didn't have the heart to waken Lady Bird then. We just flew on. Lyndon's skin was clammy and cold. I push the plane a little. Something I rarely did in that Lodestar. If I could just get a little tail wind, it would be okay.

When I landed in Rochester, I wanted to kiss that ground. I felt just like those sailors who feel that tremendous urge to get down on their knees after being out over the ocean. You have no idea how dramatically frightened I was. Lyndon had needed another shot before we arrived, and he was due for a third. I knew the danger of giving a patient too much. I held off.

Dr. Gersh Thompson met the plane with an ambulance and

took Lyndon Johnson to the hospital naked. That night they filled his bladder with water up to the kidney area, crushed one of the stones with a little lighted instrument I've seen, and fished out the pieces. The other stone, for his pain had been caused by a double-header, remained in his body for years, maybe until the day he died.

Seven days later, with not a word leaked to the press about his mysterious disappearance from the campaign trail, Lyndon was back in his district. When he won, when he became the famous "Landslide Lyndon" (a joke because his margin of victory had been so small), a reporter asked him who had done the most for him in his campaign? His only answer, then or ever?

"A woman—not my wife."

I knew Lyndon in a way no one else knew Lyndon after that experience. He used to say, "Here's the pretty gal that saved my life."

"I didn't save your life, only God can save a life," I'd answer, never knowing exactly what to call him after he became President of the United States. "Mr. President" was not what he wanted to hear from me. But "Lyndon" was a little too familiar for my tastes. We were good friends—friends to the end. "I saved your career, not your life!"

"You're looking mighty pretty today, Miss Jackie," I can still hear. And those bear hugs—he always hugged me in public. In private I spent hours as his sounding board. Civil riots, bombing the Hai Phong harbor, the Kennedy connection, his hernia—Lyndon Johnson talked. I used to listen.

After our American space exploration program was well under way, Lyndon Johnson once paid me a compliment that would send shivers up my spine.

"When I learned how to spell space, Jackie Cochran," he said, "it was you who taught me."

I'd have given my right eye to be an astronaut, and Lyndon knew it.

OUTSTANDING

The Harmon trophy selection committee named Jacqueline Cochran the outstanding woman pilot of the decade 1940–49.
—National Air and Space Museum, Smithsonian Institution, 1981

My husband was quite a mathematician. I set a record for a 2,000 kilometer run in the P-43, which was the prototype for the P-47 I mentioned earlier. I was also going to do a cross-continental in that airplane, which was a big deal in those days in the late '40s. Floyd figured that if I took the plane from 25,000 feet and let it down a steadily sustained certain number of feet per minute—without changing the throttle but rather letting the horsepower build up and up—that I would end up having takeoff horsepower just before landing. I'd be holding this terrific power for the last 10,000 feet. And I'd gain a considerable amount of speed in just handling the airplane this way over the last hundred miles.

I was the first person to fly that prototype for the P-47. It was brand-new out of the factory and I took it out to Albuquerque. On the way back I was busy running some fuel consumption tests, getting familiar with the plane, and I started the let-down Floyd had suggested. I got down to about 14,000 feet and the controls just went blah.

No control. It was the strangest sensation. Like sitting in a tin dishpan, sliding down a shallow flight of steps. That was the way it felt, and it was hair-raising. I didn't know what had happened. I pulled the throttle and still nothing happened.

The motor slows down. Starts surging. I put the flaps down about five degrees. A little stability. Then I put them down another five degrees. It's a wonder I'm not pulling them right off because they aren't made for this kind of use. Finally, the engine starts. It runs smoothly. I still don't know what's happened.

Never in my life of flying had I heard the word *compressibility*. Neither had Floyd.

During World War II, P-38s would simply disintegrate on pilots. Boys would return from combat in happy moods, successful, alive, start diving their airplanes and doing rolls over the field, and that's when it would happen: the plane would fall apart. Pilots had to be taught that every plane is built to stand a certain speed which it is dangerous to exceed.

With that prototype for the P-47—called the P-43—I didn't have any control at high speed. The stick just flopped there and I just sat there, scared. I believed the controls were broken and was shocked when I regained their use. The vibration in that dishpan had been extraordinary. Pounding the plane and me. It was an odd form of buffeting. By putting my flaps down, I had slowed myself down enough to reestablish control, but you've got to remember that at that point in the design of experimental aircraft, flaps were not used as dive brakes.

Back in Los Angeles, I went to Dr. Von Karman, a premier aerodynamicist, and Jack Northrop. I was still shaken up by what had happened. I was afraid of the plane because it felt unpredictable. I was handling it too gingerly, timidly.

"You are the first pilot I've ever discussed it with, Jackie," Von Karman said. "Compressibility."

"What's compressibility?" I asked.

"You were bucking outside forces in that plane—forces that were greater in strength than the material with which the plane was made. It was not designed to withstand that kind of buffeting, that kind of high speed." He compared the plane to a flimsy tank and the air pressure to a powerful surge of water being poured on top. "The tank can't take the weight of all the water.

It will ultimately be crushed if you pour on too much. It will simply disintegrate."

What I did when I slowed down suddenly was lessen the force.

Setting records in the P-51 later, I saw how compressibility worked time and again. In a 500 kilometer race, I had taken the plane into the trap, staying straight and level for a given number of meters before entering to get speed up. To get the record, you've got to be going mighty fast before you enter that beginning trap. So I began trying to work up some speed for it by putting the plane into a full power dive. I had souped-up that ship so it performed—for a few seconds. Then, suddenly, it started swinging as if it were a hammock tied at each end by strings higher in the sky. I knew what was coming. I didn't wait for it. Compressibility.

The British lost two or three pilots because of plane compressibility as they tried to break the speed of sound. To reach Mach 1 and go beyond, we needed a whole new class of aircraft. And men.

In 1950, Jackie set a new international speed record for propeller-driven airplanes when she piloted her North American P-51 around a 500 kilometer (311 mile) course at 715.95 km/hr (447.47 mph).

—National Air and Space Museum, Smithsonian Institution, 1981

Major General Fred Ascani

At times I think Jackie was somewhat regretful—though that may not be the right word—wistful, that she wasn't able to have better associations with women. But obviously, it would have taken a lot of time away from the things she wanted to do, to spend time mending fences in the social arena. She was always so busy. She even drove her cars like fast planes. I was with her in her station wagon in Los Angeles once when we were going fast in one direction and she suddenly wanted to go in the other, the opposite direction. She never took her foot off the gas pedal and threw that car into reverse.

My God, the rear end skidded around and she got it going the other way. I'm surprised the transmission held together. I was in the backseat and I leaned forward and said, "Jackie, that isn't going to help your transmission any."

"Fred, it'll be all right. If it's not, I'll just get another station wagon."

I was instrumental back in the 1940s in running air shows for the Air Force, and I met Jackie at one of those Cleveland shows. This was in the late 1940s and we'd all gather after a race. She knew my commander at Edwards, Al Boyd, and had tremendous respect for him. Jackie would be in Boyd's office talking about her flying projects and I'd be called in.

I learned to fly in the same time frame as Jackie and I remember my first feelings after soloing. You've worked for hours with an instructor, on dual controls. Feeling the kick in the rudder, the movement of the stick as the instructor flies the plane. Gradually, you take over, you follow through on the controls. You play games with each other. Then you solo. It's a great feeling of exhilaration. Up above an overcast, those white fleecy clouds. You're all by yourself. And no navigator. No instructor. Just you. You're up there and maybe you hear the chatter on the radio, whatever. The world is clean. It's pure. And so blue. That airplane is at your command and it does what you tell it to do. No one can interfere with you. So you do a few slow rolls, maybe a loop or two. It's so exhilarating. It's love. That's what it is. I can't find a better word for it.

You tremble after you land. In those days, the top speed was about 70 miles an hour and you landed at 30. You didn't have a feathering prop and sometimes with the propeller at idle, you'd have no forward momentum so you'd really be dead-sticking in. You didn't want to stall your plane, so you tried to keep it 2 or 3 miles faster than stall speed. But if you didn't know that, you might stall. In fact, the mark of a good pilot later was the guy who could plan his approach to where he never had to touch the throttle after approach. If you had to use the throttle to get you down after cutting back on your throttle, you weren't as good as you could be. You weren't allowed to touch it. You were literally dead-sticking it in because you had no throttle use.

There are cautious pilots who never want to know what the plane's maximum performance is, and then there are pilots like Yeager and Cochran. Yeager always pushed beyond the limits. Chuck and Jackie were alike. I think that's part of why they were really good friends. She was masculine but she was feminine. And they had similar goals, similar backgrounds. It's amazing when you consider her records in jets and remember her age at the time. She was really getting along in years when she was flying the F-86, but she never said: Am I too old for this? We seem to accept aging in men, in Chuck Yeager, for instance, but in a woman who really wasn't a part of the U.S. Air Force in the traditional or active way, it was amazing. The Air Force is a community that shares bonds, that adheres to traditional lines, but we all accepted Jackie. She formed a bond in the Air Force community and I never questioned it. In my own mind, the thought never arose: this gal's a female! That never came up. She played so many roles so well. She could be very, very feminine and she could be very hard and critical, watching her resources.

Anytime there was a discussion about goal achievement, it didn't make any difference what goals we were talking about, inevitably Jackie would inject something about her childhood, how she had learned to survive on her own. She didn't have love as a child and perhaps that's why she pushed so hard as an adult. But she responded to love and being loved. Jackie wasn't a distant person and she had tremendous respect for individuals with families. My wife, Kay, and I had eight children, and we were invited down to her ranch for weekends.

Eyesight is very important when flying experimental aircraft. To see everything, you've got to have good peripheral vision and good vision completely. I'd say Jackie Cochran was every bit as good as I was, and I consider myself a pretty good pilot. I flew with her twice in a T-33 jet. She was getting herself acclimated to jet flying at the time because she held every record there was to hold for conventional aircraft. She was making her move into the jet field and General Hoyt Vandenberg had authorized her program there at Edwards.

"Fred," he said to me, "I want this tightly controlled and it's all been set up." I thought to myself: "Don't screw this up, Fred." And number two: "Protect her at all costs." I flew with her at first and then I designated Chuck as the pilot in charge. He gave her almost all of her subsequent training in jets and upgraded her to an F-86. She knew her business, her limitations, and made it a point to learn her airplanes very carefully.

Experimental test pilots look for little signs in each other to judge performance: a little porpoising, a little wing-waving, a pilot who isn't able to level off at the designated altitude, overshooting by 100 feet or so, and then having to get back to the point. I could never believe that Chuck Yeager could make an airplane behave the way it would. But pilots are always aware of the dangers, the limitations. This goes for the *Challenger* crew astronauts. Those men and women were apprehensive at the countdown, in the final minutes. They knew what might happen. They may have been successful in keeping their queasiness from Christa McAuliffe, the teacher-astronaut. But in those experimental airplanes out at Edwards, it didn't make any difference how many times we flew them. You always knew they were experimental, that they hadn't been configured for final production, and there was always the chance something could go wrong. Always.

EISENHOWER

1952

Back in 1946, the Air Force Association, the private organization formed by Air Force pilots, was going bankrupt and its first president, Jimmy Doolittle, said, "Jackie, I think you can do some good around here." The "good" he was talking about had to be played to a tune of $185,000, in fact. They were that deep into red.

Doolittle and I had been friends for what felt like centuries, so between Floyd, Assistant Secretary for Air Sonny Whitman, and me, we pulled the AFA $12.00 into the black and put Eisenhower into the speaker's spot one night at a VIP banquet.

I fed and watered 350 people at that dinner in the Plaza Hotel in 1946, and if you had dropped a bomb on the building, there would have been little power left in the United States afterward. Everybody who was anybody was there. I remember a call from young William Randolph Hearst, Bill the newspaperman, before the party started.

"Aren't you going to invite me to this dinner, Jackie?" he asks.

"I'm not inviting anybody to this dinner. This is being run by the Air Force Association, and I just told them I'd pick up the tab." He couldn't be pissed at me. I hadn't made up the list. But I can tell you that I've never seen so many freeloaders in my life.

Everybody wanted in because Eisenhower was on the

266

podium. That was the night I suspected the general was destined for bigger things than the presidency of Columbia University.

"This man will be president of the United States someday," I said to someone sitting near me.

"Don't be silly, Jackie."

Later in the evening, Eisenhower sat down beside me.

"Why don't you run for president?" I ask. "You'd be a goody."

"Oh, no no no," he says. That was in 1946. It wasn't too many years after that exchange that both the Democratic and the Republican parties were after him to run on their tickets.

Jock Whitney, the multimillionaire American businessman, called me in 1951. "Jackie," he says, "we are looking for someone to chair a Madison Square Garden rally for General Eisenhower here in New York City. Are you interested?"

"Why me?"

"We think you can do a pretty good job," was all he said.

Eisenhower was head of NATO at that time and stationed there in France. He wasn't even a presidential candidate, but Jock Whitney and a small group of Ike supporters wanted to convince the general that he should become one—and soon. The election machinery was gearing up for 1952 and he kept repeating to his backers, "If I have a clear-cut call from the American people, I'll give consideration to it."

I took the job.

Picture this: February 1952, eleven o'clock at night, after the big fight in Madison Square Garden had ended, the place is hot, still steamy, and our people arrive, bussed and trained in from all over the United States. They're there to scream—all 21,000 of them—screaming "Holler with your dollar—we want Ike!" I remember rescuing Mrs. Jimmy Doolittle from a policeman outside. It was just bedlam—wonderful bedlam and exactly what I had wanted. Five A.M. the next morning, it was over.

We got the clear-cut picture we needed on film, the call from Americans who wanted Ike to be their next president, and I flew myself and the film footage on a TWA plane to Paris.

"The general has gone to Luxembourg for the weekend and you have a forty-five-minute appointment with him Monday morning," I'm told on arrival. I went to bed and slept the whole weekend.

Right on time Monday I'm shown in to see the general. And right on time he started talking. At last, with my satchel of film and my arguments ready, I stopped poor Ike in his tracks. "I've been here twenty-eight minutes and you haven't given me a chance to open my mouth, General Eisenhower," I said. "I came all the way from New York on behalf of a great group of people. Twenty-five thousand of them want me to tell you our story and you won't let me say a word." He started to laugh.

"You know it's true," he said then. "I've done all the talking."

I let him have it then, describing his clear-cut call, and then I said, "I've got it here in my bag, in fact."

"What do you have in your bag?"

"An awful lot of bodies on film, General. I was going to make sure I had a crowd and you won't believe this until you see it. I still have ten minutes coming to me here," I said.

He rang his secretary. "Will you change these appointments?" he asked. I knew there was some oil man from the Middle East out there. I had seen him myself, but I didn't feel bad about it at all.

Eisenhower and I talked for another two hours that day, and later I shared a front row with Mamie and the general to see the film footage of our Madison Square Garden rally.

"Would you like a drink?" he says, looking like he's about to dissolve into the floor.

"I think you need one," I answer. "And so do I."

When I left for home, he was still flabbergasted, but it had been decided.

"Go tell Bill Robinson at the *Tribune* that I'm going to run. Robinson, General Lucius Clay, and Jock Whitney, but no one else. I'm going to run."

Dwight David Eisenhower won the presidency by an overwhelming majority—seventy-two percent—and I won a friend for life. And even though he made me into the Republican I never should have been, the lifetime of experiences I had because of our association clearly made it worth my while. I remember the inaugural ball and being in a box of seats alongside General and Mrs. Hoyt Vandenberg. He was Chief of Staff of the Air Force at the time. Vandenberg and I were invited to pay our respects to the Eisenhowers up on the platform, and bless her heart, Mrs. Eisenhower said to me, "Jackie, now look what you've done to us." There were fifty million people looking on.

A beautiful young woman came up to me later and asked, "Who is that handsome man you were with?"

"He's the Chief of Staff of the United States Air Force. Would you like to meet him?"

Mrs. Vandenberg looked at me kind of funny, but I said to Van, "Dance with her. She's going to swoon she thinks you are so handsome." And he did.

After he retired from the presidency, Ike chose to call my California valley his home. He didn't live out his last days near Gettysburg, Pennsylvania. He did it in the Coachella Valley. But his house over on the Eldorado Country Club property didn't offer the kind of quiet he needed, so he accepted our invitation to use some quarters at the ranch. We converted one of the guest cottages into an office. It was quiet and the lawn around it was spacious and you could see the mountains fifty miles distant.

He had injured his knee playing football and would wear one shoe with lead in the sole, cross his legs, and swing the bad one up and down. "By jove, it's kind of hard to get up from this position, Jackie," he said to me one Sunday afternoon when I came upon him by surprise sitting behind the cottage. He could sit there for four or five hours at a time, his secretaries told me. Looking at the mountains and bouncing that leg to keep it agile.

Phone calls—did we get the phone calls for him. I had to put an extra person on the switchboard those first two years he spent out here. And the callers, some of them old friends, would never believe me when I said, "I can't transfer you to President Eisenhower because I don't know his phone number." But it's the truth. I didn't want our switchboard to have the number at hand because it would have created more of a nightmare than it already was, with the nitwits trying to get in touch with the ex-president. Walter Cronkite did his interviews with the general right in guest house number two, and when they aired, we had a dinner party to celebrate.

Roast beef, chicken cooked on a spit, spare ribs, and silence. Everything at the buffet went like clockwork that night except the dead silence which created the oddest sort of atmosphere right after Cronkite's interview with Eisenhower had aired. Bob Hope broke the spell by saying, "Well, General, you had fifteen million people in the palm of your hand for an hour and not one single laugh in the whole lot of it."

Nobody else could do something like that and expect to get away with it but Bob Hope. We all broke up laughing.

The Eisenhowers could ask Floyd and me for anything, and the feelings were mutual. Whether it was making quail hash in my kitchen on Christmas Eve—Ike did more posturing than pot-stirring—or taking care of the Pasha of Kenitra, we knew we could count on them and they could count on us. Ike told us in advance one December day that he would like to cook up some quail hash for our Christmas Eve dinner together. We had quails running around the ranch by the thousands, but it is really a preserve, so when we told Buck Chambles, our cowboy, that he ought to go shoot thirty or forty quails for ex-president Eisenhower's hash, he couldn't do it. He refused to shoot those birds because he was too fond of them. Instead, he got in his car and drove all the way to San Diego to buy quails.

"Tell Jackie if she's not too busy to pop in on me for a minute," was the message I received one afternoon. So I popped in on the general.

"I've got a little problem," he says. "President Kennedy has asked me to meet and escort the Pasha of Kenitra tomorrow, and I don't want to do it."

"Where in the world is Kenitra?" I ask.

"Camp Deloge in North Africa," he explains. "But this pasha, a cousin of the king, is arriving at the Palm Springs Airport tomorrow, Mamie is down in Phoenix for two weeks of dieting, and I've got my golf partners here for two weeks of cards and golf. I don't want to bring this pasha to my house because he may be difficult to get rid of. These people are very peculiar," he says.

"You don't dare offend them," I agree, and Eisenhower explains the significance of North Africa to certain American naval bases.

Eisenhower decided to hold a press conference the next day for the pasha, after which he would pretend to be whisked away on business and I'd take over as hostess. I was to serve this man and his entourage lunch, and as I said to Ike then, "I think I can make them happy."

The Pasha of Kenitra had a big, bejeweled dagger and the press conference went well. The place was packed. The weather was bad. I met them at the door of my home with a wet towel, a dry towel, a plate of dates, and a glass of goat's milk. The president was tickled with what I knew about North Africans, and we all had baby lamb, rice, and raisins for lunch. Then Eisenhower skipped town for all outward appearances. He and I knew differently. The pasha was pleased with himself.

After lunch the pasha put me in an awkward position.

"I'd like to see where President Eisenhower lives," he says. I stumble a little verbally and reply, "Well, his home is in a rather private area on a country club, but I suppose we can drive by. Will you excuse me for a moment so I can get everything ready?"

I tell my housekeeper to get Eisenhower's housekeeper on the phone. "For heaven's sake, call there right away and tell them to pull all the window shades down and make the house look closed up for at least an hour and a half. Don't let anyone show his face, or it will be tragic."

The pasha was determined to have his picture taken in front of Eisenhower's house, and I couldn't stop him. My heart was just beating in embarrassment.

"How about one of these other beautiful homes?" I suggest.

"No, it must be General Eisenhower's," he insists.

So we get out of the car. We are standing in front of the home when Freeman Gosden walks around to the back door of the house. Freeman was Eisenhower's next door neighbor and a close friend of mine.

"Hi, Jackie," Freeman says.

I stand stone still. Freeman and I always exchange kisses. Not this time. He looks at me kind of funny, and I turn my back.

"Who is that?" the pasha asks.

"Just one of the servants here," I say.

Jeepers, bad weather kept that entire entourage grounded there in the desert for three exhausting days. I was sick of shepherding this geezer around, sick of lamb dishes, goat's milk, and dates as well as the sight of him and his questions. At one point he had wanted to see my bedroom.

I called the Eldorado Country Club manager and said, "Look here, the president of the United States sent this Pasha of Kenitra out here, and it might make a colorful story for the club if you want to write it up. I'd like to bring him over there for dinner because I've had enough of it. What about it? Will you serve him dinner?" They agreed, and I called to warn Eisenhower away from his haunt that night. "Jackie, I am so sorry I got you into this mess."

That night at dinner the Pasha of Kenitra ordered a steak.

JETS

1953

I had planned to be in London by June 2, 1953, to see Elizabeth crowned queen, but while she was riding back from Westminster Abbey to Buckingham Palace in the royal carriage, I was still having my own rides. And they weren't ones I would have missed for anything, not even for a ringside seat at a coronation. The jet phase of aviation had been threatening to pass me by, and I didn't want that to happen. Floyd had seen me itching to try. I wanted to go as fast as the fastest men on earth, and I was riding high on the crest of official aviation in the fifties, working on Air Force projects, serving in official roles for the premier world organization, the Fédération Aéronautique Internationale, poking my nose into Federal Aviation Administration business. But it wasn't enough. I wasn't ready to retire from active duty, as they say. I wanted to keep flying faster planes, and so I started campaigning.

Everything had conspired against my setting any jet records that year. In fact, if bets had been taken, even the weathermen would have voted with the politicians, the Air Force higher-ups as well as the Canadian manufacturer of the Sabrejet I had been given the chance to test. They all would have put me in England, watching a new queen quietly from the sidelines.

But they were wrong.

Ordinary citizens don't have a snowball's chance in you know where to get themselves into United States Air Force supersonic jets. But I never thought of myself as ordinary and I was also a lieutenant colonel in the Air Force Reserve. That really didn't help much. Floyd helped. General Curtis Lemay helped. Stuart Symington helped. And the list of people I lobbied went on for miles—Boyd, Vandenberg, Canadian authorities, French representatives, General Ascani—they were all instrumental in getting me into a Canadian-built F-86, the fastest airplane in the world back then, on an official Edwards Air Force Base course and ready to attempt to break those records for 3- 15- and 100-kilometer closed circular tracks. What I and Chuck Yeager, who was training me, also knew was that this would be my chance to crash through the sound barrier as well. Breaking that barrier, with Chuck's help, was really preliminary to the test-piloting I had been hired to do for Canadair, the airplane's owner. But it was far from preliminary in my mind.

Edwards Air Force Base is north of my ranch in the desert, where the nights are cold and the days are hot, especially in late May and June. As the sun rises higher, the heat thermals start up from the desert terrain and by noon the air turbulence is at such a degree that full-speed close-to-the-earth flying is dangerous.

If you want speed records to your credit—as I did—you've got to fly in the morning when air temperatures have risen to help give you maximum speed but before excessive air turbulence sets in, as it does on hot desert days. Day after day in late May and then June, conditions had not been kind. Observation planes in the air had to be able to see your runs. And upgrading to the F-86 took weeks of painstaking work. In those days you were clocked around pylons, with a judge and a timer at each pylon to clock you with special electronic devices and to make sure you stayed just outside the black smoke markers that rose into the sky. We'd throw a couple of tires on top of each other and then, when all was ready, start a smoky fire in the middle. Twelve towers of smoke marked the 100 kilometer, for instance.

The 100 kilometer course would take in about 63 miles. I'd have to fly only 300 feet off the ground in order for the photographic equipment to catch and record me. But there were hills to one side so I'd be skimming a little up and over them. I'd get two chances—just two—to set my record because that's all the fuel the plane could carry. If all went well, I'd have a margin of two minutes of fuel after two complete passes. But could I hold that plane in a banked position of 30 degrees for a 63-mile circular flight and beat Colonel Ascani's mark of 635 mph? Edwards pilots weren't so sure. Opinions varied. And what about taking the "G's" I'd be experiencing in those sharp turns? One "G" is the force of gravity, and the turns would offer me more than one.

None of those record runs entail easy flying—100 kilometer, 15, or 3. They're possible when you've been taught by the best.

General Chuck Yeager

If I told Jackie Cochran to run that son of a bitch until it melts, that is exactly the way she would do it. When we worked together, first in the T-33 jet trainer and then upgrading to the F-86, she never gave a damn about what could happen. It wasn't that she didn't know: she'd just make up her mind to do something and that was it. She'd go all out for it. You know, red warning lights in airplanes were immaterial to her. Just like I've said before, she set records in airplanes. She didn't set women's records. She set records, period.

It makes no difference what a pilot's reproductive organs are shaped like. It's skill that matters. And the point is: Jackie Cochran had a hell of a lot of experience. Consequently, she was skilled. She knew airplanes and she was good in them.

We had known each other for several years, and her problem was always the hardware. It just wasn't readily available to women because there were no women in the Air Force on active status, flying the sort of airplanes she wanted to be flying. Later on, Northrop would hire her as a company pilot. But that was after she set her records in the F-86. And Lockheed did the same eventually. But in the beginning, to get those jet records, she had to go to Canada to get a plane to fly. Making her a company pilot, the way Canadair, Northrop, and Lockheed did, was part of the legal mechanism authorizing her to fly their company planes. She was an employee of those companies when she flew the planes. They were airplanes the companies were building or had built for the military and they'd be leased back from the military for the testing purpose or setting records.

Jackie wasn't the only gal who could have gotten these companies to hire her on. There were at least 1,200 other women who may have been just as good as she was as a pilot, with just as much experience. But when World War II ended, those other women had given up flying. They went back to running their businesses or to being housewives and mothers. Jackie would never give up. She kept right on flying fast planes.

I'd run into a few of those WASP pilots, and they were good. Some did stick with it and get into the air show business. There were some really good gal pilots. But for lack of interest or lack of financial backing, they just gradually faded out. Jackie didn't.

Sometimes I want to remind the press about Jackie Cochran. They'll be saying now, "Here's a woman flying a T-38 for the first time!" And there are gals now flying T-38s, C-5s, and C-130s. But these gals today are only doing in T-38s what Jackie was doing way back when. Hey, I want to say, "Jackie Cochran was flying F-86s and T-38s twenty-five years ago." But people have short memories.

You don't have to be superhuman to fly an airplane. The point is: we all want to blow the facts out of shape. For instance, in World War II, the better you could make the airplane you just shot down look, the bigger the hero you would be. There was an awful lot of this attitude, and it was carried forward as the Air Force expanded. Blowing things out of shape. You have to take stories with a grain of salt. Today, for instance, there's a lot of talk about flying F-14s off those carriers at night. Hey, Uncle Sam doesn't buy a piece of equipment that the average person can't operate. But if I'm flying an F-16 or an F-20, I don't discourage you from thinking I'm great.

The upshot is: you don't have to blow something out of shape if you've accomplished it. I used to irk Jackie that way when she'd be making statements, and I'd say, "Now, Jackie, that's not the way it was." But Jackie was real proud of what she accomplished. She did a hell of a good job.

A good pilot can fly anything. You know, you always look at yourself as being average or above. If you're average or above, you can handle anything that comes along. Not everybody had that kind of confidence in Jackie, though. I remember Jimmy Doolittle being worried about her cracking up that Sabrejet on Air Force property. He was staying down at her ranch and he asked me to fly down so we could talk about the program I had set up. He didn't want anything embarrassing happening. No scandal, he said. And if Jackie tore up a piece of equipment, it would have looked bad.

Hell, I told him then, she's got the experience, she can ride those airplanes really good, sitting there, running one with it wide open. I had seen her in our practice runs, in the T-33 trainer. Coming out of a trap in a test, she'd have just the right amount of fuel left. She knew what she was facing, trained for it, and knew when to put that throttle in idle and keep it there.

I told Doolittle.

We were using an Air Force F-86 to chase her, but she would be flying a Canadair Sabrejet F-86 for the records. It had been set up. There was nothing to worry about.

We had many, many hours in T-33s, the jet trainers, and many flights in the F-86. She practiced her 100-kilometer, for instance, in a T-33 until she knew it. Then I'd check her out in the F-86 and she'd fly that plane around the 100-kilometer circular course until she was proficient at it. Then we'd move on up into other preliminary work. It was during one of those practice runs that she sheared her fuel tank. She didn't know what was happening at the time, but I was practically sitting in her cockpit, watching exactly what she was doing.

"Don't get so close," she says to me.

"You forget about me," I say. "You've got a problem. I thought you were a big girl now—grown up—but you look all wet under the bottom. Pull the damn airplane up. Stop it. Cock it. Put it down on the lake bed." I don't want to scare her.

"I don't want to lose this experimental job," she says. She cuts off the power.

I tell the tower to get the fire trucks out to the lake bed. She's got a bad fuel leak. If it gets into the plening chamber, there'll be an explosion.

"Okay," I say to her, "start a gradual left turn and the minute the airspeed gets below 200, get your landing gear down. Drop the nose. Keep it to 150."

If you put Jackie Cochran in the right plane, she knew how to fly. She understood flying. Her hands were as big as mine and she was strong enough to handle the equipment. No big deal. No mental genius. Just hard work.

I remember that forced landing in the F-86. A fuel line broke. I didn't see it. Chuck did. He made a joke about it. Kept me from becoming rattled. Told me to put it down on the lake bed which would take a high-speed landing and a long roll. It wasn't until I took off my oxygen mask and smelled the fuel in the cockpit that I honestly knew why he was ordering me around. When the wheels touched ground and the roll had about stopped, Chuck wanted me to cut all those switches and jump free of the plane fast—as fast as I could.

There I stood on the plane, considering a jump that might break both my legs. Fuel is still gushing from the bottom of the main section of the left wing. It's a stream the size of your thumb and the plane is hot. I look over and see a guy, I think he's a sergeant standing there watching me, watching the plane. I've got to tell you: all people don't run toward accidents happening.

"Get over here, boy, and break my fall," I say.

"No way, ma'am."

"What are you? A man or a mouse? Goddamn," I yelled. There was no way to get down there without the ladder. Dry lake beds have extremely hard surfaces. Fuel was still draining in a stream.

Then Chuck landed and ran right over to my plane. He broke my fall as I jumped.

Mach 1 is the speed of sound, but it varies with the temperature—like the stretching and shrinking of a rubber band. Warm air temperature can increase your speed, but it also increases the speed of sound too. That's the reason why true airspeed may vary for Mach 1. In cold air it can go as low as 660, and in hot it'll be up close to 800 mph. I wanted the experience of reaching and surpassing Mach 1 almost for emotional and spiritual reasons. Chuck sympathized and understood. He

Jackie and Floyd.

Testing and pushing Lockheed
planes to their limits in the 60's.

In '61, Jackie set eight major records in Northrop's T-38 with Chuck Yeager coaching, flying chase.

Meeting Jimmy Stewart was a passing thrill but Eisenhower's friendship was a longstanding commitment.

A pack-rat, Jackie tackled
paperwork fanatically but
preferred work that would
win her first places, prizes,
aviation awards.

1975: Holding her own Air Force Academy sword for the first time in Colorado Springs.

Receiving a Harmon trophy from "Ike" as the number one female flyer while Chuck takes outstanding male pilot award.

Inside the cockpit of a plane was where Jackie best loved to be—
from the beginning of her flying days...

...to the end.

would act as my mentor. No one else need know. There'd be time enough to talk about it once the deed was done. Maybe I'd lose my nerve in the high-speed dive straight toward earth. Other men had. No other woman had tried.

The first time, I climb to 45,000 feet and it's slow going. I go all the way down to the Mexican border and leave a contrail of ice crystals as a signal to Floyd. I know he's watching. The hot exhaust vapor striking the cool air at high altitude forms water crystals which quickly turn into ice. Floyd sees me.

At the top of the world, I do a split "S" curve to start the full-power, almost vertical dive, heading straight toward the airport. This split "S" maneuver keeps the pull of gravity working on the underside of your ship. Pointing your nose over and straight into a dive up there will put you in an extreme gravitational pull and could wreak havoc with your fuel and hydraulic systems if you're not careful. I'm careful. I "S" my way over into the most exciting ride of my life, heading straight down—and I do mean straight—keeping my throttle at full power. This is where pilots lose their nerve. I don't.

I read the meter aloud for Chuck to hear...97...98...99...

You're part of the plane on a flight like that. Attached to it in ten different ways. Strapped into your seat, to your parachute, to the oxygen system, to your radio for listening, talking, reading the Mach meter aloud. Chuck listens. If there's an emergency—well, the speed heading straight down like that is just too great to do anything single-handedly. I'd never get the canopy open using just my body force against such outside forces. I can see the lever to pull which will set off an explosive charge and blow the canopy open. There's one lever to blow me into space as well.

I was hanging face downward diving at Mach 1 with my blood surging into my brain, not looking forward to what pilots call a "red-out" (the possibility of blood vessels bursting), feeling the kinks in my abdomen from old surgical scars complaining and the arteries in my legs—never perfect anyway—wishing, if arteries could wish, that I had worn a "G" suit. It would have corrected some of the problems. I hadn't bothered to put it on. I had a "G" suit available, but the "oldsters" there at Edwards never wore them. I followed suit—stupidly.

I pulled out of that first dive through the sound barrier exhilarated, exhausted, and before getting to 18,000 feet. The pull-out slowed my speed and I went back past the barrier. The shock and turbulence were familiar.

"Tell me what you're feeling," Chuck says.

"Shock waves look like rain," I answer. Flying inside an explosion I want to say, but I can't find those words. You hear just fine up there, but you don't hear the sound of your plane. That sound passes behind you because you are going faster than sound can travel.

You can take a piece of knitting yarn, stick down one end of it with ordinary glue, and the yarn will stay flat. When you get to supersonic speed, the shock waves coming off the airplane make the knitting yarn stand up and bend forward. It's just incredible. You think you are seeing things.

Back on the ground, after that first time, I couldn't find my feet. I felt like I was two feet off the ground. Friends all around. Congratulations and kisses.

The control tower didn't catch it, Jackie, someone is saying. Do you want to break it again, just for the record? I'm asked.

"I sure do," I say. "When?"

"Right now."

An hour later I went up again—a little higher on the rubber ball that time. Believe me, breaking the sound barrier and being the first woman to do it was the greatest thrill of my life. The bulletlike shocks left the black and blue imprint of the shoulder straps on my body. And two weeks later Chuck and I performed a barrier-breaking duet on a Sunday afternoon, for a Paramount Pictures film crew. The film footage would have been fantastic. The sonic booms broke the camera.

There was a Major Simon who went up as high as 150,000 feet in a balloon. He could sure talk about seeing stars at noon. It doesn't always happen though; even at 50,000 feet you don't always catch the stars out. You have to have certain conditions. But when you do see them, they are just as brilliant as they can be from my ranch lawn on a clear night. Most pilots—even the ones who fly that high—don't look up. They want to look down all the time.

In those long weeks of May and June 1953, I set new world's records, going 653 mph around the closed 100-kilometer course, bettering Ascani's mark of the year before, shattering the women's record of 540 mph held by the premier French female pilot, Jacqueline Auriol, capturing other firsts and simply having the time of my life, cementing what would become one of the most remarkable friendships in my life.

The only complaint: the low-swooping Sabre on one of those record flights stampeded a couple hundred chickens on a nearby ranch. The chickens herded into a corner and some smothered to death. Why was it that dead chickens kept turning up in my career—first over Flat Pass Air Force Base and then over Edwards?

"Produce the dead chickens," I told the owner, "and I'll pay for them."

President Eisenhower presented Jacqueline Cochran with the Harmon Trophy for the outstanding female pilot of 1953 in a ceremony at the White House. Major Charles E. Yeager received the male pilot trophy.
—National Air and Space Museum, Smithsonian Institution, 1981

OTHER VOICES:

Glennis Yeager

I still have the last dress Jackie Cochran had made for me. It's a lovely thing she had designed and sewn in Hong Kong but it was too big at first. I'm a size 4. When she saw it on me, she knew it was too big, so we went to Saks in Palm Springs to the alterations department and to the same woman who altered her clothes. We bustled in and she said, "Make this right for Glennis." Jackie was a clotheshorse. It was nothing for her to take thirty to forty suitcases along with her when she was traveling.

If you really analyze it, I would never in my life have left Grass Valley, California, if it weren't for Chuck and Jackie Cochran. I'd have stayed right here and been just as content as I could be. I don't need to travel. I don't care about fantastic adventures. But you couldn't have peace or quiet with Chuck or

Jackie around. They were regular catalysts for one another and they made me go along. They just wouldn't let you alone.

"You've got to do this," one would say.

"Now, you really should," the other would insist.

"You just must," they'd say.

And if Jackie or Chuck decided to do something, they'd do it. She was very determined. Like Chuck. She was so tenacious, she would never ever drop anything. If she decided she was going for something, there was no stopping her. Forget it. And anything negative would just never get talked about. She'd just walk away from it.

But it was the adventure that kept Chuck going off with Jackie. If it hadn't been done before, they'd say, "Let's do it." And he got to fly, of course. It was the flying that made it especially important to him. He flew with her on so many of her record flights, always on her wing, right alongside, telling her what to do. They had great times. They were alike.

She did a lot of good—a tremendous amount of good—and between Jackie and Floyd, they probably accomplished more in their lifetimes than anybody. Jackie especially was often able to use people without their really knowing they were being used. She was always talking about adopting children, and she was the godmother to an awful lot of children, but she may have been entirely different if she had given birth to her own children. Motherhood might have changed her.

I remember when the four of us—Jackie, Floyd, Chuck, and I—were staying in the ritzy Beverly Wilshire Hotel in Los Angeles because we were going to attend a dinner in honor of Floyd's work with the Arthritis Foundation. The "bird's nest" was in vogue then—"bird's nest" being the name of the hairdo that was all the rage. Well, I had long wavy hair and I could do it up miles high, so I did. It was just beautiful—or so I thought.

Jackie took one look at me and said, "What the hell have you done with your hair?"

I didn't even want to go to the dinner in the first place, and she destroyed my confidence just like that. I'm not particularly given to tears, but, oh, I was angry. I said to her, "Okay, if that's the way it is, go to hell. I'm not going to the dinner."

But I went. I didn't want to embarrass Chuck by not going, and I thought the world of Floyd. But I could have killed her.

POLITICS

1956

I became a Republican because I loved Eisenhower so and hated what Roosevelt had been doing to our country equally so. My decision was probably a mistake. But it did make me more comfortable on visits to the White House when the Eisenhowers were living there.

I remember the night Queen Elizabeth came for dinner and Prince Philip stifled a yawn during her toast.

Floyd had to enter a hospital because of a gall bladder attack, so I called Ann Whitman, Ike's secretary, to express my disappointment about not being able to attend.

"It isn't serious, but Floyd's too sick to come tonight, so I presume this cuts me out of the pattern," I said, using one of our aviation expressions.

"I don't think so, Jackie," she explained. "The Eisenhowers want you here. Let me check it out and I'll call you back. I'm pretty sure it can be arranged." And it was.

The only prominent Democrat present was Lyndon B. Johnson, a senator then, and I would be sitting between him and his wife, Lady Bird, my good friends, and State Department Under Secretary Christian A. Herter, a former governor of Massachusetts who was quite crippled with arthritis, the nasty disease that made my own husband's life so miserable for so many years.

The room was packed tight that night. Mamie and her staff

had squeezed ninety-two people into the state dining room which would ordinarily hold a max of sixty.

There was a terrible storm outside. It was just awful. Howling and blowing, making a racket, and the room became quite hot. The air-conditioning system had gone off.

The queen spoke above the noise of the wind and rain and addressed the crowd with a little speech that reminded me of a little girl talking. She was charming. She always reads her speeches. Watching Prince Philip, however, who was exceedingly bored, was the funniest part of the dinner. His yawns were nearly contagious, as yawns can be in a crowd of people.

Suddenly, we were all wide awake. There was a wild noise. Not thunder—but a noise that reminded me of a Gatling gun going off. Every person in that room jumped. An assassination attempt—we all believed we were in the middle of an assassination attempt. The room became charged with the electricity of human emotion. People dropped forks, spoons, and dessert dishes of fresh pineapple and sherbet clattered. There were a few screams.

Eisenhower never flinched. He blanched, but never once hesitated. My eyes went to him immediately. But as they did, that room filled with more Secret Service men than I could believe possible on such short notice. They came from behind French window curtains, doors, out from the kitchen exits— everywhere. It makes you realize how inconspicuous they can be when they want it that way. When they don't, it's a different story. And this evening, it was that sort of story.

The hot buzz continued for what seemed like an eternity. No one moved much.

Then there was a release.

One of the Secret Service men had cracked a door to let in the cool breeze, and the wind caught it, slamming it closed to create the Gatling gun effect.

I looked over at Herter and noticed that a big glop of sherbet had been spilled down the lapel of his coat in the confusion. Without thinking twice or asking anyone's permission, I grabbed my knife, reached over, and scooped it up and off.

Johnson leans over and says in my ear, "You certainly are quick on the uptake."

Yvonne Smith

I first met Jackie in a political atmosphere. She had become interested in politics after helping in the Eisenhower campaign for president and she began to be more active. In 1955 she decided to run for Congress from her district around Indio and the Coachella Valley. She came to me because I had been involved in politics in El Centro and she wanted someone like me, with my background, and being a woman, to help in the campaign. I took a year off from my job and we ended up working together day and night for the duration of the campaign— until the bitter end.

We were gone from dusk till dawn trying to meet all the people in the district: farmers, crop pickers, everyone. She had her speeches prepared on six-by-eight cards, but most of the time she'd end up speaking extemporaneously, taking questions from the crowds. Her mind was always at work; she was always thinking on her feet, responding to some pretty prying queries. I remember the teetotaller who wanted to know whether or not she drank. Yes, Jackie drank. What would she say, I wondered.

"Well, sir," she says, "yes, I drink, but just two years ago I flew an airplane faster than the speed of sound, so I guess I don't drink too much."

There was a sweet little black man who stood up at one rally and said to her, "Miss Cochran, I am a weeder in the agricultural fields and I want to show you something." He began demonstrating how he worked in the fields and explained that he had to use a very short hoe. "Do you know why we have to use such a short hoe, Miss Cochran?" he asked.

"You know, I don't know, sir," she answered, "but I'm gonna find out." And from there she went to discuss the matter with all kinds of farmers to find out why they couldn't put longer handles on their hoes. Most told her that the longer handle would prohibit the weeder from getting close enough to the weed. The handle would get in the way, but I don't think any answer ever sufficed. Jackie and I were in Europe a decade later, driving down a road in Austria, and she looked out into a farmer's field and said to me, "This reminds me of that little man back in California. I wonder if they have longer hoes here?"

I was there for Jackie Cochran's first real, first big, and first serious defeat. She was like a sister to me over the years, but she lost that election, and I believe she would have made a fantastic congresswoman. Floyd took the failure almost harder than she did.

———

In 1956, Jacqueline Cochran made an unsuccessful bid for a congressional seat from California. She campaigned by piloting her own plane around the district.
    —National Air and Space Museum, Smithsonian Institution, 1981

I should have run as a Democrat; leaders of the party had actually approached me in 1951 about running for election. At the time neither the party nor the timing was right. Floyd kept telling me that politicking might not be my strong suit. Perhaps I should have listened, but I had been dreaming of a place in Congress and by now you know that I am not one easily daunted by cautions or precautions. If I want something, I go for it. And I wanted to be one of the few women ever elected to a seat in the House of Representatives.

I saw the loss coming. My opponent was a Hindu, born in the Punjab, India, and I always suspected him of being a communist, here in the United States on a fraudulent visa. I'd almost bet his passport belonged to his uncle.

"Well, it's going to be nice to have you in Washington, D.C.," Eisenhower said to me about three weeks before Election Day in 1956.

"I'm not so sure we'll be seeing each other back east," I admitted even then. "I'm going to lose by about 1,500 to 3,000 votes. I think I'm outnumbered."

Eisenhower called twice on Election Day but I had gone into a corner to lick my wounds. It's no fun to spend nine months campaigning your heart out and then lose. It was devastating at the end.

Stuart Symington

Running for Congress was a mistake Jackie made. The people out there in her district didn't understand her, a woman as driving and as competitive as Jackie Cochran. She didn't make sense to them. You know, there's an expression politician Al Smith had. Al Smith, who ran for president of the United States and lost, could be the greatest politician this nation has ever seen, and he had an expression he used at least once. "You don't tell people in a campaign," he would say, "you sell them." Jackie Cochran didn't know how to sell herself to the voters. She'd tell them. I suffered from this problem myself because I spent so many years in business running my own companies, telling others what to do. But Al Smith said, you can't operate like that in politics.

Eisenhower tried to involve me in politics in other capacities. Sometimes it worked. Sometimes it didn't.

The phone rings one morning at the ranch and it's a request from Eisenhower. He wants me to spearhead a drive for medical supplies, clothing, and food to be sent to Korea because we were in the midst of the strife over there and blatantly in support of a character named Syngman Rhee, the president of South Korea.

"You'll be perfect, Jackie," Ike's man says to me.

"Well, I'm afraid I'll have to decline on the basis of personal disgust," I explain. He's pretty taken aback by my comeback. So I explain further, "Look, let me tell you what happened between Syngman Rhee and me about three months ago. Maybe you'll understand then."

I had been invited along with General John Cannon to make a tour of American bases in the South Pacific. As a lieutenant colonel in the Air Force Reserve as well as my being ex-director of women pilots, I was asked on several occasions to take part in such activities and to offer my insights. It was no big deal and I enjoyed General Cannon, as well as his wife, LaVon, immensely. We were in Korea and the general and I were invited over for tea with Rhee along with our American ambassador. We sat down in a garden. That's when it started.

"I'm very happy to meet you, Miss Cochran," Rhee says. "I know you very well by reputation and I happen to know that you are an outspoken person. So maybe I can get my thoughts across to you today," he continues, making me a little nervous about what thoughts he has in mind.

"Well, I'll do what I can, Mr. President," I reply. "What is on your mind? What thoughts can't you get across to other Americans?"

"Your country, the United States of America," he explains, "is harboring and fostering communism. I think you are doing a thoroughly dishonest job of handling the problem within your own borders."

I was astonished. And this is the truth, because I retained a file copy of the letter I wrote to him after I returned home. I was furious then. He continued: "I think you are yellow as a nation and not worth anything."

"What do you do with communists here in Korea?" I ask, trying to remain as polite as I can possibly be with my blood boiling over.

"We find them in the morning and shoot them at night," he says.

"Without due process of law to find out whether the allegations are valid, you shoot them?" I say with that question in my voice.

"We get rid of communists," he replies.

The conversation continues in this vein for a few more

minutes and then I've had it. Cannon and our ambassador are just sitting there. Neither knew what to say.

I say, "If you weren't an elderly man, Mr. President, and if I were strong enough, I'd knock you right on the nose. I won't sit here any longer. I love my country and I'm leaving. You are a nasty-minded, dirty old man. Good day."

I walked out on the street by myself. I didn't care if he was the president of a nation friendly to the United States. He was a creep.

So when Eisenhower asked me to help him out, I backed out. "I wouldn't lift my finger to help that man or his country. He's a senile, dirty, dishonest politician."

Mrs. Wendell Willkie, wife of the man who ran for president and lost to Franklin Delano Roosevelt, spearheaded the Korean drive, and two very serendipitous things happened. One: I got a telegram from her, directly asking me if I would be co-chairman—a request I politely declined. And two: I was in Washington, D.C., the evening they kicked off the campaign and ended up stepping out of an elevator and into the presence of Syngman Rhee. Not a word was spoken by either of us. He probably didn't even remember me because his mind was such a mush ball. But I wouldn't ever forget.

RUSSIA

All Russia exudes the same smell—musky, sour-sweet, all-pervading, yet indescribable. It's not the smell of, say, China or Turkey, and it isn't the smell of Finland. But it hits you at the border and stays until you have departed into other lands. I went to Russia twice; once as a guest of the American ambassador and once on official business as president of the Fédération Aéronautique Internationale. I took a train the first time in 1950. Chuck flew as copilot with me in my lucky Lodestar in 1959.

Lettuce was bought by the leaf in 1950. An egg cost me ninety cents and bread for the employees of the American embassy cost almost $400 dollars a month. The lovely roll I admired in the window of a bakery turned out to be wooden. The women wore a strange orange lipstick and the Kremlin was off limits to the likes of me, even though I was there on very unofficial business with my good friend, LaVon Cannon, General Cannon's wife.

One-thirty in the morning. It's quiet and dark and I'm trying to read a Gorki play in anticipation of an evening at the theater. That's when I first heard the roar of several jet afterburners. The pilot in me overshadows the tourist, and the next day LaVon and I get permission to take an embassy car with a Russian driver to the town of Zagorsk, where the writer Tolstoy lived, about 150 miles outside the city.

"No stopping along the way," we're told. "No picture-taking. Sight-seeing only." But my appetite was whetted with anticipation of airplanes. What kind did they have? Were they into jets the way Americans were into jets in 1950? I had seen a few at the Moscow airport, but I wanted to see more.

The whole Russian countryside is sprouting radio towers and I can just make out barbed wire barricades back from the side of the road. A group of jets fly overhead. We've been riding for a half hour.

"Excuse me, sir," I say to the driver who speaks English. "I have a problem here. I must use a toilet. Please stop."

He slows the car peevishly. Finally he stops, because he can see no choice. The American woman has him cornered—for want of a bathroom, you might say. I either wet my pants or he lets me climb out by the side of the road and go into the woods to use the kind of facilities only nature affords.

That "powder room" alongside the barbed wire fence offered me only glimpses of a long runway, at least 10,000 feet long, and nine Delta winged airplanes. This was about eighty miles out of Moscow. But I made mental notes of this and other pieces of information, and back home I was debriefed by several U.S. congressmen who didn't want to believe even what little I described. Even Symington didn't want to believe my story about the Deltas. Lend-lease airplanes had littered certain airport landscapes, and in a shipping channel along a fifteen-mile naval yard I spied docks crammed with enormous cranes unloading cargo, more than thirty-two submarines and ships of all kinds packed closely together like sardines. There were destroyers, two aircraft carriers, and several other warships.

At least twice in my life, "going to the bathroom" when there was no real bathroom around has put me in pretty funny circumstances. That first time along a Russian highway, it was pure fakery, of course. The next time with Chuck, it was no joke, though he wanted to make one of it.

Chuck Yeager

I'll never forget the trip Jackie and I took in a T-33 over Switzerland. I was a squadron commander, and a group of us had just
come back from Tripoli in North Africa. We landed in Torino,
Italy, and I saw an emblem I recognized on the tail of a plane.
"Who's here?" I ask.

We're supposed to be in Torino only long enough to refuel to
make it on into France, but there it is, a two-star flag on that
plane and it can belong to only one guy: General Albert Boyd.

"Where're you going?" he asks as we shake hands all
around. He's eyeing up my F-86 and the others. They're all
smoked up because we've been shooting a lot of gunnery and
working really hard. I've got at least three lieutenants with me
and we're all brown and lean and dirty.

"Where're you guys coming from?" Boyd asks.

"Libya. We've been in Libya for a month," I answer.

"I've got to go to Naples to pick up Jackie Cochran," he
explains. Then he stops—obviously he's working out a new
plan. "Chuck, why don't you go to Naples to pick up Jackie and
I'll take your F-86."

"Yes, sir," I answer.

My lieutenants were bug-eyed. You know, I put a two-star
general in my cockpit, start the engine for him, and told those
guys, "Get going. Don't let that old man out of your sight. Get to
full power now before he takes off." Two-star generals don't fly
F-86s ordinarily, but General Boyd was different, and those
guys had just figured it out. I got into Boyd's T-33 and went to
get Jackie in Naples to take her to some big deal in France.

A T-33 is a two-place jet. She's sitting in the back of one
when we leave France to return to Italy. We're on a direct flight
over Switzerland, which is illegal. It's neutral territory, and we
are in a military plane. What I had planned to do was to fly so
high no one need ever know. So much for the secrecy.

Just as we're crossing the border into Switzerland, Jackie
says, "I've got to go to the bathroom."

"Use the goddamn relief tube," I answer, kind of smiling, knowing the military never has been able to get it right for a gal.

"You know they don't work for women," she says.

"Well, that's a personal problem."

"Chuck I've got to go to the bathroom. Land," she says.

We are at about 45,000 feet going over Geneva and she's ordering me to land. I'm smiling.

"Hey, we can't land in Switzerland," I explain. "This is a military plane. These people don't allow military planes on their property."

"Well, I'm going to wet my pants," she says, still insistent.

"Hang on, Jackie," I say, "we'll land in Sorino, in the southern part of the Swiss Alps. It won't look as bad there."

She's bitching and moaning back there. I'm laughing. I let down in Sorino and say to her, "This is going to cost us. There'll be a landing fee."

"I don't care what it costs. I'll pay for it," she says.

The problem was: Sorino didn't have a jet starter unit for a T-33, so I had to land, taxi right up to the front of their operations building, raise the canopy, and let Jackie out of the plane. I couldn't shut down my engines. Guards came out, asked us for ten bucks, and were happy when they saw U.S. dollars. They couldn't believe their eyes when this good-looking blonde gal got out of the plane, went into the bathroom, and simply climbed back into the plane to take off. They were all watching her. A whole mess of them. I was laughing out loud.

Back in the air, I say to her, "Jackie, if you are going to act like a fighter pilot, you've got to live like one."

No answer from the back.

Jackie and I flew into and over other countries together. We took her Lockheed Lodestar to the annual convention of the FAI in '59 when it was held in Russia, the year she was president of the organization, and I copiloted because she knew she'd get herself into trouble flying in strange countries with strange procedures and the possibility of bad weather. She needed me. I had been stationed over there by then and knew the scene. She flew us into Kiev, and believe me, those Soviets were really surprised we made it. An old dirt strip, bad bad rain, heavy, gusting winds, and a crazy Russian navigator. But Jackie could take care of herself.

That plane trip to Moscow in May of '59 wasn't without risks. We wanted to leave on the twelfth. In the long run, it was worth it because of the international aviation rules and regulations we were able to straighten out, but even the insurance company recognized the danger inherent in that flight. My domestic company dropped me and my plane's policy just days before we were to leave. Lloyds of London finally came through for an exorbitant amount of money—figure this in '59 dollars: $6,000 for six weeks of time plus $1.00 for every two minutes of airtime over Russian soil.

I packed everything: twelve tubes of lipstick (a medium red), salt, pepper, a small peppermill with some whole peppercorns, two small watermelons, canned soups, dried fruits, canned crackers as well as canned chicken, and lots of clothes. Oh, and I remember asking Margaret Ann Currlin, my secretary back then, to make sure to pack dental floss, umbrellas, and raincoats. It was a nightmare getting ready on all fronts. Even the passports didn't come easy—and we needed six Russian visas for the six people in our party.

Before crossing into the Soviet Union from Budapest, we were assigned a Russian navigator with the foulest smelling breath imaginable. Garlic. Even from several feet away the garlic was strong enough to knock your socks off. Chuck and I commandeered him into the cabin behind the cockpit. I beat his ears off about the delays and disappointments the Soviets had caused me. I was so irritable.

We had been given permission to land first at Lvov and then proceed over to Kiev for a sight-seeing excursion. Moscow was on the next day's agenda. The city airport of Kiev had been listed as our alternate stop, just a back-up in case of bad weather. And bad weather it was once we were in the air. We're flying an "Aeroflot route" never used by a foreigner before. Chuck tells me that he's just learned that Lvov has only a grass strip 3,000 feet long for landing my big Lockheed with the lucky

13 on its tail. And we have only a few radio frequencies available for our use. It's not going to be easy. And my irritation is still mounting. This navigator, pretending little command of the English language, hangs there behind me, looking pale, worried.

The weather is stinko. We are at 7,000 feet and I see a pass in the mountains through which we should reach Lvov. Mountains on either side reach at least up to 9,000 feet. A big black thunderstorm is straight ahead. Even if we make it to Lvov, the question remains, can we put the plane down on water-logged grass in a driving rain?

Just then the navigator rushes up to hang over my shoulder and breathe in my face. God! Our interpreter tries to catch his nervous drift. He's saying, "Hold! Hold and circle until clearance from the ground." But with few frequencies available to us—Americans—there's not a sound from the ground. This guy grabs the microphone and tries to talk into the wrong side. I wasn't so sure he was who he said he was—a navigator? But if he's not here for navigating, just what is he doing aboard? He changes the frequency, asks us to go to 11,000 feet, above the mountains, shaking the mike, jerking it and reminding me of a scared monkey in a zoo.

We hear some Russian jabbering and this "navigator," who knows no English, suddenly says to me quite clearly, "Get to 13,000 feet." Honestly, I wondered what the Soviets were up to. And what they thought we were up to.

The grass strip at Lvov was completely unsafe for a plane weighing more than 20,000 pounds like mine, and with the rain, the field would have been even more treacherous. Chuck and I decided to give up on Lvov and head toward our alternate, Kiev, but when we told our Russian spy, he practically jumped up and down. He wanted to call Moscow, wanted us to keep circling for hours, wanted to save his own skin, I think. I thought he was going to hit me on the head with the mike.

"Get back there, boy, and strap yourself in right now," I ordered him. I just wasn't much of an international politician at that point. I was too irritated.

Chuck and I locked him out of our cockpit. When we arrived at Kiev, I understood why he was worried. The main runway was out of commission, and I had to put us down on a rather short dirt strip. It wasn't as slippery as grass would have been. Later, the mayor of Kiev told me the runway at Lvov was paved and long. What was even stranger still was the view of Kiev from the air: airports surrounded that city, and I had been forced to land on a dirt strip. My irritation at Russian hospitality remained at an even, unwavering pitch for weeks.

I frightened our navigator to death on the way into Moscow two days later. It was overcast and cold and I was pretty sure I had a couple of thousand feet of ceiling below me as we let down into the air over Moscow. I didn't turn on the de-icers. I let this guy watch the windshield frost over—minute by minute—through 11,000 feet. The guy is sweating it. Chuck is smiling at me. Finally, the ice is so thick that it's whipping off the propellers, beating a tattoo on the sides of the plane. You can hear it. I can see the anxiety in the garlic-lover about to explode.

He screams, "Get to 3,000 feet."

Chuck says calmly, "Want to turn on the de-icers?"

"In a minute," I answer slowly—very slowly.

The navigator is green. I can't get any radio communication with the Moscow tower, and that's when he hands me a list of other frequencies he's been carrying in his pocket all the time.

I taught him a lesson about American women in red lipstick, not orange, not bold red, just a nice American red, that I bet he still hasn't forgotten. And when we landed that day, I put us down smoother than he'll ever experience again in his life. As we deplaned, he looked at me as if he had met the devil herself and it was me. We never saw him during the rest of our doings in Russia.

I was in Russia with an esteemed group of American delegates—Jimmy Doolittle, C. R. Smith, who was head of American Airlines then, people from General Dynamics, and scores of important aviation execs. Speeches, toasts, exhibits, a visit to a Russian aircraft factory (which was soon replaced by a candy company), an air show, a mass parachute jump, and talks with the Russian Aero Club were all on my agenda. There were enough Russian military men and their medals at that conference to sink a supertanker. And they were all abysmally ignorant about the United States of America. They were also deceitful, crazy for power, and jealous of each other. They seemed to like western Scotch whiskey and western cigarettes. And night after night the same banquet food was displayed for guests, who were never given a chance to take a bite. Seriously, I stood in countless crowded gatherings where chest-high tables of food, looking more than vaguely familiar from the very night before, remained untouched while speeches, lack of silverware, and hordes of dignitaries kept us from getting too close to the tables. The rule was "bottoms up" at every toast, and the same cold fish kept coming out from the kitchens over and over again.

Something strange occurred in Bulgaria, strange enough to interrupt our meandering schedule—Turkey, Italy, Spain had been on our agenda—and head us toward home sooner than planned.

Russian authorities had promised us permission to cross Bulgaria, a Soviet state, and head on into Turkey, where I knew some of the authorities. When we were ready to leave Bulgaria, though, the authorities suddenly changed their tune.

Just a case of crossed signals, Chuck and I said to each other, trying to rid ourselves of the anxiety. But we couldn't shake the feelings. And we didn't like the smell of things. So we decided to go fishing and not in Turkey. A couple of days in Iceland, fishing for salmon cured my case of espionage jitters. The ice cap, the snowy mountains, glaciers, blue lakes, and ice floes were awesome as well as the salmon we caught and ate.

CHUCK KEEPS A DIARY

1961

Chuck Yeager

There was nothing available for Jackie to fly after she had that opportunity in the F-86. I left Edwards Air Force Base in 1954 to go to Germany, and up until 1960 or so she never had the right opportunities. We kept in touch, running into each other, or else I'd get messages from her through friends in high places— ambassadors, generals, people like that. "Tell Colonel Yeager I'll be in Madrid on such and such a day. Or tell Colonel Yeager I'll be in Paris." These people would track me down and I'd fly to see her in an F-100 or something. Sometimes I'd have an empty seat in a two-place jet and I'd take her for a ride.

I remember landing at a British base and asking her if she wanted to go to Spain with me. "I've got the seat but if you want to go, ship your trunks via commercial air," I told her. She always had a baggage problem, always loved flying jets. She'd get a charge out of seeing how we hit tankers and had she been trained, she would have loved to have been exposed to combat. But Jackie knew combat was no place for a woman. She had traveled around the Pacific. She knew what the score was, what conditions in those war camps had been. Hell, her opposition to

298

women fighting wars had nothing to do with moral issues. If I were a soldier running a prisoner of war camp, and you were my prisoner and a gal, I'd romance you every time I had the urge. Jackie knew this about men. It's that simple and she didn't want to see women ever exposed to those kinds of conditions. She wasn't dumb. She had a tremendous amount of old-fashioned instinct and she could discipline herself to fit a situation.

She did it in the F-86, in the T-38 jet records, and later in the F-104 for Lockheed.

From August 1, 1961, until October twelfth that year, we worked together nearly every day at Edwards. Past fifty years old then, she still wanted to fly those fast planes and had gotten Northrop to hire her as a company pilot. Norair, a division of Northrop, had built T-38s for the Air Force. They leased one back from us for Jackie to fly.

In 1961, Jacqueline Cochran set eight major speed records in a Northrop T-38, including speed over a 1000 kilometer closed course, 1023.01 km/hr (639.38 mph), distance in a straight line, 2387.82 kilometers (1492.39 miles), and sustained 17,090.68 meters in altitude (56,071.80 feet high).

—National Air and Space Museum, Smithsonian Institution, 1981

Chuck gave me the notes he had made almost daily during our work on the T-38, one of Northrop's finest. The diary says more about my work even in its clipped format, full of aviation jargon, names, places, people, and brief bits of praise from the greatest pilot in the world than I could ever conjure up by myself.

August 1 Jackie arrives at Edwards in Lodestar. Moves into Lt. Colonel Burt Rowen's house.

August 2 Introduced to Northrop people at 9 am. Got cockpit time and made one hour flight in backseat with Lou Nelson at 11:30. At 3 pm taken to altitude chamber where mask was fitted and a run in the chamber takes her to 41,000 feet. Okay.

August 3 Call from Pentagon about Jackie flying. No clearance yet....

August 4 All T-38s grounded for canopy checks. Clearance for Jackie arrives. I flew with her. Trouble with earphones. Fine touch and go landings. Looks OK. She flies Lodestar to Indio for weekend.

August 7 Jackie returns to Edwards 9:30 am. Takeoff 11:30 for flight to Yuma. Flew first leg of 1000 km. 4 touch and go. Good flight. Return to Edwards. T-38 grounded because of gear-up landing at Randolph Air Base. Communications good between cockpits.

August 8 T-38 still grounded. Held meeting at 1:00 pm for all people concerned about records. Yeager, Guy Emminger, H. E. Gardner, Jack Farley, Northrop, Larry Green, DeWitt, Keith Markham, Maj. MacConnell. Lieut. Col. Smith, Walt Pegee. Got a call from Bert Rhine on barographs.

August 9 Called Gen. Bradley about grounded aircraft. Doubt in Northrop's mind about leased T-38 being ready for records by 17th. 12:30 pm aircraft ungrounded. Two flights with Jackie. Climb to 40,000 feet. 1.2 Mach speed, stalls, shuts down one engine and restarts. Four touch and go landings done very well. Second flight afterburner takeoff practice run on 15–25 kilometer course. Two landings. No trouble. Dinner at Jackie's (steak) with Andy (Bud Anderson), El (Eleanor Anderson), Burt, and myself.

August 10 Skip records this week. Will try 15–25 kilometer record on 24th or 25th. In Jackie's first flight she climbs to 40,000 and chases Cmdr. Peterson in X-15. Good altitude control on runs.

August 11 Flew two 15–25 km with radar. 4 touch and go landings. Good flight. Second flight without radar. West-east run. Jackie departs for Indio. I drive Ford station wagon home to bring Glennis back to Edwards for party Saturday night.

August 14 One flight on 15–25. Radar OK. Leak in static system and left engine leaking oil.

August 15 She looks ready for solo. First solo flight takeoff at 2:30 pm runs 15–25 without radar. I chased her in F-100. Very good flight pattern though a little big. Jackie needs a little work on radio position reporting in landing pattern. General Branch and Col. Hall meet Jackie after solo. She has dinner with General Ascani.

August 16 One flight—15–25 kilometer run—course and heading good. Little altitude trouble on turn but Jackie is okay in trap, finishing 15–25. Flew at .9 Mach. Weather was good and all check points were visible. Good landing.

August 17 Climb to 36,000 feet to start 1000 km run but ran into broken clouds east of desert center and decided to abort the run. Made a run on the 15–25 km and returned to base. Jackie is a little mixed up on the downwind leg for runway 22 and lined up on 24 of south base. Should concentrate a little more. Second flight was good. Takeoff and climb to 36,000 feet and lit the afterburner 40 miles out. Went through the trap at 1.1 Mach. Average speed was 747 mph. Run looked good. Good landing.

August 18 One flight today on 15–25 course. Average speed 742 mph. Very good altitude and heading control. Same trouble with her pattern. Rolled out 30 degrees on down wind. Knows aircraft quite well and stays ahead of it. Departed for Los Angeles to pick up Floyd.

August 21 Jackie flew one flight today on 1000 km course. Visibility on course good so all landmarks were observed. News releases readied.

August 22 Flew aircraft on test hop to 51,000 feet. Left afterburner out at 45,000 feet; right afterburner at 50,000. Speed 15–25 km at 36,000, 1.3 Mach each way, average speed 863 mph and finished with 450 pounds of fuel in left tank, 550 in right. Very good flight. She had no trouble with runway line up on downwind leg.

August 23 One flight today. Tried to get F-100 for chase but radio is inoperative. Timers arrive and hold meeting for all concerned with record attempt.

August 24 Big day! First solo in production. Jackie took off in Northrop T-38 for 15–25 record attempt at 9:00 am. I chased in F-100. Flew good pattern and lit afterburners 50 miles from west outer marker. Jackie held good altitude through trap and made a good procedure turn. Lit afterburner 40 miles out on return run and nailed the altitude down perfect. Average speed was 844 mph. All the officials were pleased and the record was confirmed. One down and nine to go.

August 25 Held press conference at Northrop-Air (Norair) for Jackie. Jimmy Allen and Charles Barr emceed and it lasted from 10 am to 11:30. CBS filmed considerable amount of Jackie in cockpit. Flew one flight in T-38. 1000 km at 30,000 feet. Course time was 58 minutes, average speed 637 mph.

OTHER VOICES:

Charles Barr
(NORTHROP PUBLIC RELATIONS EXECUTIVE)

I remember the day distinctly. Jackie was making runs in Northrop's twin jet T-38 and her attempts were being clocked by the NAA—the National Aeronautic Association. It was a very hot day, just as it usually is out there in the desert, and there were press people who wanted to take her picture sitting in the cockpit. It wasn't going to be feasible for her to get out of the plane and go into the ladies' room to fix her face and hair, so she asked for a few moments before they lined up to get close-ups. Someone brought her a little red parasol and she sat there in the plane with this umbrella, putting her makeup on, combing her hair.

You have to imagine how hot it was out there. She finally got out of the airplane, and her flight suit was soaking wet from top to bottom. There was a great deal of strain making some of those flights. The shortest circular run, 15–25 kilometers, was very difficult to do at high speed. I believe she went the fastest it has ever been flown. And there is a real limitation on how accurately you can be making that kind of flight in a high speed plane. The heat wasn't the only reason she was perspiring heavily. The strain of all that added to her.

Northrop had a large staff out there at Edwards, and Jackie was there to show what a high performance airplane could do, to set those records for us. We were engaged in making a plane that was even better than the T-38. It would be the fighter version of the T-38, or the F-5, and we wanted to market that F-5. The records in the trainer would help. Eventually we sold F-5s in large quantities. Jimmy Allen was the director of the company then.

August 28 Flew the 500 kilometer this afternoon. Climb to 40,000 feet, light afterburner at the pylon and accelerate to 1.1 Mach. Cut back afterburner nozzle to 50 percent and hold 1.1 the entire flight. The fuel worked out very close at the end. Good landing from a straight-in approach.

August 29 Weather forces a cancellation for 1000 km run. Flew 500 again and had a perfect run... Average speed of 691 mph. Jackie made a good landing from a straight-in approach.

August 30 Northrop T-38 out of commission for fuel tank repair. One flight in F-l00 to check out pylons at Beatty, Nevada, Lone Pine, Calif. Jackie and Floyd to have dinner with General Branch. Their household goods arrive today. Meeting with National Aeronautic Association (NAA) timers.

August 31 Jackie makes a practice run on the 500 km course in the T-38. Fuel system checks out okay. Official run is flown at 1:30 p.m. and Jackie cuts it a little close, landing with 0 fuel in left side and only 100 pounds in the right. Average speed: 659.4 mph. I go dove hunting with Gen. Branch. Back Sept. 3.

September 5 Jackie on one flight at 2:00 pm on 1000 km course.

September 6 Jackie took off at 11:00 am for 1000 km record attempt. The beacon had slipped frequency and radar lost her on her turn. Flight was aborted. Tried again at 2:30 pm but she cut inside the start pylon at 2,000 feet and aborted. 500 km scheduled for tomorrow. Lots of static about timers. Jackie on phone until wee hours of the night. Tony Mahlman (an old friend of JC's) is coming tomorrow.

OTHER VOICES:

Jack Farley

(FORMER TEST PILOT AND BASE ADMINISTRATOR FOR NORTHROP AT PALMDALE-EDWARDS AIR FORCE BASE)

I was concerned about the timers because we were putting so much effort into the flights, and if a timer missed one marker, we would disqualify everything. These timers have to visually spot the plane and it's pretty hard to get all the people working together on something like those records. I told Jackie, "We are working with civilians, and out there in civilian life this kind of accuracy isn't asked for. Besides, we're sending these people out into the wilds to watch. They are separated from each other. This could be a big problem."

Chuck and I were at her house there in Edwards and we were discussing all this over Scotch or something. It's late. It's been a long day and she says, "Wait a minute. I'm going to get Tony Mahlman on the phone in New York. He can help."

"It's eight o' clock our time, Jackie, it's got to be late back in New York," I tell her. She doesn't pay any attention to me. She dials and says, "Tony, we've got some trouble here. Get on the next plane to California and get here." And he did.

The whole time I was there at her house I kept saying to Jackie, "Listen, I've got to get home. My wife will be worried." By this time it's nine o'clock and I hadn't called home yet.

Jackie says, "Oh, don't worry about Shirley, Jack. I know Shirley. I'll take care of her."

When I finally left about ten o'clock, she says, "Here, take this with you, ring your doorbell, and give it to Shirley with my apologies." It was one of the largest bottles of her famous perfume.

I liked Jackie Cochran.

"Bud" Anderson

(LIFETIME FRIEND AND
FELLOW AVIATOR TO CHUCK YEAGER)

When Jackie was flying the T-38, I chased her around the pattern a couple of times. She was a good pilot and she sure didn't let her age bother her. She wasn't young then. In fact, one night over at her house discussing problems, I remember being there when she laughed and said, "God, I must be pretty old to have accomplished all this." She really didn't know how old she was, never having known her birthday. She did have a big ego, but she could be straightforward like that. We were always being invited down to her ranch for weekends and parties.

September 7 Re-run 500 km. Good run. Observers miss her at Lone Pine, Calif.

September 8 A good 1000 km flown today with a speed of 642 mph. Jackie gave a talk to 400 officers at a "dining-in" at McClellan AFB about trip to U.S.S.R. She went to New York for NAA meeting.

September 13 Jackie landed at 4:15 am. We flew the T-38 on the closed course distance. Takeoff at 2:15 pm and climbed to 40,500 feet for initial cruise. Fuel checked out very good. I was amazed at the way Jackie handled the aircraft at high altitude. Everything looked good on the entire flight. Landed a little short of oil in left engine. Weather was bad over Kingman, Arizona. Cruise climbed at 96% rpm and .87 IMN to 46,500 at end of run. We were in the air 2 ½ hours.

September 14 We tried cold fuel today. It gave us an additional 170 pounds at the end. Was a very good flight. Held meeting with NAA people about tomorrow's run.

September 15 Flew closed course distance for record today and had a good run. Jackie did an excellent job even with bad weather. I chased her in an F-100 all the way.

September 16 Flew today with Jackie and exceeded 49,000 feet. Landed at Palmdale where Jackie will depart for point to point record.

September 18 Jackie took off from Palmdale at 10:00 am for attempt to set records from points to points. I took off from Edwards in an F-l00 with 275-gallon drop tanks. During climb Jackie reported rough engine and poor performance. Also the fuel flow inoperative. Jackie returned to the field where I finally found her takeoff flaps were still down. Also her navigation lights and beacon were on. I was rather disappointed. She's a little cocky in the airplane. She landed back there at Palmdale with 1500 pounds of fuel in each side and made a good heavy-weight landing. The aircraft is refueled and another takeoff was made at 12:30 pm. Everything went smooth on this flight. We ran into clouds at the edge of Utah which lasted until the edge of Cheyenne, Wyo. Clear the rest of the way. Jackie landed with 250 pounds of fuel in each side. Made a beautiful landing and turned off after a 4000 foot ground roll. Bob White returned the F-l00 to Edwards.

September 29 Edwards AFB. Flew the aircraft today to include a practice run on the 100 kilometer course. Jackie did a fine job at 1.2 Mach. Looks like this will be a piece of cake. Aircraft was okay. Average speed 742 mph. Jackie was in the altitude chamber today with the pressure suit (CSU 4/P). Everything went fine and maximum altitude was 65,000 feet. This was the first time a woman was taken up in the chamber in a pressure suit. CSU 4/P was the type of suit.

October 3 Tried a run today but weather moved in from 26,000 to 37,000 feet. Very good landing. Airspeed system iced up and Jackie stalled the aircraft at 35,000 feet. Made a no-sweat recovery.

October 4 Ran the 100 kilometer for record at 1 pm. The first run wasn't too good but had an average speed of 763 mph. A pylon was cut so the run was voided. Second run was 740 mph. Very poor. Another flight was made at 5:30 pm but both runs were pretty sorry. Jackie was a little late on all of the corrections. Jackie doesn't seem to be in too good a physical or mental state.

October 5 I flew in the backseat of the T-38 with Jackie on a practice run of the 100 kilometer. I talked her around the course 2 times with a little help on the stick. First run was 782 mph and second run was 787 mph. I think I know what has been Jackie's trouble on the 100 km. During the flight as she starts gaining a little altitude, she lets off on the back pressure on the stick to stop climbing and this causes the turn to become larger. Jackie and I spent two hours talking this over. She finally understands that in order to fly a constant circle, if the airplane starts to climb, she must increase the angle of bank and let off on the back pressure a little and let the nose drop but still hold the same rate of turn. This is what makes the 100 km so hard to fly. Jackie still has a touch of the flu.

October 6 Jackie felt a little better today and after a delay caused by communication trouble, she flew one of the most perfect runs that has been flown on the 100 km course. She learned her lesson well. The record speed was 784 mph. She held 1/4 mile outside of the course the entire trip. I was very pleased to watch the reaction of the timers and radar people. I think they expected another 10 or 15 trips like the F-105 tricks. She made one hell of a good flight.

October 9 Jackie flew the N-156 today. I chased in the F-100 with Lou Nelson in the back. She did a beautiful job running stalls on the airplane and ended up by making a landing on the lake bed and deploying the drag chute.

October 10 Colonel Anderson and I flew the T-38 and everything checked out okay. Maximum altitude was 55,000 feet with no blowouts. Jackie and I started a flight with the CSU 4/P suit, but since she had no vent air, it became too hot and we aborted. We fitted Jackie with an MC-3 suit and the mission was flown OK. Maximum altitude was 55,000 feet. Good landing.

October 12 Jackie took off at 9 am in the T-38 using afterburner. Bud Anderson and I chased her in the F-100. It was an excellent flight with everything working perfect. Jackie entered the course at 55,800 feet at .93 Mach and accelerated to radar. At the end of the run Jackie pulled up to 56,800 and then pushed over. She cut the right afterburner at 52,000 feet and the left one at 50,000 feet. At 12,000 feet she removed the face piece from her pressure suit and made a perfect landing on the lake bed.

Northrop-Air (Norair) presented Miss Cochran with one dozen yellow roses.

A very tender ending to a wonderful program and a fitting token to a wonderful lady—a pilot who gave Norair much more than they expected.

—Charles E. Yeager

I am often asked what my sensations were when flying at Mach 1 or beyond way up there, about ten miles above the earth's surface. Well, I've got to admit that you are too intent on the job at hand to have any particular impressions of the moments. There isn't any fear. There's a confidence you feel. There's a great alertness about what is happening to your plane and what has to be done about it. At sonic speed it takes less than a minute to reach the ground from the start of a vertical power dive. That means the earth is moving toward the nose of your plane very fast indeed. There's a really warm feeling of accomplishment and I always want to find Floyd fast.

There's another feeling, however, one of humility and trust. I am a strong believer in God. I'm not a fatalist, because I really believe that God helps those who help themselves. But up there things come into proportion. The people on the earth have disappeared. You have left them behind you and are on your own, impressed with the immensity of space—so close to space and those noonday stars, convinced there must be a divine order of things.

On October 18, 1962, President John F. Kennedy presented to Jacqueline Cochran her 14th Harmon Trophy.
—National Air and Space Museum, Smithsonian Institution, 1981

STARFIGHTER

1963–64

On May 4, 1964, flying a Lockheed 104 jet Starfighter, I established a women's international speed record over a 15 kilometer straightaway course of 1429.297 miles per hour. Such international records are always supervised and controlled by the Fédération Aéronautique Internationale which has fifty-eight member nations, and general offices in Paris, France. I was president for a time.

On June 1, 1964, in the same plane I set a new international speed record around a circular closed 100 kilometer (about 62 ½ miles) course of 1303.241 miles per hour.

On June 3, in that same superfast plane, I set the women's international speed record about the 500 kilometer closed course (about 312 miles) of 1127.394 miles per hour.

Tony Levier
(CHIEF OF LOCKHEED TEST PILOTS)

When Jackie wanted to break the world's speed records in 1963, she had to come to Lockheed because we had the fastest airplanes in the world. I helped her get started, hired her as a pilot in my program, and even gave her a pay rate. I was her boss.

"Tony," she says to me, "I want Chuck Yeager to be here."

"Jackie, he can't. We are a commercial firm and he's in the military. He can help, but he can't direct your program."

"But Chuck and I get along so well," she argues.

"Chuck Yeager can help, but he's got a job over there with the Air Force and we're civilian. Don't worry, Jackie," I tell her. "You're going to have the time of your life. I'm going to set it all up. If anything at all doesn't suit your fancy, if anything upsets you, you come to me and I'll correct it. Is that fair enough?"

"Fair enough," she says.

Well, I took my group of 104 pilots aside, into my office, and I said to them, "We are going to have Jackie Cochran around here. She's here to check out this airplane and we are all going to make her life as pleasant as possible. I don't want you guys so much as looking cross-eyed at her. Do you understand?"

There was a lot of grumbling in the room, a lot of mumbling about an old dame trying to do their jobs. They were all young guys and ex-military fighter pilots and put on the whole bit, the chauvinistic routines.

"I'll have your hides if I hear anything bad," I told them.

I selected "Snake" Reeves as her trainer, the best pilot for the job, and I got the ground school pilots and engineers into the act too. "She's the only one in this class now," I warned them.

Right off the bat she just fell in love with the whole damn bunch of us and the feeling was mutual. She rented a home in Lancaster, California, near our base, and cooked every bloody working day. Jackie Cochran would fix us a picnic lunch—fried chicken and stuff like that—and bring it to the base in a great big wicker basket. She was a great cook and we'd have everything. I used to make sure I was around for those lunches, and sometimes it meant driving up from Lockheed's offices in Burbank, California.

But it wasn't just the cooking that made the difference with those men. Jackie went right into this Starfighter program and broke records that aren't easy to break. A lot of men have never been able to break her records, even today. There were military pilots who liked to pooh-pooh her, but they couldn't fly as well as she could. It was very steep flying, being directed by a controller on the ground, going around an imaginary course by radar, and in order to break the records you had to be right in there, skimming these pylons—imaginary pylons in the sky—curls of smoke, that's all they are. Jackie had to follow directions, tighten up on the turns, holding, holding, losing, and keeping that plane in the right altitude, not yoyoing higher or lower. You had to come out of the course a little higher than where you went in. Anyway, those circular courses were big too. God, they were big and the altitude had to be down low. You flew right down there near the ground—1,000 feet or so off. Going into the trap, entering the course, you had to come in just so, make a turn, and fly very precisely or you would run out of fuel—not to mention missing the record mark. The next year she came back and broke some of her own times flying an Air Force single cockpit 104 that had just come off the production line. That one had a little more fuel capacity and was a little faster. She was also able to have Chuck work with her because of the more clear-cut Air Force connection.

But my men in the 104 Starfighter program in '63 ended up having a lot of respect for that woman. She was demanding, but understandably demanding, and she could be very kindly. She liked pilots, especially hot pilots. It didn't hurt to know Jackie Cochran either. We all had such good times at her ranch meeting senators, bigshots, even the President of the United States.

I was the first person to fly the Starfighter. It's not hard to fly if you know what you are doing. You had to understand the plane.

Major General Fred Ascani

I flew that bird, the F-104 Starfighter. It's scary and fast. Tony Levier has a tendency to play down the danger. But if you want to get an idea of how dangerous that plane is, you should dig into

the German Air Force's accident records for the 104 and count
the fatalities. They attribute them to pilot error, but it wasn't the
case. I think they lost something like eighty-five F-104s in the
first 1 ½ years of flying them. Eighty-five? That's more than
two killed a week during some weeks. They blamed it on the
pilot, but the plane had a nasty tendency to pitch up under certain conditions and there wasn't much you could do to save
yourself under those conditions. There was no wing area there
to recover. Tony, being the naturally great pilot he is, would
pooh-pooh the dangers, but the F-104 was a tricky airplane to
fly. I took it to Mach 2 and I guess that's the fastest I've ever
gone. You had to be extra careful in the slower speed ranges and
getting it back onto the ground. It wasn't, and still isn't, a very
forgiving airplane. It will not forgive a pilot the slightest error
and you get into fatally hot water so fast. Dangerous airplane.

But I think I gave Jackie the F-104 challenge at a banquet up
at Edwards when we were celebrating her success at breaking
the sound barrier. Pancho Barnes was invited. And Jackie
Cochran was the guest of honor at the officer's club. It could
have been a disastrous combination because the two hated each
other.

We were sitting at a U-shaped table, with Jackie on one end
of the U and Pancho on the other. They glared daggers at each
other the entire evening. Jackie didn't like Pancho because she
believed Pancho was the most uncouth woman alive. And she
did have a mouth on her you couldn't believe possible in a
woman. Pancho didn't like Jackie, perhaps, because of Chuck.
Chuck was friendly with both of them.

Anyway, as I sat there that night at dinner, I decided to
make a little toast to Jackie Cochran. It rhymed. I can't remember it word for word now, but the essence was: "Here's to
Jackie, who pierced Mach 1, and to the day Mach 2 is done."

Jackie Cochran was so delighted with what she had done
that week that I felt a little guilty about planting such a notion for
the future. But not too bad.

The fact is: I flew the Starfighter a distance that would have
taken me around the world at the equator. What I was trying to
do was to familiarize myself with the flight characteristics of the

plane in 1963. To know it well was crucial. Some of my practice flights were made with movie cameras mounted in the cockpit to give me Mach numbers and the temperature of the engine. My flights enabled engineers at the General Electric power plant to evaluate the plane about what its optimum maximum speed actually was. That was my purpose really. And I got more speed than anyone expected. I pushed that engine to temperatures that had been prohibited by operating manuals. The engine inlet temperature had been a limiting factor on the speed.

When a certain maximum temperature is reached in any jet plane, a red light goes on in the cockpit and you've got to pull back on the power. In my forty flights in 1964 in the F-104G, I exceeded the allowed temperature of 121 degrees centigrade. And in the record flying, I got as high as 151 degrees centigrade when the full afterburners were lit. The chase planes couldn't keep up with me, even Chuck Yeager's.

People don't listen up when we talk about speed these days. They are so used to discussions about satellites traveling through space at speeds up to 17,000 miles per hour and rocket planes like the X-15 going 4,000 mph, reaching altitudes of 300,000 feet above earth, that my speed flights might look pale by comparison. But you've got to realize that missiles, satellites, and rocket-powered vehicles have only a minute or two of power to shoot them to those high speeds. After that the vehicle is flying as a result of inertia. Flying an airplane 1,430 miles an hour for 47 seconds, or three minutes, or 16 ½ minutes and even longer makes for rough, hairy rides. Real satisfaction came from those accomplishments.

I remember thinking about the leading edges on the wings of that airplane. They were so sharp they could cut you if you happened to lean against one. As sharp as the blade of an ax.

It would touch ground at 225 miles per hour, and to slow down, I had to eject a parachute from the tail of the plane. You had to keep the power up to 92% coming in for a landing until the wheels touched ground. If the power failed when you were still in the air, the sink rate of the ship was about 11,000 feet per minute. You'd be dead. The wings were only seven feet long. It was more like a manned—or womaned—rocket. But it sure could perform.

Making the plane was big business. It was manufactured not only here in the United States but under license by Lockheed; they put it together in six foreign countries. By the fall of '65 international production on the Starfighter put dollar figures into the billion range. At peak production there were more than 100,000 people involved in production. The plane was going to be a multi-mission fighter-interceptor and it would work for Germany, Japan, Canada, Belgium, the Netherlands, Italy, Norway, Turkey, Greece, nationalist China, Pakistan, Denmark, and Spain as well as the U.S.

Picture in your mind a rectangular tunnel, 300 feet high, a quarter of a mile wide, and extending 20 miles long through the air at an altitude of 35,000 feet. I had to fly through that tunnel at top speed without touching a side. There were no walls to see but radar and ground instruments let me know my mistakes immediately. Up there at 35,000 feet the temperature would be about 45 degrees below zero. Not pleasant but perfect for what I was doing. Inside the plane you are hot because of the friction of speeding through air like that. The cockpit was air-conditioned, but when you descend, things happen so fast the plane's air-cooling system can't keep up with it. I was always hot and perspiring back on the ground.

The 100 kilometer closed course was so damn difficult. Imagine an absolutely circular racetrack, about a quarter of a mile wide, on the ground with an inner fence exactly 63 miles long. Now, in your mind's eye, leave the track and get into the air at 35,000 feet. Fly it without touching the fence in the slightest. It's tricky because if you get too far away from the inner fence, trying not to touch, you won't make the speed you need to break the record. And if you get too close, you'll disqualify yourself.

Eyes are glued to that instrument panel. Ears can hear the voice of the space-positioning officer. You are dealing in fractions of seconds. And your plane isn't flying in flat position. It's tipped over to an 80-degree bank to compensate for the circle. That imaginary inner fence may be to your left, but you don't head your plane left. That'd lose you altitude. Instead, you pull the nose up a bit and because the plane is so banked over, you move closer to the inside fence. You turn.

But I had been flying these measured kilometer courses for so many years. Way back in the forties I made a 100 kilometer record that still stands in both men's and women's categories for propeller driven planes.

If I had to choose the most exciting adventure I've ever had in the air, I'm sure I couldn't. But flying the Starfighter ranks right up there.

During 1963 and 1964, Jackie set several new records in a Lockheed F-104G. In the spring of 1963, Jackie set two speed records: 15–25 kilometer (9–12 mile) course, 2036.974 km/hr (1273.109 mph); 100 kilometer (62 mile) course, 1923.897 km/hr (1203.686 mph). In 1964, she broke three more records in the F-104G, two of them her own: 15–25 kilometer (9–12 mile) course, 2286.875 km/hr (1429.297 mph); 100 kilometer (62 mile) course, 2083 km/hr (1302 mph); 500 kilometer (311 mile) course, 1816 km/hr (1135 mph).

 —National Air and Space Museum, Smithsonian Institution, 1981

SPACE FOR WOMEN
IN SPACE

"All this talk about brains and dames in space is bunk. If there had been a scientist on my flight, I don't think we would have gotten him back. As for the ladies, to date there have been no women—and I say absolutely zero women—who have qualified to take part in our space program." This was in 1963. And that was the way Gordon Cooper, one of our astronauts, expressed himself.

Of course no woman had qualified, Cooper. No woman had been allowed to test her mettle against the men up to that point. And of course, no scientist would have gone up with a Mercury astronaut because the capsule had room for only one person. No scientist would have gone along with Orville Wright on his maiden voyage there at Kitty Hawk, North Carolina, either. But that was no reason to assume that passenger planes wouldn't exist one day in the future. One swallow does not a summer make. And women wouldn't be left behind in the space race for very long.

I had every intention of following my high performance aircraft adventures with a trip into space. So I got myself teamed up with my good friend Randy Lovelace, M.D., working at the Lovelace Clinic in Albuquerque, New Mexico, to test women for astronaut abilities. I also got appointed as a consultant to NASA space chief James Webb.

Maggie Miller

Just for the heck of it Jackie put herself into the same tests—
medical and emotional—that they gave the astronauts back then
in the '60s. Then, she had a whole program set up with Randy
Lovelace, designed to prove just how capable women were. She
and Mr. Odlum put up the seed money to start all the space medical research in the United States.

Every time there was a space thing happening, she was right
there glued to the news reports. Right after NASA had successfully completed their moon shot, she received a letter from them
saying that a small piece of moon geography had been dedicated
in her name. I couldn't believe it. She just filed away the letter.

Back in 1960 Randy Lovelace and I went through a list of the
99s, the prestigious women pilots organization, and invited
members to become part of an aerospace medical experiment.
The first step in weeding out unsuitable male applicants to the
space program had been a medical test, so Dr. Lovelace and I
believed it would be interesting to put women through the exact
same tests. And we did. I covered their travel and maintenance
costs and Dr. Lovelace and his staff did the rest. Twenty women
pilots responded enthusiastically and twelve made the grade.

Jerrie Cobb, Mary Funk, Rhea Hurrle, Mrs. Philip Hart, the
wife of Senator Hart of Michigan, identical twins Jan and
Marion Dietrich—these were just a few of the first group of
women to become part of aerospace medical history in our program. That women would be just as good astronauts as men was
something we wanted to prove and we'd prove it on private
foundation funding if that's what it took. In addition to the thorough medical check-up, we tested the women in response to
various stresses. One was the tilt-table test in which the candidate was tilted on a table, held at about a 60-degree angle while
pulse, respiration, and blood pressure were taken down. The

efficiency of the vascular system can be checked in this way. Any abnormalities in blood vessel function are immediately apparent on the tilt table. Then there were endurance tests. They pedaled bicycles uphill, for instance, while we measured and watched. *Life* magazine did a feature on the program.

No applicant was obligated to proceed into any future program. The point was to prove that women, while physically slighter, would not be disadvantaged by their size or strength for space travel. In fact, size should have been a positive determining factor when you considered the size of those little capsules. It was a launching pad for women and we were anxious to have it succeed.

After a testing period at the Lovelace Clinic in Albuquerque, New Mexico, candidates were to proceed to Pensacola, Florida, where the program would move one step further in a Navy medical laboratory. That's when NASA, in the midst of the Mercury space flight program, put the cabosh on our women's astronaut program. And that's also why I ended up testifying before a congressional committee about whether or not women were being discriminated against by the National Air and Space Administration (NASA).

Yes, they were discriminating, but not directly, I said. NASA never did deny women entry at first. What they did was to limit candidates to applicants who had experience as jet test pilots (and what woman except me could claim that on her resume) and to individuals with heavy engineering backgrounds and certain age brackets. The age factor eliminated me immediately.

Women were not eliminated because they were women, by any means, and I told the investigating committee so. But there was also no reason to stop the medical research on women surviving in space either. I was sorry to see it end that way because we could have offered valuable findings at little expense and little cost to the astronaut program back then. The committee was worried that women in the program would slow down the race into space. There could be no further involvement by the Navy's Pensacola operation.

Congressman George Miller from California was chairman of the House Space Aeronautics Committee then, and we became great friends. Miller asked me to write a report on the space program and I told him I'd do it if he promised not to put it in his file number 13—what I used to call my wastebasket. He laughed.

I used to think that it was ridiculous of our government to take seven men, our first seven astronauts, put them in an expensive public relations basket for seven years, and spend a fortune on them without preparing the basis for a much wider-based space program. NASA needed a much wider outlook. They needed more scientists, medical doctors, astronomers, and a whole array of people on which to build. They didn't have it then. Miller was fascinated with my ideas.

"Jackie," he says to me one day after studying my thesis, "I think I'd better hire you as my assistant."

"Well, I'd be honored to work with you, Congressman, but I'm not for hire. I'm kind of busy." I was about to sell my cosmetics company to a larger company. Floyd was pushing me to do so, and he was right, I couldn't handle the high pressure of the beauty industry long distance any longer. I'd stay on as a consultant, but that was it. They could have my name but not much of me.

My interest in space doings has always been keen. Back in 1953 I was asked by a committee headed by Jimmy Doolittle to help commemorate the first powered flight by man up at the United Nations. Doolittle and his team wanted me to make some predictions then about space, who would orbit first: the Russians or the Americans.

My talk took four minutes, and having seen those Delta monsters over on Soviet tarmacs, I told them the communists would put a satellite into orbit before us. If they had as much thrust as I had seen in 1950, I knew doggone well that somebody over there would put it together and into orbit.

I remember a luncheon Lyndon Johnson threw to honor some sergeant who had volunteered for a space research program. They put this poor guy in isolation for weeks and weeks to learn from his reactions. They were trying to simulate conditions in outer space. There were going to be some other men there from Congress who were on the space committees, and Lyndon knew how I'd love such an affair.

"You come to my Senate office first, Miss Jackie," he says. "I'll take you myself." He was in the Senate at the time, so it's got to be about 1958, and it was just like Lyndon to offer his hand.

The luncheon was in the Senate dining room and there were 250 men and one woman. On Lyndon's left was the Secretary of Defense. On his right, there was me. I looked down at my plate and wondered what was going on.

The meal consisted of steak and salad and we were to start right off with the main course, to move the proceedings right along.

Leaning over to Lyndon, I say, "Since when have you fallen in love with Russia?" I thought he knew something I didn't know for a change.

"What are you talking about?" he asks.

"Well, that's a map of Russia," I explain, pointing to my steak.

"No it's not," he insists. "These steaks have all been cut and shaped to the state of Texas."

"Look again, Lyndon," I say.

Sure enough, the steaks were all upside down on the plates and when you turn a map of Texas upside down, it looks a lot like Russia.

Lyndon got up out of his seat, came around the table, and turned my steak around. He started walking around the tables, turning steaks to look like Texas.

"Jackie tells me that this steak looks like Russia and I'm telling you that it's supposed to look like Texas," he says. "I want you all to turn it around before you eat it."

Airplanes like the X-1 and the X-15 made space exploration possible in this country from a research point of view. And yet, the men who flew those airplanes 50 miles into space hadn't even been considered astronauts. That made me angry and I decided to use my friendship with Lyndon Johnson to do something about it. He was vice-president at the time. And I was in Washington, D.C., on business for George Washington University, where I was a member of the board of directors. I called Johnson's office early one morning on a whim, more than a particular plan. Lyndon got right on the phone.

"I've got something to see you about," I say.

"Well, come right over," he says, startling me with his lack of formality.

"I can't. I'm still in bed," I explain.

"Well, I wish I were there with you," he says, joking. "When you are ready, come on over."

I met with him later that morning and after we chitchatted about Floyd and Lady Bird, I said to him, "I've come to ask you to do something that must be done."

"Anything you ask me to do, I'll do," he says.

"Now, wait a minute, Lyndon, I haven't explained what it is yet. Don't be so quick to agree."

"What is it?" he asks, intrigued by now.

"I want you to give three men astronaut wings—three men who aren't technically part of NASA's astronaut program—three men who have moved our space program way up there because of their accomplishments."

He wanted to know all about these men and what they had been doing out at Edwards Air Force Base. Then I explained to Lyndon that the boundaries of space had yet to be defined, that NASA had no lock or key on the research, and that others were working mighty hard—so hard that they deserved some formal recognition. He agreed immediately and put his staff at my disposal.

He'd always laugh good-naturedly at the way I approached this kind of project, but he was 100 percent behind me. "Jackie, go to it," he said to me that day. And I did. We even flew their wives to Washington, D.C., for the award and made sure the director of NASA, James Webb, was there for the occasion.

It was just too bad that the Vietnam War played such havoc in Lyndon's life—as well as his funding priorities for space exploration. In the end, it was his administration that shut down the space research out at Edwards, but Lyndon, always my friend and I his sounding board, never felt easy about making such difficult decisions. I know because I watched him sweat some of them out.

Vi Strauss Pistell
(COCHRAN-ODLUM RANCH HOUSEKEEPER)

Johnson was always tracking Jackie down. It was funny at times the way he could find her. Sometimes the call would come to her when she was in an airport, sometimes at a luncheon, any-where. Once in Santa Barbara she was in the middle of a big affair and he wanted her to fly to Washington, D.C., immedi-ately. "I just can't come now," she told him. "I'm going to send a plane for you," he answered. And he did. And she went.

When we were driving through Texas together one time, our car broke down and the Johnsons came to the rescue. We stayed at their ranch, a homey place. That night at dinner Lyndon told Jackie and me, "We're having a home-grown product for dinner tonight." Jackie says, "What's that?" And when he answered, "Catfish," I knew she was about to die. She ate it though and I wasn't sure she'd be able to stomach it. And brussels sprouts too. Jackie absolutely deplored brussels sprouts. After dinner we sat on a couch and Lyndon was lounging, leaning up against me, practically resting his head in my lap. Jackie was about to die laughing. He was using me like a cushion. Later, we'd say to people, "The President of the United States used to *lean* on me a lot."

TWO PRESIDENTS
AT A TIME

1967

I have had a great life filled with friendships with great people. How many other ordinary Americans can claim to have played host to an ex-president of the United States—who was a Republican—and a current President of the United States—a Democrat—at the same time in the same living room on the same Sunday afternoon?

I had played golf on Saturday and put in a hard week of work. I was exhausted, but then again, I was always pushing myself to the point of exhaustion. I told the housekeeper at our ranch that Floyd and I didn't want to be disturbed on Sunday and to plan some scrambled eggs or milk toast for supper. Nothing special. No interruptions, I insisted.

The phone rings. I've greased my hair pretty good and I'm still in bed, not really dressed, reading, hoping to hear from no one but Floyd. It was rare for us to be alone like that.

"The President would like to come over to pay a social call," one of General Eisenhower's Secret Service men is saying to me.

"You mean the general," I correct him. It's so easy to make slips of the tongue about ex-presidents.

"Yes, General Eisenhower and the President would both like to come over, Miss Cochran," he says. "Would it be convenient within the half hour?"

"Who wants to come over?" I ask. And he repeats the

request: Eisenhower and Johnson are over at the Eldorado Country Club, playing cards, considering a golf game, and insisting on a visit to my house.

"Can you give me more than a half hour?" I ask.

"No problem," this very nice Secret Service man says. "I think they'll play a round of golf anyway. They're still debating."

"Will you call me back when they are on their way?" I ask.

OTHER VOICES:

Aldine Tarter

Johnson was a maverick like Jackie. She called me one Sunday afternoon to say, "The President's coming for tea, Aldine. You and your husband are invited. Get here quick. Hurry. Good-bye." That was it.

I looked over at my husband and he glances at me. "I've got work to do; I'm not going over there to fool around." But I didn't want to miss it. Jackie was in a dither. Everything had to be perfect. The housekeeper—it wasn't Vi Strauss then—wanted to be part of the scene and kept getting in Jackie's way.

I had known that President Lyndon Johnson was going to be at Camp Pendleton in California, not too far from us, but I had no idea he'd want to see me. Jeepers, I hoped the Secret Service men would hold them off long enough for me to wash my hair, pull my clothes together, and get some refreshments ready. The housekeeper was doing nothing, standing stock-still, she was so stunned. "Get some fresh dates," I was yelling at her when Aldine arrived.

I ran to wash my hair, put a headband around it when it was still wet, and hoped it would curl right. The temperature was about 75 degrees and you could see for miles. Not a breeze but just fresh and beautiful. I called the Secret Service people back. "Tell them not to come to the back door. For heaven's sake, make them walk in the front door." Everybody always came around to my back entrance, and I didn't mind an ex-president acting casually, but somehow, for history's sake I suppose, I wanted the President of the United States to do it right.

The cars pulled up—two of them. Secret Service men were in one and Eisenhower and Johnson in the other. I ran down the front steps, and by that time, the general had already taken off his golfing shoes. He was going to march around in his stockinged feet and that made me laugh. Lyndon left his rubber-soled shoes on. He's not a very good golfer. I'd be surprised if he ever broke 100. Eisenhower had shot a hole-in-one at Seven Lakes Club shortly before, and he was still proud of it. I accused him of cheating, of course, told him that his caddy had kicked it in for him, that he had used a magnetic ball or something. I was just teasing. He had shot it fair and square. We all exchanged a lot of sly remarks about the golf game at first and I thought the visit would be limited to ten or fifteen minutes.

Lyndon did all the talking. There we were—Floyd, Eisenhower, me, and a few people from the household. Eisenhower was very attentive, and Lyndon was going on and on about Vietnam. At one point Johnson even asked Eisenhower, "What do you think?" And that surprised me. The general said, "I don't see how you could have done it any other way."

Lyndon asks me, "Can you show me around this ranch, Jackie?" We had 800 acres and the house was almost in the geographical center. I had a nine-hole golf course out front and a big Olympic-size swimming pool heated especially for Floyd. Out back there were some garages, and that's where I was headed to check about a car. I wanted to drive Lyndon around.

Eisenhower says, "Jackie, why don't you use my car? It's right down there at the bottom of the steps."

Lyndon and I begin to walk out, leaving Floyd and

Eisenhower to chat. "Would you like to go home now, General?" I ask. "No, this is just fine, Jackie." We had been talking for at least an hour by this time, and sometimes I got nervous leaving Eisenhower and Floyd alone. Neither were very well.

The President and I walked down to the car and I leaned in to ask the driver to step out. I was going to drive because I liked to drive.

"Nobody's going to shoot this man here," I say, smiling over at Lyndon. Lyndon looks at the group of men and announces, "All of you, stay away." We climb in and off we go roaring along, over the golf course and all around the ranch. Secret Service men and cars trailing behind in a flurry of dust and grit. It was just beautiful, with a view of Chocolate Mountain.

Four o'clock on a Sunday afternoon on my little golf course can be pretty busy ordinarily, but there had been a tournament earlier in the day, the crowds had thinned, and I had telephoned the manager of my little golf course to make sure the place wasn't packed with people and to shoo the hangers-on off. By the time Lyndon and I landed on the scene, it was nearly empty. But not quite.

I spied a golf cart and a man about to get out to hit a ball. I knew that General Eisenhower's car had a special shatterproof windshield, but I still didn't want to test it out with the President of the United States sitting right there in the front seat. I started blowing my horn to beat the band and this golfer turns around to stare at me as if I were crazy. Then I jumped from the car.

"Don't you dare hit that ball, Mr. Ray Rummonds," I yelled. He was playing with his wife, and I knew them both well.

"Why not?" he wanted to say but never got the chance.

"Would you like me to introduce you to the President of the United States?" The two of them stood open-mouthed for only a moment, and then they came over to the car. Mrs. Rummonds was dumbfounded and could hardly budge from her seat in the golf cart.

Mr. Rummonds wasn't believing me for a second. Then he looked in the window and said, "Well, you *are* the President." To which remark Lyndon said, "I sure am." They shook hands and Rummonds said, "I'm glad I didn't hit you with that golf ball."

I'll bet Ray Rummonds has told that story at least 150 times.

Lyndon and I headed back to the ranch house, where he was

interested in additional refreshment and I was in for a battle with the general.

Aldine Tarter

Eisenhower cornered her and I heard part of it. "Jackie," he said, "you've just broken protocol here." She asks, "I have? How?" He answered, "Yep. No private citizen ever drives the President of the United States anywhere, and you just did. You've broken protocol." He wasn't happy about what she had done, and he wasn't going to give in easily.

"Well, goddamn it," Jackie said, kind of surprised, kind of peeved. "Lyndon got in the car and he didn't have to."

Then Eisenhower grinned. He still wasn't happy about what she had done, but it didn't change his feelings about her. He liked her a lot, but what I could never figure out was why Mr. Odlum and Jackie spent so much money taking care of the Eisenhowers. They must have spent up to $30,000 some of those seven years he had his office on her ranch. Military people can be such moochers.

For days after the big presidential "summit" there at the ranch, local newspapers speculated about what had gone on out at the Cochran-Odlum ranch. Jackie didn't want or need the publicity. But finally, Mr. Rummonds wrote a letter to the editor to insist, "I was standing on a green at the Cochran-Odlum golf course last Sunday afternoon, about to hit my ball, and I'm here to tell you that the President of the United States and Jacqueline Cochran came by in an automobile. Jackie rolled down the window and said to me, 'Don't you dare hit that golf ball. The President of the United States is in this car.' And darned if it wasn't Lyndon B. Johnson himself who shook my hand."

Jackie was so proud of herself.

RECOGNIZING LIMITS

1970

OTHER VOICES:

Tony Levier

We had this hot helicopter at Lockheed about 1970. It was pretty damn fast and had a lot of potential. Jackie knew it and thought, "By God, I'm gonna break some records in a helicopter." I was flying helicopters at the time myself, so when she convinced the Lockheed Corporation to set up another deal for her, I brought a helicopter down to her ranch and gave her the first helicopter ride she'd ever had.

At Lockheed we figured she was upwards of sixty years old at the time. Jesus, nobody that age is flying things like hot helicopters. Nobody but Jackie.

She did a surprisingly good job for a while. I checked her out in it, but a more experienced helicopter pilot took over her training.

Helicopters are funny vehicles. They are hard to fly. You have a collective stick and you have a cyclic stick. What you have to be able to do first of all is get the helicopter straight up off the ground. Eventually, you can take a copter off in a running start, but at first, it's straight up. And to do that, you've got to have coordination of both this collective stick and this cyclic stick. By lifting up slightly, you increase the thrust on the main rotor blade, and using the other stick, you keep the chopper from not moving laterally, either forward or backward, as you're lifting up. When you are checking out a new helicopter pilot, you let him fly one stick while you fly the other. You lift up really gently and teach the pilot to hover and how to handle the ground effect right there at eight or ten feet in the air. You just stay there. You've got to make sure the copter doesn't move sideways, forward, or backward. Then you swap sticks while the new pilot learns how to use the thrust and lift up, cranking a throttle at the same time. Theoretically, after a pilot has learned both sticks individually, he can use his knowledge to work both together. But what works in theory doesn't always work in reality. Coordinating the two motions isn't easy. It can be like riding a bicycle. After maybe ten flights it comes together. But what frustrations in the meantime.

Jackie came back from her first solo practice flight in this damn hot helicopter, and something happened to her. I don't know what it was. But she was apparently scared to death.

She was trying to land it, and as she set it down, lowering it to the ground with the collective, something disturbed her. She got out of phase and began to bang it down on the ground. Banging it up and down—hitting the ground harder than hell—then popping up and banging down again—losing control and then smashing it down so hard, she smashed the landing gear right off.

An engineer rushed out under the rotor system and climbed in to grab hold of the controls. He kept it down that time, or else she might have pushed that collective back up to go up again. Finally, she got out.

She was ready for me when I arrived at the ranch a couple of days later to talk about her project. We were both getting along in years, and she knew what I was going to suggest.

"Good God, Jackie," I remember telling her, "can you imagine how Lockheed might feel if something happened to you while you were in one of our helicopters? What's going on with you?"

Aldine Tarter

The damn dog scared me to death. Mr. Odlum would sleep with a dog in his later years, in the early seventies, and Jackie had a bedroom across the hall. I went in to wake Mr. Odlum because I thought Jackie was dying and that's when the dog scared the hell out of me.

"Mr. Odlum, Jackie is having seizures and she wants to go to Albuquerque to the Lovelace Clinic. Let's get the doctors on the phone and let's not scare her to death. She doesn't think it's serious. But I know it's serious. It's bad." He got up and put a robe on and came into her bedroom. She had had another blackout.

Together the three of us called the clinic and talked to the doctor there. He didn't want Jackie to fly after we described her symptoms. I did more listening than talking, and his suggestion zapped my first thought: we'd charter a plane and get her right over there. Albuquerque was at least two days' driving away. My mind started working. We'd make up a bed for her in the back of one of the ranch station wagons. Two of the men could take turns driving. They'd be on the road within the hour. It was going to be okay.

"Floyd thinks I'm going to die, Aldine," she said to me when Mr. Odlum had gone back into his room.

"He's old and he's scared, Jackie," I said.

"That's funny," she answered. "After all these years of his being so sick, he thinks I'm the one who's going to die."

"I think we need to get you to Albuquerque today," I said, trying to avoid the issue. I agreed with Mr. Odlum about the seriousness of her seizures. She kept passing out, then coming to, as if nothing were the matter. She seemed unfazed by it all, but she didn't argue with me about going to the hospital.

I got Mr. Odlum alone. "Now, calm down," I said to him. The last thing I needed was for him to scare her to the point where she'd have a more serious seizure. I didn't know what was causing them, and I figured her own calmness had to be helping at least a little. He didn't need to start mourning her before she was dead.

This all happened in the morning—nine o'clock in the morning.

By four o'clock in the afternoon they still hadn't started for

Albuquerque because Jackie had spent hours packing suitcases, ordering boxes of grapefruits and dates loaded onto the roof of the car, and filling the back of it completely. That was the day she insisted on frying chicken they could eat along the way. God, I was so mad at her.

"Where in hell do you think you are going to lie down in that car?" I asked. "Why do you have to take all this luggage? Please tell me why. Please leave it here." She was so stubborn.

"No," she said. "I'm taking it all." You couldn't argue with her. The fruits were gifts for the nurses and doctors at the clinic. She'd sit in the backseat, she insisted, in a small space she'd allotted herself for a thirteen- or fourteen-hour car drive. I couldn't believe her.

Finally, Jackie was almost ready to go. "Now, Mr. Odlum," I said to him when we were in his bedroom. "Don't say things that will make her think she's in serious trouble. She needs to leave here with confidence that she is going to be all right. Okay?"

"Okay," he says.

I kept saying she was going to be all right, but I had no idea where the seizures were coming from—and they kept coming. "Help me send her off feeling confident," I asked. It was a confidence I didn't have at the time. I honestly didn't know whether or not she would make it all the way to Albuquerque. And we had wasted an entire day getting her ready to go. The two men who could have been napping to prepare for a night of driving had been loading the car and working. Golly.

We're at the front door waiting for a golf cart to be brought up so she doesn't have to walk down to the loaded car. She turns to me. "Do you think your husband would mind if you stayed here tonight with Floyd? I'd feel more comfortable if someone were here with him, Aldine."

"Of course I'll stay."

Floyd turns to her, looking positively stricken.

"Oh, Jackie, don't die and leave me."

THE PACEMAKER

1971

I was never a healthy woman, but I was never a hypochondriac. My reasons were real for being in and out of hospitals all my life.

Jeepers—from that first botched surgery for appendicitis back in my teens to the series of major abdominal operations, eye surgery to save my pilot's license earlier in my life (eye muscles were stealing my depth perception), and foot surgery in England—my body simply wouldn't behave. Twice I miscarried the children Floyd and I would have loved to raise. And Floyd would get upset but I always dismissed his worries. There was no use wasting worry on something over which you had so little control. He never asked for arthritis. I didn't ask to be childless. But Floyd would worry anyway. Once I even lied to him about my whereabouts when I knew damn well I was going to be in a hospital. I felt if I let my health stop me, it would be all over. And I wasn't going to allow such an end. I never saw myself as any older than twenty-five. I suppose that's why it killed me to get older.

In the summer of 1953, after I had stupidly broken the sound barrier without first putting on the "G" suit designed especially to protect me from the shock, I snuck into Albuquerque, where Randy was going to perform what he called a "noble plication," or the operation to end all my abdominal operations. There had been six on my tummy up to that time.

On arrival in New Mexico, I called Floyd's secretary at his

Los Angeles office and told her to inform Mr. Odlum that I was going up into the mountains to interview an old Indian and I'd be with Dr. Lovelace. Nothing to worry about, but I'd be out of touch for at least a day and a night. Technically, it wasn't a lie. The nurse on duty in the operating room was an American Indian and Randy was going to be with me when I reached into the heights of anesthesia.

By 1970, I couldn't hide the state of my health from Floyd. He was there when I fell over with drink in hand. He was there during my seizures and I worried about him. That man had run his businesses out of wheelchairs and out of agonizing pain for decades. He lived by sheer grit, walking on raw bone when he had to get up and walk. He had no cartilage in his feet in the end—bone and skin—that's all. He'd hobble in utter pain.

Arthritis is a terrible disease and more frightening than any disease I know. It destroyed my husband and stole the marriage we had planned right from my grasp. Floyd could hardly bear to be touched—by anyone.

Cortisone helped, but it also hindered. At a special dinner one evening for the Arthritis Foundation, of which Floyd was a primary contributor and fund-raiser, the cortisone robbed him of the right to shake the hands of the people who loved him. Putting a thumb on his hand would make him bleed. Something as simple and as vital as the warmth of human touch was denied him for more than forty years of his life. He ended up in bandages that night.

I called Aldine from the Lovelace Clinic to tell her that I had arrived safely, had suffered only three more seizures along the road but had been free of them since settling into the hospital room. I didn't want Floyd to worry. I did want her to know that the doctors suggested a pacemaker. I didn't want her to tell him. Then I found myself blurting it out to him anyway. I had my heart to blame for the seizures. My pulse rate had been dipping dangerously low.

OTHER VOICES:

Aldine Tarter

Jackie came home with a pacemaker implanted, but her life was far from over then or there. She lived with one or another kind of pacer for more than ten years. The doctors kept trying new ones out on her, and I believe she ended up with eight or nine varieties. In fact, Mr. Odlum used to accuse her of not having the right kind because she didn't go any slower but, in fact, tried to go faster than she had before.

She had a big three-wheeled bicycle for riding around the ranch, cycling back and forth to her vegetable garden, sometimes insisting that I climb on the back. There was a platform on the back, and she had a special stainless steel box for her picked vegetables. God, I used to think, "You could have a heart attack right here, Jackie Cochran, with me riding along on the back of your bike." It was at least a half mile down to the garden. But it never stopped her from yelling to me as she pedaled past my office, "Come on, Aldine, let's go." Or from running around the golf course, trying to hop fences that were waist-high or throwing parties for more than 100 people. That was on Mr. Odlum's eightieth (that would have made her somewhere in her late sixties) and it was a real wing-ding.

———

Randy Lovelace had been placed in charge of aviation medicine at Wright Patterson Field in Ohio not long after I proposed him for the Collier Trophy during Roosevelt's tenure. He became one of our country's greatest authorities in aviation medicine and was involved in the space program. We were friends for years and years. He loved everything about airplanes and flying. His uncle had been very successful in the medical community in New Mexico and had invested in real estate there. This was the uncle who put Randy through medical school and was always asking him to come back to Albuquerque to practice. But there was too much going on elsewhere.

Randy was married to a wonderful woman, Mary, and they had two little sons when I first knew them. One of their boys contracted polio during that horrible epidemic and died within a few days. They brought their son's body to Albuquerque for burial, and while they were there, the other boy came down with polio. They believed that their only hope was to get him to Hot Springs, Georgia, which had the polio center funded and fostered by Roosevelt and the March of Dimes. I flew Randy, Mary, and their sick little boy to Georgia.

It was no help. Their second son died.

I remember how crazed people were about polio and how we worried about the contagion. Before leaving Hot Springs to return to the ranch, I removed every piece of movable cloth from the plane and had it burned, as well as my clothes. The plane was fumigated too.

Randy and Mary were absolutely devastated, as you can imagine. That's when he told his uncle he'd return to New Mexico if he could found a clinic dedicated to research. Floyd helped and even served as chairman of the Lovelace Foundation for a while. I believe that Dr. Lovelace was a fine surgeon, and I'm sure he saved my own life at least once.

American piloting equipment is so far superior to anything the Russians had in the Korean War that it saved lives and it's because of doctors like Randy that we've got the stuff—and they don't. I remember the first bail-out bottle. Dr. Lovelace was the first man to bail out with it at 42,000 feet. As I recall, he carried this bottle strapped to himself so it wouldn't get loose. Nowadays, you sit on your oxygen supply, and if you bail out, your oxygen mask goes right with you. I used to be on the functional clothing board in World War II. We tried to think of everything a pilot might need. Randy was there with me thinking. Funny, though, when it came time to save his own life, he didn't even have an overcoat.

In 1966 Randy Lovelace and his wife, Mary, were in a medium-sized charter plane being flown from Aspen, Colorado, back to Albuquerque, when the pilot took the wrong canyon out of Aspen. When he reached the dead-end and had no room to make a 180-degree turnaround, they crashed high up in the mountains, and then froze to death before help could arrive. They were among my closest and dearest and I was, quite simply, devastated.

Well, now it seemed I was looking at the end-game for myself. Whenever I'd want to get a proper perspective of man's place here on earth, I'd go out onto our ranch lawn and look at the moon, planets, and stars through our rather large-sized telescope. The moon is so near that its light reaches us here on earth in less than two seconds. I used to look at it closely with landing fields in mind. Then I'd take a look at one of the distant stars and realize that it might have been extinct long before man here on earth came into being. It takes the light from some of those stars millions of light years to reach us as opposed to those seconds from the moon. When you start to consider the billions upon billions of balls of fire called stars going on and on in accordance with a pattern, you've got to feel small. But not too small. For I'd then consider how smart we were, how much we knew and how the mind of man had gradually taken ascendancy over so much.

I possess a rather simple-minded approach to religion. The universe is so ordered and so divinely planned that there must be something more. It's that simple. It doesn't have to be complicated. I'm satisfied that if my body goes back to nourish and create flowers, then I'm part of an infinite, divine plan. It's only human to believe in an afterlife where your personality is important and you'll continue to do and love the same pleasures you pursue and love here on earth.

For a long time after returning from Albuquerque, I couldn't look up into the sky without bursting into tears. Then I began thinking: this is stupid. And that was that. In fact, I decided that if I couldn't fly high-performance jets any longer, then I'd take up soaring, flying airplanes without engines. My body could stand the pressure of altitude up to about 7,000 feet, so I applied for my permit. I could see no reason why I couldn't soar alone, particularly when I planned to fly in remote areas where I couldn't possibly hurt anyone but myself. And at least I'd be in the air again.

Maggie Miller

I was at a dinner party one night at Jackie's house and there were several couples present. Her house was arranged so nicely, and after dinner, we'd all retire to the sun porch for games, cards, or conversation with after-dinner drinks. There were several people sitting at the backgammon table, but I was opposite the table along with Jackie and a young fellow whose wife was absorbed in the game. Jackie was facing the table, but this young husband had his back to his wife. To make conversation, he says to Jackie, "I'm very interested in pacemakers, and I've done a little reading about them. I wonder if you should be smoking?"

She has a cigarette in her hand. She always enjoys her smokes and gin.

Absolutely deadpan, she says, "Oh. What do you know about pacers?" She could really pull the shades down on people when she wanted. "Do you know where they implant a pacer on a woman?"

"Well, not exactly," he answers.

"Right here," she says to him, putting her hand on her breast. "Want to feel it?" she asks him. "Go ahead," she invites, egging him on. He's so embarrassed. He doesn't know what to do, and I'm certain he was wondering where his wife was. Jackie could see the doings at the backgammon table, but he couldn't.

His face turns red and he stalls for a minute. There's a twinkle in her eye. "I'll take your word for it, Jackie," he says, trying to dodge the issue. But she won't let him off the hook.

"Here, feel the pacer," she insists.

You devil, I thought, but I didn't say it to her right then. Her sense of humor often came to her rescue.

When the Lovelace Clinic doctors had told Jackie that her flying days were over, her whole roof caved in. It hadn't dawned on her until that very moment that the seizures, the heart trouble, and finally the pacemaker would actually put an end to her aviation career. She wanted to sit around feeling sorry for herself for a while. She'd go out at night and look up into the desert sky, counting the stars, wishing she could fly again. But she couldn't. For once, her dreams were bigger than what she could accomplish.

But she bought a big recreational vehicle, a real motor home, and she drove it like an airplane all over the country. I took one trip with her, and we were barreling along through Colorado when I looked out the back window and saw black smoke pouring out of the rear end.

"Shut it down, Jackie," I said. "We're in trouble."

She stopped right there on an exit ramp going off the highway, and that big RV blocked the way completely. I went out the rear door to take a look, but I couldn't do much all by myself. There was a gas station about a half a mile away, so I told her—she was still sitting in the driver's seat—to "stay put, I'll go for help."

It took me a while to arrange for someone to drive back to survey the situation, and by the time the mechanic and I returned, the traffic trying to get off the highway via the ramp we were blocking was piled up for miles. There was this dumb motor home and I glanced in the window at the driver's side and discovered that Jackie was sitting as calm as you please, filing her nails.

"Maggie," she says to me, "the first thing they teach you in training is to keep calm in a crisis."

I laughed and then we were towed to the side of the road. Because I had friends not far away in Denver, I went in search of a telephone to rustle up a car for our use. She stayed behind in the van again, and this time, on my return, she was cooking us a duck for dinner. Nobody could cook duck the way Jackie could. I haven't had duck like that since she died.

FLOYD DIES

1976

OTHER VOICES:

Yvonne Smith
(POLITICAL CAMPAIGN MANAGER AND OLD FRIEND)

It was a happy forty-year marriage because both Floyd and Jackie were so darn independent, so strong-willed, so naturally intelligent. He was a tycoon and his name had been giant-sized in the investment industry for decades. But he idolized her. He couldn't fly the way she could. In return, she idolized him. You could see it when they were together, when they were discussing a project, disagreeing, testing each other. She told me that when she first saw him, she thought, "Now, there's a man I could really be attracted to."

Floyd was about five feet eight and a half inches tall, wiry when I knew him in the 1950s, and he always looked about ten years younger than he was in actuality. He had a balding head, with patches of graying hair at the back and a crop of freckles on his head from all that time spent in the sun, in the pool, on the telephone much of the time. He never gave off those airs of big-time stand-away-from-me businessmen. He never lost his small-town background as far as I could see. He was wonderful. He'd wear a white bathrobe covered with orange palm trees, an old straw baseball cap, and slippers by the pool. And he'd sit in a beach chair—beach chair and the two ordinary swimming tubes strapped around each of his arms completed the picture of Floyd Odlum at work. He never liked desks, even when he was spending his time at his office in the Wall Street area. I think Atlas was on Pine Street. What a genius.

Jackie and Floyd communicated constantly during their fantastic, interesting marriage. They would seem so separate, but they were actually inseparable, in a sense. I'm convinced Jackie was capable of extrasensory perception. There is no question in my mind about it, but she didn't like to talk about it.

Floyd had so few enemies, and that amazed me because of the incredibly shrewd way he had operated in his business dealings. He used to say, "I don't care what the rules are as long as someone tells me what they are so I can act accordingly." In his day he could cripple his competitors when he wanted to do so. At the end of his life there were some bad business decisions made—not all of them were Floyd's—but that never would have happened when he was in his heyday. He had been almost psychic in his business sense.

Floyd Odlum

Looking around for a deal a few years ago, I came across a startling fact in our studies—the stock of almost all oil companies was underpriced. Just multiplying the amount of proven oil reserves they had in the ground by the price of crude oil gave me a higher figure than the companies were supposed to be worth all together. In addition, they had the equipment, refineries, distribution, and good will as assets.

It isn't something an ordinary investor can profit by, but I figured that if I could buy control of these companies, I could resell them to their competitors at a more realistic price. I looked around and settled on Barnsdall Oil. It had no refining or distribution, but it did have 140 million barrels of oil in the ground. There were two million shares out, which meant each one was backed by $70 worth of oil. But it was selling on the market for $22—a rare bargain.

It took me a year and a half, until 1948, to buy it—a little at a time, so as not to force the price too high. It went up to 46 before we were finished, but that was still cheap. When we had 28% of the company the management found out what we were doing.

They didn't want me to take over and indicated they would buy stock themselves to stop me. When I heard that I figured, hell, I wanted control. I called the New York Stock Exchange and said I was paying $2 over the market price for Barnsdall Oil. Everything I needed came in the same day.

We held Barnsdall only until 1950, a little over a year. It made its greatest profit that year, $15 million. All the oil companies have always known their stocks were underpriced, but it would be a violation of the antitrust laws for one to buy out the other directly. So when they heard I had Barnsdall—Shell, Gulf, all the rest of them came to me.

I finally sold to Sunray Oil. The whole thing took place at the ranch from Saturday to Wednesday, the fastest big deal we ever had. Sunray brought in twenty experts, and we put them up at the guest houses (two bathrooms, Hollywood style, and large stone fireplaces). The place was mobbed. The deal was closed on the lawn and we got $44.3 million—$12 million more than I paid for it—plus an option to buy 719,000 shares of Sunray at $12.

Meanwhile Barnsdall helped Sunray's strength and the price of Sunray shot up. We picked up the option and just sold out in 1952 at a higher price. We made $9 million more on that end of the deal. Actually, I'm sorry that Sunray got such a bargain, but we can't hold on to these things forever.

Glennis Yeager

What I remember most about Floyd and his relationship with Jackie is the way he would do anything for her—anything. He wanted her to have everything and anything she wanted. He wanted her to set those records and was always disappointed when she didn't make one. He walked with a cane when I first knew him, but he could get around pretty well. Later he always had a wheelchair. He was her business counsel and they would argue about decisions at times.

Oh, how he suffered. People would make him wait and that hurt him to be on his feet. And shaking hands was even a worse proposition. When people squeezed his hand, he'd never say a word but I'd know how much it hurt.

Floyd loved to get money moving for others. He told Chuck and me what to do with our money for years. He knew when to sell and when to buy. Just for the fun of it, he'd handle other people's money, to play with it. Jackie was extremely dependent on Floyd, I think. He was such a fabulous person. I thought the world of Floyd Odlum.

Louise Rosen

Mike and I went to visit Jackie and Floyd once a year for a vacation out there at the ranch for as long as we were married, about twenty-seven years. It broke Jackie's heart to give up the big ranch. They moved across the road into a very pretty house, a big house, but it wasn't her ranch, the one she had built. In those final years Floyd would often be so sick that he hardly came out of the bedroom. Poor guy. Jackie used to say to me, "Sit down here, Louise, and look out at those mountains, those gorgeous mountains." And we'd sit together. I loved her dearly.

There had been lots of guest houses on the ranch, at least six or eight of them, and those beautiful gardens and orchards with the grapefruit trees, the dates—just oodles of them—and all these exotic birds. Cages of them were all around the ranch. Her flowers had been simply magnificent.

Mike Rosen

Selling the ranch was a great sacrifice for Jackie. She had loved it so, and Floyd's surviving son—the other one had already died—made some bad business decisions there for a while. Together, Floyd and his son, Bruce, lost lots of money in a desert real estate decision. What happened was that Jackie had always owned rights to only parts of her ranch. Floyd wanted to finance his son, who wanted to build homes and condominiums out there on the property. They had at least 800 acres. So Jackie deeded her rights to the ranch over to Floyd, and Floyd's son lost the money.

If it had only happened two years later, it wouldn't have been so bad. Two years after the father and son real estate venture went bankrupt, the desert land boom really took off. It was devastating. They went ahead and built 150 houses on the property and never sold a one that I knew of. Not everybody can manage money the way Floyd had done in his business career, and his son was more of an artist than a financier. Floyd may have wanted to offer his son a financial stake in life because he knew his own health was really failing then. It was a bad idea to build those houses, and someone had been feeding Floyd's son bad business advice. It ruined everything. Jackie and Floyd were never the same because they gave up something—their ranch home—they had loved very much. Then Bruce Odlum committed suicide.

Every time I think about the house that Jackie built being a country club restaurant, I get the chills.

Jackie and Floyd weren't ruined financially. They still had some money, but the well was running dry.

Yvonne Smith

He died on a Monday or early Tuesday morning in Jackie's arms. I had been there on the weekend and I was happy about that because when I was there, Mr. Odlum could be carried out of his bed. He spent most of his time in bed the last two years of his life and he'd trust only me or Chuck to pick him up and put him in his wheelchair. I'm a strong woman. I'd arrive on Friday evenings, driving up from El Centro where I was working as Administrator of Imperial County Health Department, and he'd say to me, "By golly, you're here, Yvonne. Can you get me up?" So I'd get him up to have supper with Jackie and me. He knew I wouldn't drop him. So fragile, he had lived with that arthritis for so many years and it had left him brittle, fragile, so breakable.

The weekend before he died, he had been out of bed for all three evenings—Friday, Saturday, and Sunday.

Indio, Riverside County, June 18, 1976

Industrialist and financier Floyd Odlum, founder of the Atlas Corp., a giant holding company, died yesterday at his home here. He was 84.

Odlum had suffered from arthritis for many years and was bedridden at his ranch. He and his wife, aviator Jacqueline Cochran, had hosted many famous persons, including President Dwight D. Eisenhower.

I held Floyd in my arms when he died. It was June 17, 1976, and he had suffered so long that it was time it stopped. I tried to comfort him. I was there.

When I gave speeches in the early 1960s, I used to quote from an Abigail Adams letter to her husband, John, who was hard at work in Philadelphia trying to wrench the country free from its colonial English bonds back then. Abigail was up in Boston, out of the heat of the political battles being fought over Revolutionary War issues, but not out of her husband's earshot. I was never away from Floyd either. Abigail was a strong woman and was powerful because of her strength, her own thoughts, her own opinions and because she had her own life, I think. Here's the passage I would read in my talks. She had written it on March 31, 1776. "I long to hear that you have declared an independency. And by the way, in the new code of laws which I suppose will be necessary for you to make, I desire you would remember the ladies and be more generous and favorable to them than your ancestors. Do not put such unlimited power into the hands of husbands. Remember, all men would be tyrants if they could. If particular care and attention is not paid to the ladies, we are determined to foment a rebellion and will not hold ourselves bound by any laws in which we have no voice or representation."

Floyd had understood what I needed in a marriage from the very beginning. He made life better for so many people, especially me.

OTHER VOICES:

Maggie Miller

After Floyd died, Chuck Yeager found the sealed envelope with the information that had been dug up about Jackie's background. Chuck told me this story. He asked Jackie, "Do you want to open this?" She said, "No." Then he said, "Is there any reason to keep this letter around?" She said nothing. So he burned it.

Vi Strauss Pistell

That's right. It was never opened.

ADVENTURE

SUMMER 1980

In 1948, Harry Bruno was head of the New York Adventurer's Club and he asked me to give a talk that would focus on an outstanding adventure. It was almost impossible to do, even back then before I broke through the sound barrier, had my day in the Starfighter, or saw stars at noon. I couldn't choose then and ended up talking about my childhood, learning to fly, getting caught between the mountains in that Waco, flying the bomber to Britain.

In 1954, *Guideposts* magazine asked me to write about adventure again. "I have found adventure in flying, in world travel, in business, and even close at hand. There is adventure for me in such a simple pastime as my helping the wild quail on our ranch lose their fear and come trustfully close to me.

"Adventure is a state of mind—and spirit. It comes with faith, for with complete faith there is no fear of what faces you in life or death."

In truth, I ended up living a life of continuous adventure. I think it was Peter Pan who said, "To die will be an awfully big adventure."

OTHER VOICES:

Yvonne Smith

Jackie was an avid reader and remembered what she read. Her collection of children's books and fairy tales was incredible. And you know, her own life had been a little bit like a fairy tale. There was a beginning, a middle, and then an end.

I get very emotional when I tell this story.

I went to the Air Force Academy in Colorado with her in 1975 when they honored her with the permanent exhibit of her memorabilia. She's the only woman they've ever done this for. And that was when they gave her the sword.

The cadets at the Air Force Academy presented Jackie with an official Air Force cadet sword, and she was simply flat out with shock and pride. The sword is the one item a cadet may own, and here were these people, these people she had worked so hard for and with, giving her something as significant as their sword. She was thrilled.

There is a big hall there in Colorado Springs and an oval staircase that sort of winds around and around up to the higher floors. I went upstairs for something and I was returning to the main floor when I looked down these winding stairs and caught sight of her blonde head in a sea of handsome cadets. She was standing directly in the middle of a huge crowd of young men who all wanted to talk to her. I just gasped. She was right where she wanted to be, talking pilot talk with the cream of our nation's new pilot crop. The whole scene from above where I was standing very still reminded me of one of those yellow flowers she cherished. She was the center.

"When I die, Yvonne," she said to me later, "I want to be buried with my sword and my doll."

"Why do you want to do that?"

"I want to take this sword with me if I go to heaven and, well," she says, pausing, "if I go to that other place, I'll be able to fight my way out."

Aldine Tarter

That was her request: to be buried with the sword and her doll. She'd talk about it all the time, especially after Mr. Odlum died. And I tried to talk to her. "It's nice to be buried with things you love, but I think it would be nicer if that sword went back to the Academy, where it belongs, with all your memorabilia."

"Nope, nope," she'd insist. "I want it with me."

She'd be grinning, though, and I think she just wanted to tease us. Fighting her way out of hell was not really the approach to death she could have been taking. There were more important things to think about.

But all along, there was no question about the doll. Before the end came, she had a change of heart, or so she said, and altered the will to indicate that the sword should go back to the Air Force.

The doll stayed.

Father Charles M. Depiere

I was known as the "flying priest of Washington," and Jackie Cochran and I met because of our mutual interest in aviation and because of her deep faith in Catholicism. We were friends for forty years. I used to use a plane to get around my parish, one of the largest in the state of Washington, so that's where my nickname got started. I'm from Belgium originally, but Jackie and I met initially in New York City.

She wasn't a flamboyant Catholic, but her trust that there was a God up there was real. She used to tell me that she was especially aware of his presence when she was flying—way, way up there. I knew all about each of those flights. God was right there beside her, she said.

Her health was not good at the end. Everything failed her, her heart, her lungs, circulation—just everything. Those last summer months in 1980 dragged on for her. Such a slow, peaceful exit might have been fine for someone else, but she was bored, and time dragged on. Being tied down by her body like that was the most unpleasant experience, she told me when I came to see her to administer the sacrament of the sick, the last rites, as we call them. She received Holy Communion and I do think it gave her the strength she needed for that final adventure.

"It means a lot to me, Father. Imagine flying down here from Spokane just to see an infirm old lady like me," she said. We laughed and then recalled the psalm story. It's a funny one.

Jackie and I had traveled to the University of Colorado together, where she was going to give a speech to open the new department of aviation. We talked about what she wanted to say and she wanted to use a passage from a psalm which talks about man flying into the unknown, a last frontier. "As it says in the palms," she'd say as we practiced the speech. And I'd correct her, "No, Jackie, it's not *palms,* the word is pronounced *salms.* The *p* is silent." But she couldn't get it quite right.

Then I decided to fix the cue cards for her. I'd spell it s-a-l-m-s, so she'd remember to say it as *salms.*

We were sitting on a podium and next to me was a professor at the university, a woman. She glanced at the cue cards but didn't say anything at first. Jackie gave a wonderful talk and at the end, *salms* came out as *salms,* not *palms.*

The professor sitting next to me clapped along with the others, but when things had quieted down, she turned to me to say, "Father, I'd like to call your attention to the word *salms.* I think you've misspelled it there on the cue card."

"Ahh, and so I have," I said simply. Jackie winked at me.

She did not want an elaborate funeral service. There was to be no big scene, she insisted. A simple pine coffin, a few very close friends and relatives who had been by her side to the end, her rosary beads, and her doll. She was buried with her doll. It was a closed casket with yellow roses covering it.

On the sunny morning of August 12, 1980, under the clearest blue sky you can imagine, with several jets streaking above us by sheer accident, not design, Jackie was laid to rest, surrounded by Chuck Yeager, Stan and Wendy Odlum (Floyd's grandchildren), Aldine and Jack Tarter, Vi Strauss Pistell, Yvonne Smith, Maggie Miller, Mike Rosen, Ann Wood, Tony Marimon, Charlie Shibata, the golf course superintendent, and his wife Jeannie.

It hadn't been planned that way, but there were thirteen people present and it struck me as a sign of very good luck. I'd like to presume that there was some divine pilot guiding her heavenward even then.

EPILOGUE

Upstairs at the National Air and Space Museum in Washington, D.C., the offices, the secretaries' cubicles, the Xerox machines, the word processors, typewriters, and the buzz of people busy with office business is pretty typical of government scenes. The prevailing mood isn't, and the work being done by these Smithsonian Institution employees is hardly routine.

These are people who know and love airplanes and who understand the flyers who knew those planes. Curator Claudia Oakes has been with the museum for more than seventeen years—"right out of college," she admits. Her special interest at the museum has been *women in aviation*.

"The 1930s—the decade Jackie began her flying career—marked a positive change for aviation in general, of course, but for women in aviation, it was a real turning point. Amelia Earhart, the most famous female pilot in the history of aviation, defined for the decade what women were trying to prove by their flying: it was a dual message—flying is safe, and women make good pilots. But Jackie Cochran turned out to be the *standard bearer* for all women pilots.

"The two female entries in the 1935 Bendix race—Earhart and Cochran—were the best-known women in aviation in the thirties and perhaps to this day. When her friend Amelia died, Jackie acknowledged that Earhart had 'placed the torch in the hands of others to carry on to the next goal, and from there on

349

and forever'. Cochran may have used the plural 'others' in that speech to the Women's National Aeronautical Association, but in her heart, she was the 'other.'"

In that highly competitive sphere of air racing, Jackie Cochran always wanted to be first among men—not women. Why? Because "women's records are invariably broken by men in higher performance aircraft," she told Claudia in an interview in 1979. She had to be first—with no qualifications, please.

When World War II put a temporary stop to the major air races, Jackie Cochran put her skills and her savvy to work for the war effort and accomplished more than most any other American woman can match in retrospect.

In her test-piloting—when women test pilots were unwanted and nearly unheard of in a highly competitive male world—she was paid one of the highest compliments a professional can earn: the acceptance of her peers as well as their admiration for her skill. Her being a woman was simply beside the point. She was good at what she did.

Her vision and stubborn persistence in so many areas makes me reel with empathetic exhaustion. I am fascinated by her power to get difficult tasks accomplished against overwhelming odds. Look at her:

—manipulating her way through the United States military establishment after World War II to lobby for a separate Air Force;

—pushing aviation medicine into recognized existence and nurturing it along with money and love;

—seeing the need for women to be there at the birth of the aerospace industry as well as the space for women in space (and getting her knuckles indirectly rapped in a congressional committee investigation for trying too hard);

—recognizing the inestimable value of the American missile program and supporting it, along with her husband, when all bets were off and all odds were against its success;

—climbing into the cockpit of an airplane that could go faster

than the speed of sound and then diving it straight at the earth
(never losing her nerve or control where many others had);

—flying one of the most unforgiving airplanes ever designed—
the Lockheed Starfighter—and pushing it past 1,400 miles an
hour for two summers in a row at an age when most of us
would prefer to be sitting in a beach chair reading a good book.

Jackie never lost sight of her main objectives—living the
good life, and always aiming for the very top in any endeavor—
nor did she even begin to doubt that if she tried hard enough and
fought hard enough and maneuvered hard enough, she would
not only achieve what she most wanted, but could even affect
the course of history—and have one hell of a lot of fun doing it.
As indeed she did.

—Maryann Bucknum Brinley

OTHER VOICES:

Chuck Yeager

Sometimes even Jackie Cochran couldn't believe what she had
accomplished.

APPENDIX

1932—Earns her first pilot's license.

1934—Enters the MacRobertson London-to-Australia race.

1935—Jacqueline Cochran Cosmetics begins manufacturing and Jackie enters her first Bendix race.

May 11, 1936—Married to Floyd Bostwick Odlum in Kingman, Arizona.

1937—Wins first place in women's division of Bendix and third place overall; becomes first woman to make blind landing, in Pittsburgh, Pennsylvania; is awarded her first of 15 Clifford Burke Harmon International Trophies of the International League of Aviators as the outstanding woman flyer in the world.

1938—Takes first place in Bendix transcontinental; receives the General William E. Mitchell Memorial Award as the person making the greatest contribution to aviation that year.

March 24, 1939—Establishes a women's national altitude record, and in September 1939 breaks the international open-class speed record for men and women. She wins the William J. McGough Memorial Award from Air Service Post 501; the American Legion honors her with its award; New York Mayor Fiorello H. LaGuardia presents his trophy for winning the New York-to-Miami Air Race in '39.

April 1940—Breaks the 2,000 kilometer international speed record and the 100 kilometer national record; wins the Minneapolis Aquatennial Air Classic Award as the outstanding woman pilot and receives her third of four trophies from the Women's National Aeronautical Association as the outstanding woman pilot for '38, '39, '40 and by the next year, '41.

June 1941—First woman to pilot a bomber across the North Atlantic; organizes a group of twenty-five American women to fly for Great Britain in the war effort.

1941 to 1943—President of 99s, an organization of women aviators founded in 1929.

September 11, 1942—Appointed director of women's flying training for the United States.

July 1943—Appointed to the general staff of the U.S. Army Air Forces; directed all phases of Women's Airforce Service Pilots (WASP) program.

1945—Receives the United States Distinguished Service Medal; travels to the Far East as correspondent for *Liberty* magazine; first American woman to enter Japan after World War II.

After the war, Jackie continued to participate in air races and to establish new transcontinental and international records. She still holds more international speed, distance, and altitude records than any other pilot.

1949—Decorated in France with the Legion of Honor.

1951—Receives the French Air Medal as well as the Lady Drummond-Hay Trophy; other foreign decorations include Wings of Air medals from Belgium, Spain, Thailand, Turkey, pre-communist Rumania. She is voted one of the 25 outstanding businesswomen in America by the Boston Chamber of Commerce.

1953—Flying a Canadian-built Sabrejet F-86, she is the first woman to exceed the sound barrier; receives the Gold Medal from the Fédération Aéronautique Internationale, the only woman ever to have earned this award. Her book *The Stars at Noon* is published and merits the annual book award from the Secondary Education Board of Boston. She is called "Woman of the Year in Business" by the Associated Press poll of newspaper editors for the first time. She wins that title again in '54.

1954—Is offered the Frank M. Hawks Memorial Award of Air Service Post 501, American Legion.

1955—National Association of Manufacturers gives her their Golden Fleece Award. She receives honorary degrees from Russell Sage College, Elmira College, and later from Northland College.

1957—Receives the Air Force Association Award for distinguished civilian service, the only woman to have been so honored. The United States Air Force has already cited her in '49 and '51 for recruiting service, and she continues in '57 to hold rank of command pilot in Civil Air Patrol. Also in 1957, she travels to Nicaragua as personal ambassador to President Dwight D. Eisenhower.

1958–59—President of the Fédération Aéronautique Internationale, the only woman ever to hold that office and to be reelected for the 1960–61 term.

1962—Chairman of the National Aeronautic Association.

1962—Establishes 69 intercity and straight-line distance records for Lockheed in a Jet Star; first woman to fly a jet airplane across the Atlantic. Also in '62, Jackie sets 9 international speed, distance, and altitude records in a Northrop T-38 military jet aircraft.

April 12, 1963—Sets 15–25 kilometer course record in Lockheed F-104 Starfighter—1,273.109 mph.

May 1, 1963—Breaks 100 kilometer course record with a speed of 1,203.686 mph.

May 11, 1964—Begins resetting her own records in Lockheed's F-104G Starfighter: for 15–25 kilometer course, a record of 1,429.297 mph; for 100 kilometer course, 1,302 mph; for 500 kilometer course, 1,135 mph.

September 16, 1965—Presented with Pionierkette Winderose decoration by German government.

May 1969—Awarded Distinguished Flying Cross with two oak leaf clusters by Chief of Staff, U.S. Air Force.

May 31, 1970—Honorary Doctor of Science degree from Notre Dame College, Manchester, New Hampshire.

June 16, 1970—Presented with Legion of Merit by Secretary of the Air Force.

September 18, 1971—Named Honorary Fellow of the Society of Experimental Test Pilots.

December 17, 1971—Enshrined in the Aviation Hall of Fame in Dayton, Ohio; the first living woman to have been so honored.

Other titles, significant dates, and honors:

Director—Storer Broadcasting Company.

Member—Board of Councilors, University of Southern California, Institute of Safety and Systems Management.

Director—Air Force Academy Foundation.

Trustee—Air Force Museum Foundation.

Vice-President—Air Force Historical Foundation.

Board of Trustees—Donald Douglas Museum and Library.

Member—Honorary Board of Directors of the American Hall of Aviation History of Northrop Institute of Technology.

Permanent Trustee—International Women's Air and Space Museum.

September 10, 1975—First woman to be honored at the United States Air Force Academy in Colorado Springs, Colorado, by having her memorabilia dedicated as a permanent display in Arnold Hall.

1975—Private papers donated to the Dwight D. Eisenhower Library, Abilene, Kansas.

August 9, 1980—Jackie dies at her home in Indio, California.

November 6, 1980—Memorial service for her is held at the United States Air Force Academy, Colorado Springs, Colorado.

INDEX

355